Cookies

Cookies

Simon St.Laurent

McGraw-Hill

New York   San Francisco   Washington, D.C.
Auckland   Bogotá   Caracas   Lisbon   London
Madrid   Mexico City   Milan   Montreal   New Delhi
San Juan   Singapore   Sydney   Tokyo   Toronto

McGraw-Hill

A Division of The McGraw-Hill Companies

1 2 3 4 5 6 7 8 9 0   DOC/DOC   9 0 2 0 1 9 8 7

ISBN 0-07-050498-9

The sponsoring editor for this book was Michael Sprague and the production supervisor was Claire Stanley. It was set in Janson Text by Patricia Wallenburg.

Printed and bound by R. R. Donnelley & Sons Company.

McGraw-Hill books are available at special quantity discounts to use as premiums and sales promotions or for use in corporate training programs. For more information, please write to the Director of Special Sales, McGraw-Hill, 11 West 19th Street, New York, NY 10011. Or contact your local bookstore.

 This book is printed on recycled, acid-free paper containing a minimum of 50% recycled de-inked fiber.

Dedication

For my parents, who were delighted
to hear I was writing a book
with a title they could understand.

Acknowledgments

I'd like to thank Michael Sprague, for realizing that cookies deserved a book and encouraging me throughout the writing process. Tracey Cranston helped me get through the writing, even when the code wouldn't work and the skies were gray. Patty Wallenburg did a wonderful job of turning a late manuscript into a nearly on-time book.

I would like to thank Dave Kristol for his time and help in explaining RFC 2109 and its implications. I would also like to thank my employers, Joe Hunt and Sarah Glover, for the patience that helped this book get written.

My mother, Mary St.Laurent, deserves all credit for the fine cookie recipe.

Contents

Contents

Chapter 3

Chapter 4

Chapter 5

Chapter 6

Chapter 7

Chapter 8

Chapter 9

Chapter 10

Chapter 11

The Importance of Maintaining State

Cookies address a major deficiency in the structure of the World Wide Web. When the Web first arrived, it seemed like a glorious new way to communicate. Hypertext Markup Language (HTML) was simple, clean, and easy to learn. Setting up a Web server was a minor challenge for a UNIX system administrator, but creating sites was easy. Hyperlinks gave developers a new way to connect and organize information cleanly, without layered menuing systems or difficult lookups. Documents could cross international boundaries with ease, without the need for onerous password systems, expensive application programs, and impossible file directory structures. It was all amazingly easy, deliberately simplified to the point that the average high school student could create an extensive site in a weekend.

The Web also broke all the rules. Programmers who had spent years developing applications with more traditional Graphical User Interfaces (GUI) interfaces (Windows, the Macintosh, and X Window Systems) found themselves having to start over when clients called and asked them to build applications using the Web. The old security systems, the old interfaces, and the old program structures all began collapsing when the tidal wave of the Web hit the world of computing. HTML was not a programming language; it was more like a formatting language with an odd GOTO function for moving between files. The interfaces for creating Web pages from structured (database) information were primitive, complicated, and difficult to manage. Faced with the overwhelming popularity of the Web, developers had to learn to adapt, creating new techniques and interfaces to replace the rubble the Web had made of their previous grand designs.

One of the greatest losses was state maintenance. A Web page does not care whose computer it is on, what country that computer is in, how that computer reached this page, who is currently typing and clicking on that computer, or even how long ago the page was loaded. From a Web page's perspective, it is just as good to have arrived ten minutes ago as ten hours or ten microseconds ago. Every connection to a server is a separate event, unconnected to any previous events. There are ways to make the client computer and the server computer keep track of what they have been doing, but these arts have been covered only slightly in the technical press and maligned greatly in the popular press. Although the asynchronous nature of Web pages makes it difficult to create connections (beyond simple links) between pages, the tools are there and have been for years—a very long time in the world of the Web.

Cookies are one key answer to this problem, allowing developers to keep information stowed away between Web page retrievals and create transactions with context. Cookies have been accused of malevolent invasions of privacy, virus-mongering, and security breaches. As we will see, they are mostly innocent, if only because they aren't capable of most of what their accusers have charged; but they do not provide a complete solution to the developer's needs, either. We will see they fit in the toolkit, and how they work with other tools. Along the way we will discuss how to manage cookies, inspect their contents, and take alternate routes when users hostile to cookies have turned them off.

Why Maintain State? The Complexity of Transactions in the Real World

One of the most difficult things that Web developers have had to do is communicate to their clients how the stateless nature of the Web interferes with things that seem incredibly simple in the real world. Buying a drink from a vending machine seems like a very easy thing to do, but implementing it over a Web connection is a lot more complicated. The Web does not provide the supporting infrastructure that even a vending machine has. In the following sections, we will look at a variety of transactions from the extremely simple to the remarkably complex to see what kind of supporting infrastructure they require. After our tour of the real world, we will examine ways to recreate that infrastructure in cyberspace.

Level 1: The Vending Machine

The classic vending machine provides the simplest possible transaction experience. You put in some change, push a button, and your goods and change tumble out of the machine. Even this transaction has a few steps, though—you put in the money, the machine verifies that it is really money, and you make a selection. After you make your selection, the machine has to calculate if you get change, and dispense it as necessary. The process is anonymous, as the machine keeps no record of who bought what when, and if you lose your money in the machine, it is usually pretty difficult to retrieve.

Figure 1-1 provides a simplified portrayal of this transaction. We are not concerned here with the machine's ability to verify coins and make appropriate change—what matters is making sure that the customer has paid before dispensing a fine drink.

This flowchart is hardly the classic breakdown of every step in the process—it merely indicates key points in the transaction, including the position at which the customer is allowed to make a purchase. The Insert/Verify/Return Change box conceals many steps, including the decision of whether or not to allow the user to enter into the "Payment Acceptable" state. This state diagram, and others like it, do not portray the rules and requirements of crossing from one state to another. Instead, they illustrate dependencies among tasks and states. The large gray box will be a common feature in our later work, indicating the areas where we need to maintain the context of a transaction.

Level 2: The Grocery Store

The grocery store is considerably more complicated than the vending machine. The store stocks thousands of times more goods, carefully arrayed to attract your eye as you wander the store with your shopping cart. The cart is an important part of the shopping process, allowing you to buy more than you can reasonably carry and making it easy to choose and return goods throughout your tour of the store. Most goods come prepackaged, but there are areas of the store (the butcher shop, for instance) where you can make special requests and negotiate for goods. You can also purchase some food in bulk, selecting your own quantity and paying by weight instead of by the package.

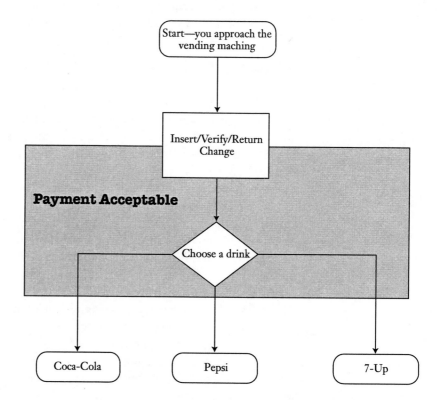

Figure 1-1
Payment Context
in a Vending
Machine

When you come to the cash register, you have a whole new set of obstacles to negotiate. With the vending machine, every item is a separate purchase, but in the store the clerk at the register will scan in all of your goods before charging you for them. You also have the opportunity to present coupons, and the register will make certain that the barcodes on your coupons match the barcodes on the products you have purchased. Stores have also introduced discount cards—in exchange for information about you, like your address, you can have a card that entitles you to extra specials and (with another bit of information about your financial situation) check-writing and check-cashing privileges. If you do not use these cards, your purchase is recorded anonymously; the store will use that information for its inventory management and also check to see what combination of goods you bought. If you do use the card, the store has a record of which person bought what, allowing management to track sales over time: buying habits, coupon use, weekly needs, and a much broader picture of which goods are purchased together. This kind of consumer information (usually stripped of the name and address) can be resold to third parties, making extra profits for the grocery store in a transaction that takes place long after the customer leaves.

Because of the use of a shopping cart, the context for this transaction is considerably more complex than that of the vending machine. Acceptance of payment is only one factor in the grand scheme of a grocery store, as illustrated in Figure 1-2.

Figure 1-2
Payment,
Statistical, and
Shopping
Contexts in the
Grocery Store

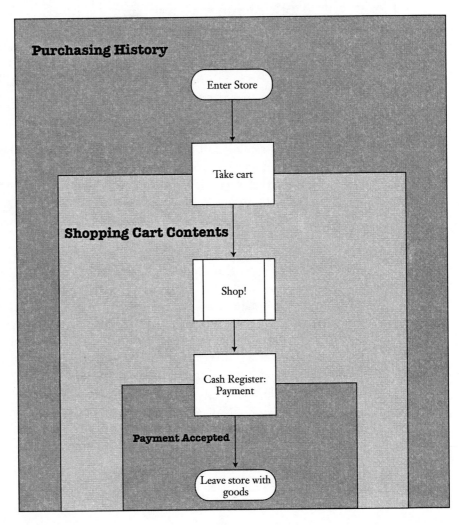

As you can see, there are three different contexts maintained here. The outermost context is overall shopping history—the kind of information the grocery store collects when you use their discount cards. The next is the shopping cart itself—all the goodies you collect as you stroll up and down the aisle. The final context is the payment context—you are not allowed to leave the store until you've paid at the cash register. These contexts continue through your departure from the store. Your overall purchasing history still surrounds you, the contents of your cart are (you hope) the same as they were inside the store, and either you have paid for the goods or the security car is chasing you through the parking lot.

Level 3: The Telephone Transaction

Ordering by phone has exploded over the last 20 years, allowing catalog marketers to take a significant portion of the market for goods from clothing to computers to auto parts to fruit. Unlike at the supermarket, you don't have your goods when you leave the store. Most purchases are made with credit cards rather than checks or cash, though C.O.D. is sometimes a possibility. You never go to the store and browse the shelves; instead you browse a catalog and choose the items you want. When you have a list of what you want, you are ready to call the vendor.

Your telephone call is similar to a visit to the cash register, but with some important differences. Because the store will be shipping you the goods, you must give them your name, address, and phone number, assuring you of a lifetime supply of catalogs. When you provide them with the list of what you want, it is not always certain that the goods will be in stock—you may have to back-order items and wait for them to be shipped separately. Once you have negotiated which items will be arriving when, it is time to present payment information, usually your credit card. Sometimes your credit card will get cleared while you wait on the phone, but other times it will be cleared later. Once your transaction is settled, the operator will usually give you a transaction number that uniquely identifies your order in case something goes wrong and you must call back. After you hang up the phone, all you need to do is wait for the goods to arrive, unless of course you ordered them C.O.D. If you did, it will be time to pay the postman soon.

Phone transactions look somewhat similar to the grocery transaction, with a few more parts, as illustrated in Figure 1-3.

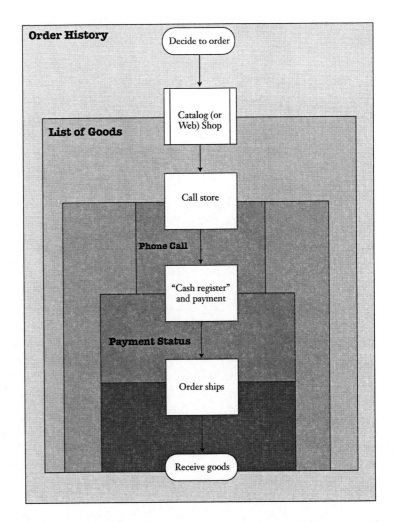

Figure 1-3
Shipping,
Payment, and
Statistical
Contexts in
Catalog Ordering

The list of goods and the shopping cart contents are similar, as are the grocery purchasing history and the order history at the mail-order vendor. The cash register part is much more complicated, however. The checkout of the grocery cart is simple, but the telephone operator must create a pick list of goods for your order that someone else will have to find in the warehouse. Payment can be more complicated as well. All payments to a grocery store are charged immediately, while many mail-order houses wait until your order ships before billing your credit card. You cannot just take your goods and walk out the door; you are dependent on the good graces of a shipping company as well as the mail-order vendor. Telephone transactions have many more complications than ordinary grocery shopping, and are a better model for the kinds of systems needed by commercial enterprises on the Web.

Level 4: Buying a House

Buying a house is the most complicated financial transaction average Americans are likely to encounter in their personal lives. The charming parts everyone likes to think about are the shopping and the moving into a fresh new, house. The parts in the middle, unfortunately, can be extremely complicated and require a serious of frequently difficult relationships between the homebuyer, the seller, and a variety of others who manage these transactions.

Most house purchases are still done through real-estate agents. The agents interview potential home buyers to find out what they want in a house, and try to match up the desires with a series of homes they then show. Once the buyers settle on a house, the financial transactions begin. Most buyers need a mortgage, which requires convincing a bank of their ability to pay for the house. After they have disclosed all of their personal information to the bank, along with information about the house, the bank decides whether or not to fund their dreams. When the buyers do get a mortgage, they still have a few hoops to jump through, like getting insurance for the house—banks will not pay the money out until there is proof of insurance. After they have arranged all this, the buyers must sit down with the sellers, the agent, the bank (sometimes two banks if the previous owners still have a mortgage), and a lawyer or two for the closing, where the title finally transfers. When the purchase is completed, the buyers must arrange for services such as electricity, water, gas, and garbage collection, move in, and wait for the mortgage payments to come due and the tax bills to appear. As Figure 1-4 demonstrates, home buying is complex because it includes a number of interdependent states, all of which must be sorted out before the transaction can close.

Buying a house requires transactions with many different people, usually including a real-estate agent, the owners of the house, an insurance agent, a bank, and probably lawyers at the closing. (I have left out the lawyers and the service hookups to keep the diagram from turning into a maze.) Most of the states involved here are relationships—the initial agreement with the agent, the declared intention to buy a particular house, an insurance policy to cover the house, and a mortgage to pay for it. The last two states carry on beyond the date of the transfer, as the bills will arrive continuously once the buyer owns the house. The mortgage approval process itself can be extraordinarily complex, as the bankers determine the potential lender's creditworthiness and the value of the house as collateral. The difficulty of making all of these transactions come off at the same time helps keep the real-estate agents in business, providing their services as catalysts to a chain reaction that might otherwise fizzle out in the financial maze.

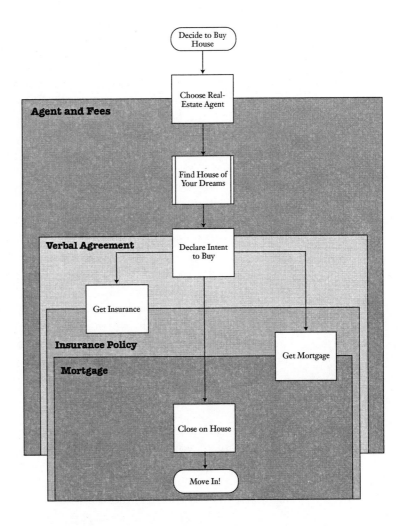

Figure 1-4
More Complex
Contexts—Home
Buying

Level 5: Border Crossings

Border crossings are always complicated. They may be international borders, borders within a building, security clearances for a job, or borders within a computer security system. The form of the transaction is always similar—you have to prove your identity and your right to go to the place you're headed. Frequently, you need to apply for that right in advance. While you are there, you need to carry the documents that gave you permission in the first place, because just crossing the border is never enough. If you are visiting a foreign country, you need a passport, a visa, and a stamp (or other evidence) that indicates your date of entry. Within a corporate campus, you may need a badge of some kind that identifies you and lets you past certain checkpoints to get to your office and other places you need for work. In a computer security system, you can enter a username and password to either open a session (like telnet) that the host can easily monitor, or check in to receive a token of authentication that your computer will present as needed to get to the resources you're using. In all of these situations, crossing the border is part of the process, and the place you're most likely to get stopped, but being on "foreign" territory demands that you keep a token of your crossing while you are on the other side.

Even when you are not in foreign territory, you most likely carry the documents that present the official versions of your identity—your driver's license, your social security card, your credit cards, bank cards, employee badges, supermarket check-cashing cards, and maybe even your passport. All of these documents have different levels of "officialness", and perform different functions. However well your passport may establish your identity, it probably will not serve in place of a credit card, while your video club card is not going to help you when you cross international borders. Still, each of them provides you with a "state"—in these cases, the right to certain privileges. Smart cards, which allow authorized persons to change certain information, will soon offer more flexible tools for maintaining and combining these functions, as well as those of your wallet.

Figure 1-5 shows an old-fashioned international border-crossing scenario, including the documents that currently establish citizenship and rights of entry.

This diagram assumes that you already have a passport, which provides overall proof of your identity throughout this process. After you have decided where you're going, you very likely need to apply for a visa to go there. The visa will have specific terms and conditions that apply to your stay in the foreign country, and must be checked with your passport when you cross the border. When you enter, the border patrol examines your passport and stamps your date of entry, to make it easier for them to keep track of whether you have violated your visa terms. While you are in the other country, you should keep your passport close to you at all times. You may not ever need it, but foreigners are always subject to inspection of their documents, especially if they must visit a police station or conduct official business. Your visa and passport also typically last beyond the time of your trip; even if a visa only allows you to stay in a country for two weeks at a time, it may be good for months or years, allowing you to make multiple visits without having to reapply each time. These contexts extend beyond the duration of the trip.

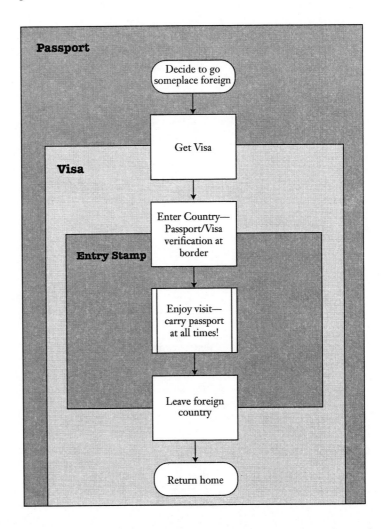

Figure 1-5
Border-Crossing
Context

Why Statelessness? State and Network Communications

If state is such a valuable tool in the real world, why did the designers of the original Web protocols deliberately choose to ignore it? Overhead is the main reason; maintaining a connection can place a heavy burden on computing resources when too many people are using a tool. Also, because people browsing the Web are not likely to spend their entire session reading pages from one server, it does not make much sense to keep open a connection that may not be needed again. By making it as simple as possible for a Web browser to retrieve documents from any Web server, the HyperText Transfer Protocol (HTTP) made the hyperlinking features of HTML clean, workable, and friendly.

Statelessness has already proven to be a problem for at least one aspect of Web communications. When the Web was originally built, Tim Berners-Lee and the other developers pictured a browser that downloaded and displayed a single document at a time. The early browsers displayed text—graphics were supported by links, but not as an immediate, in-line part of the document. Page retrievals were simple and reasonably quick, even over a slow link, as shown in Figure 1-6.

Figure 1-6
HTTP 1.0 and the
Original HTML
Browser Model

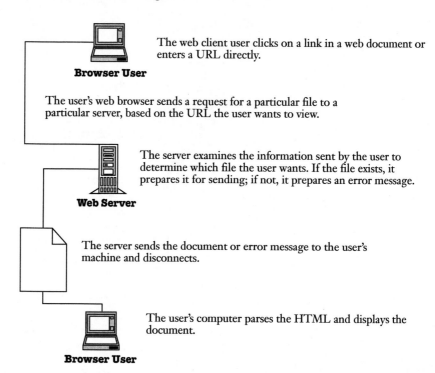

The web client user clicks on a link in a web document or enters a URL directly.

Browser User

The user's web browser sends a request for a particular file to a particular server, based on the URL the user wants to view.

The server examines the information sent by the user to determine which file the user wants. If the file exists, it prepares it for sending; if not, it prepares an error message.

Web Server

The server sends the document or error message to the user's machine and disconnects.

The user's computer parses the HTML and displays the document.

Browser User

The development of Mosaic and other graphical browsers changed that situation dramatically. By making graphics appear on the same screen as the text, browser developers created a new medium for communications and design, but put new loads on network connections and the servers providing the files, as shown in Figure 1-7.

More recently, the World Wide Web Consortium (W3C) has released standards for HTTP 1.1. The new protocol is something of a departure from the older model, allowing the session between the browser and the server to remain open until the entire page, complete with all the graphics from that server, is loaded. As you can see in Figure 1-3, this reduces a lot of the overhead involved in loading graphical pages.

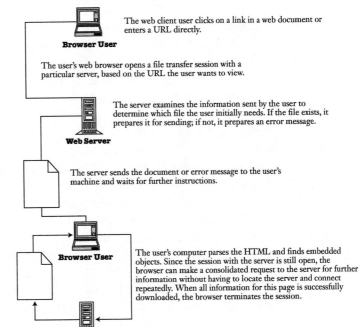

Figure 1-7
HTTP 1.0 Loading
a Page with
In-line Graphics

The web client user clicks on a link in a web document or enters a URL directly.

Browser User

The user's web browser sends a request for a particular file to a particular server, based on the URL the user wants to view.

The server examines the information sent by the user to determine which file the user wants. If the file exists, it prepares it for sending; if not, it prepares an error message.

Web Server

The server sends the document or error message to the user's machine and disconnects.

The user's computer parses the HTML and finds embedded objects, requiring it to re-contact the server and create additional sessions for each one.

Browser User

The entire cycle repeats, with the browser creating new connections to the server for each object needed. The graphics, applets, and other objects are downloaded. This process can add up to 25% to the time required for download.

Web Server

Figure 1-8
HTTP 1.1 Loading
a Page with
In-line Graphics

The web client user clicks on a link in a web document or enters a URL directly.

Browser User

The user's web browser opens a file transfer session with a particular server, based on the URL the user wants to view.

The server examines the information sent by the user to determine which file the user initially needs. If the file exists, it prepares it for sending; if not, it prepares an error message.

Web Server

The server sends the document or error message to the user's machine and waits for further instructions.

The user's computer parses the HTML and finds embedded objects. Since the session with the server is still open, the browser can make a consolidated request to the server for further information without having to locate the server and connect repeatedly. When all information for this page is successfully downloaded, the browser terminates the session.

Browser User

Web Server

This solves one major problem—download time for pages. It still does not address the state issues we faced in the real-world examples presented above, though. HTTP 1.1 keeps the connection open while the page is loading, but the kind of information Web developers building interactive applications need to collect and save is spread over several pages. The issue still needs to be addressed in a way that works after the page is loaded.

State and Programming Structures

In a "normal" GUI operating environment, programs frequently have to surrender control of the computer to the event loop, managed by the operating system. Although, in a sense, the program has exited, all of its data and programming structure remain intact and awaiting a call to action. At a Web site, the program "ends" every time a page finishes downloading. Client and server are connected only sporadically, when the user loads a new page or submits form data. This requires a different style of programming, one that seemed to end with the rise of the PC and the demise of the terminal.

To save programming cycles, many terminal interfaces were written as a series of separate programs, each of which concluded by refreshing the information on the user's screen. When the user typed in new information, such as a command or some text to search for, the terminal sent to the mainframe the new input and the contents of the screen. The central computer examined the screen, and figured out which program to run to handle the new input. The easiest way to make this work was to add a small code to the top line of the screen that did not interfere too greatly with the user. The user never had cause to notice that the terminal was not always in communication with the central machine, and the central machine was spared the hassle of managing user interfaces and waiting for input. This system worked very well with simple hierarchical menu systems, but was not a great model for the new tasks that the more immediately interactive PCs were good at, like spreadsheet manipulation and word processing.

Web pages behave in a somewhat similar way. Instead of codes at the top of the screen, Web pages can send Uniform Resource Locators (URLs), some with extra data for programs on the server side to process. Between page downloads, the server does not have to do anything, though tools have sprouted to help servers keep track of the users they are managing. The main problem, though, is that there are not many convenient ways to keep the server and the client in sync during this "silent period." As we have seen, real-world tasks demand multiple transactions connected by a consistent set of circumstances—a consistent state.

Cookies and Other Crumbs

Netscape created the "Netscape Cookie" in 1994 as part of the feature set of Netscape 1.1. It passed without much notice until Netscape 2.0 arrived—with the option to turn off cookies. Cookies are a small piece of text stored in a file (`cookies.txt` in Netscape, separate files in the cookie directory in Internet Explorer) on the user's machine. They cannot grow to over 4K, and no domain name (**netscape.com** or **microsoft.com**, for instance), can have more than 20. Cookies stay on the user's machine until they are removed by expiration, explicit request of the user, or just by being the oldest cookie around when the limit of (approximately) 100 cookies for the machine or 20 for the domain is reached. This gives them a significant advantage over the other state-management techniques available when cookies were created—they survive beyond the session in which they are created. Users can turn off their machines and the cookie remains, waiting to be used again the next time the user visits the site that created it.

Cookies are an old programming concept, originally used for quick hacks. A programmer who couldn't make two parts of a program (C++ objects, for instance) communicate with each other, could create a "magic cookie", a small text file containing the material that needed to move between the two routines. While not usually the most efficient way to write a program, it had the clear advantages of being reasonably easy to work with and very easy to debug. If it didn't work, the programmer could always look at the text file to figure out what had gone wrong. Most GUI programs use a cookie of sorts to keep track of their preferences—the classic `.INI` file in Windows is a kind of cookie, as are Macintosh preferences files and Windows 95 and NT registry entries. They are not called cookies but they serve the same basic function, providing continuity between the times programs and operating systems are run, even if the machine has been turned off for a week, a month, or a year.

There are other ways to implement cookie-like behavior that do not write files to the hard drive, but none of them has the permanence of a cookie. If you are a user who doesn't want the Web sites you visit to know anything about you, these techniques will undoubtedly be your preference. If you are the kind of user who doesn't want to have to type in all your information every time you want to download beta software from a particular company, cookies will undoubtedly make you happy. We will cover several ways to create cookie-like behavior in your sites, helping you make certain that the users who choose not to accept cookies can still explore and use your sites. As helpful as they are, cookies cannot do everything. We will examine the latest improvements to the cookie standard as defined in the

Internet Engineering Task Force (IETF) RFC 2109, the upcoming Open Profiling Standard (OPS) proposed by Netscape, Verisign, and Firefly, and endorsed by Microsoft, IBM, and Sun among others, as well as the privacy initiatives under consideration at the W3C. Digital signatures and encryption will also get some attention as ways to verify user identity in situations that require more security than the average username/password and cookie combination can provide. All of these tools are designed to help developers create sites with the kind of functionality we've outlined in the real-world examples above.

The good news about cookies is that they work on most browsers, and compatibly at that. Cookies are one Netscape standard that Microsoft has endorsed with resounding enthusiasm. Perhaps too much enthusiasm—Microsoft's site seems excessively fond of dropping cookies all over the browser at every visit. Their tools on the server side are significantly different, but still use the same set of standards for cookies. As we will see, you can use both sets of tools (as well as others) to accomplish similar tasks. The difficulty with cookies is not the usual incompatibilities between browsers; instead, the minefields lie in incompatibilities between your site and supersenitive users. We will examine a few paths through those minefields, and develop solutions that let users conduct successful transactions without giving away more than they want to.

CHAPTER 2

Cookie Anatomy

Before we continue our examination of the pros and cons of cookies, we need to take a detailed look at their contents. The information contained in most cookies is trivial, but is still enough to make programmers' and marketers' dreams conceivable and give privacy advocates fits. Despite their tremendous power, cookies perform these grand tasks using only a tiny amount of information, making this opening tour quite brief.

Remember, cookies are not supported the same way in all browsers. Throughout the rest of this book, we will be exploring the Netscape and Microsoft implementations of cookies, but not all browsers implement those particular models of this technology. Lynx, for instance, implements cookies (including much of the new RFC 2109 cookies) but "gobbles" all of them when the user exits the program. Some browsers you might not expect to support cookies, like those created by Spyglass for embedding into appliances, also support cookies this way. Older browsers, like Mosaic and the early AOL browsers, do not support cookies at all.

Looking into Cookies

After several years of remarkable stability, the cookie standard is in flux. Netscape originally created cookies, but is handing them over to a standards body. RFC 2109, a proposed IETF standard, will transform some of the basic mechanisms of cookies and add extra features to the current standard. Most of the examples in this book will use the older Version 0 (Netscape) cookies, as RFC 2109 is not yet widely supported, but notes along the way will point out ways to improve your cookie development with RFC 2109. In this section, we will cover both kinds of cookies, starting with the current but older standard. For now we will cover only the contents of cookies; tools for creating and managing them will get full treatment in subsequent chapters.

The two varieties of cookie have much in common, and provide similar services. Browsers and servers that can handle RFC 2109 cookies still work with the older versions as well. To maintain compatibility with the widest range of browsers, the authors of RFC 2109 recommend using both kinds of cookies and allowing the browser to decide which to use. Later we will examine techniques that developers can use to manage this transition. For now, we will cover the contents of both kinds of cookies to give you a sense of where cookies are now and where they're headed.

RFC 2109 has been published, but the proposals it makes are receiving new revisions that reflect difficulties, both technical and political, vendors have had in implementing the standard. RFC stands for Request-For-Comment, which is something of a misnomer. While most standards begin as proposals and have a name change to standards at some point, an RFC remains an RFC even after the commenting process is complete. If RFC 2109 receives two implementations from different vendors, i.e. a compatible client and a server, then it will be given the more prestigious title of Internet standard. Even if it achieves that lofty position, however, there is no requirement that vendors implement the new standard. RFCs provide the detailed standards for much of the basic infrastructure of the web. Unfortunately, they are not always as stable as other standards, and can be superseded or made obsolete by later RFCs. In RFC 2109's case, it is already being supplanted by working drafts, which may eventually turn into a new and improved RFC, and, with any luck, be implemented in the mainstream browsers.

Cookies Today: Version 0

Version 0 (Netscape) cookies have six parts: name, value, domain, path, expires, and a secure property that determines whether the cookies can be transferred unencrypted. Each cookie is supposed to be limited to 4K of information. Not all browsers enforce the 4K limit, but development beyond that point is not recommended even if it is possible because of performance issues. Uploading and downloading a 20K cookie would definitely annoy the average user on a modem connection. If you really need to push the envelope, your site could create and use as many as 20 cookies, all of which were smaller, but there are usually easier ways to manage information.

Table 2-1
Structure of a
Version 0
(Netscape) Cookie

Part	Value
Name	Value
Domain	domain name
Path	path information
Expires	date (in GMT)
Secure	No value—cookie is transmitted securely if attribute is listed.

Name

The name is a sequence of characters that uniquely identifies the cookie. The name is required, and cannot contain whitespace, semicolons, or commas. If you create two cookies with the same domain, path and name, the cookie that was there first will be obliterated by the newcomer.

Value

Once you have gotten past the required cookie header material, this is the area developers can use to store information. A value is also required, and cannot contain whitespace, semicolons or commas. Many times developers will use escape encoding to get around this restriction; see Chapters 6 and 7 for encoding techniques in CGI and JavaScript applications.

Domain

Only the pages from the domain which created a cookie are supposed to be allowed to read that cookie. Microsoft cannot read Netscape's cookies; IBM cannot read cookies from Dell. This field contains the domain name from which the cookie was created. Cookies from IBM's top-level domain will have a domain value of **.ibm.com**. As we'll see later, not all cookies actually come from pages in the domain listed, but as a general rule this simple protection can at least keep unwanted readers out of the cookie jar.

By default, the domain is set to the full domain name of the Web server that made the request or provided the page that created the cookie. A developer can use a smaller portion of the domain name to share cookies among several servers sharing a top-level domain. For instance, **myserver.mydomain.com** could request that the domain for its cookies be **.mydomain.com** instead of the full **.myserver.mydomain.com**. This way **hisserver.mydomain.com** and **herserver.mydomain.com** could both read and use those cookies. You cannot, however, request that a cookie have a domain of **.com** or a similar top-level domain; that would make it too easy to create cookies completely open to prying eyes. The domain limitations on cookie access are shown in Figure 2-1.

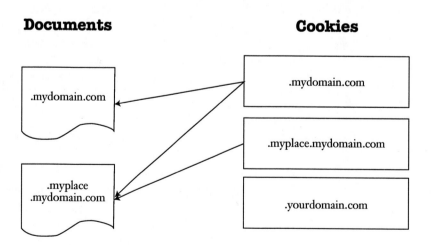

Figure 2-1
How Cookie Access can be Limited by Domains and Subdomains

Documents   **Cookies**

.mydomain.com

.myplace
.mydomain.com

.mydomain.com

.myplace.mydomain.com

.yourdomain.com

All domain names are prepended with periods to meet a requirement Netscape created for security—all domains must include at least two periods (for domains in the top-level **.com**, **.mil**, **.gov**, **.edu**, **.org**, **.net**, and **.int** domains) and possibly three (for all other domains). This prevents developers from creating generic **.com** cookies or even **.ny.us** cookies that can be read by a large number of servers.

Path

The Path value is similar to the domain, but restricts cookie usage within a site. By default, the path is set to the path for the page that creates the cookie. Only pages in the path specified by this part of the cookie can read or set the cookie. Suppose a developer creates a mall site that contained many different stores. All of the stores use the same shopping cart software, but do not want to share shopping carts because they need or want to have their own private cash registers. Each store could receive its own private cookie, kept separate from the others by a path, while sharing the general user information stored in a cookie for the site without a path specified. If the domain were **mymall.com**, then there could be one cookie for **mymall.com** with no path specified, and separate cookies for the paths `/storea` and `/storeb`. Store A could not read Store B's cookies at all, allowing competing shops to share a web server politely, but both stores could get general information from the cookie without a specified path. Figure 2-2 shows how path information can restrict cookie access.

Figure 2-2
How Cookie Access can be Limited by Path

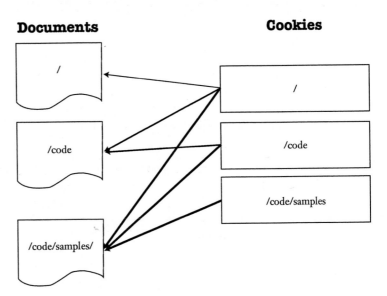

You should always set the path explicitly if you specify an expiration date for a cookie. Set the path to **/** if necessary. Netscape 1.1 will delete all cookies without a specified path when the user exits the browser.

Expires

Much like real cookies, browser cookies don't last forever. Some cookies disappear when the user quits the browser, while others can hang around for months or years. Most of the cookies detested by privacy advocates are of the more pemanent variety, allowing developers to track users between sessions. This variable holds the expiration date for the cookie, expressed in Greenwich Mean Time (GMT) in the format:

```
Wdy, DD-Mon-YYYY HH:MM:SS GMT
```

Wdy is the weekday (optional), DD is the date, Mon is the month, YYYY is the year, HH is the hour (in 24-hour time), MM is the minute, and SS is the second. If you leave this value blank, most browsers will hold on to the cookie for the duration of the session.

Some browsers, including Lynx, will delete all cookies when the user quits the browser no matter what the expires variable requests.

Secure

The Secure option allows developers to create cookies that are encrypted in transit, using HTTPS, SSL, or another means of providing security for all communications about this cookie between the server and the browser. This attribute has no value; unless it appears when the cookie is created, the cookie wll travel without any security.

At least in current browsers, the Secure option has no effect on the way cookies are stored on a user's machine. They remain unencrypted and available to anyone with access to the cookie files. Developers who need to keep cookie information away from prying eyes must implement their own encryption schemes.

Cookies Tomorrow: Version 1 and RFC 2109

Although the cookie technology in Version 0 is primitive, it has proven capable of a wide variety of tasks. RFC 2109 proposes to extend cookie abilities and provide extra information that will make it easier for users to manage cookies. RFC 2109 is in flux and there is no browser yet available that supports all of its features, but the basic structures are worth exploring. The general structure is similar to that of the original (Netscape) cookie, but many of the details are different. The following outline is an introduction to the improved cookie—later chapters will provide more depth on how to apply these tools.

Table 2-2
Structure of
Version 1 Cookies

Part	Value
Name	Value
Comment	Text that will be displayed to users considering whether to accept cookie
CommentURL	Site with more information on cookie
Discard	No value—cookie will be discarded upon browser quit if present
Domain	Originating domain name
Max-Age	Suggested lifetime of the cookie, in milliseconds from time of creation
Path	Path information for cookie
Port	Port information for cookie (0-65535)
Secure	No value—cookie will be transmitted securely if present.
Version	Should be 1 in all RFC 2109 cookies

Name

As it was in the older standard, the name is a sequence of characters that uniquely identifies the cookie. The name is required, and cannot contain whitespace, semicolons, or commas. If you create two cookies with the same domain, path, and name, the cookie that was there first will be obliterated by the newcomer. The only innovation here is that names beginning with the dollar sign ($) are reserved and may not be used by applications. These$4U is an acceptable name, but $4U is not.

Value

A value is a required part of the cookie. RFC2109 does not explicitly restrict the use of semicolons and whitespace, but developers will probably find it easier to stick to the old encoding for easier compatibility with the older cookie standards.

Comment

The Comment attribute is an innovation that allows developers to tell users why they are creating cookies. Although it is optional, I strongly recommend that developers use the comment to provide clear information about the purpose behind a cookie. If users have set their browsers to ask them before accepting cookies, this message will appear in the dialog box. The comment can give users a clearer picture of the cookie they're considering, and perhaps the comment will be persuasive.

CommentURL

CommentURL gives developers an opportunity to provide users with a more detailed explanation of what a cookie is supposed to do. If a user needs more information than the basic comment provides, and the browser displays this URL, the user can visit the site to get a clearer picture of why a particular cookie is attractive. It is unclear how many developers want to give away the secrets of their trade, or how many users will be interested in reading Web programming diagrams, but it is certainly an additional opportunity to communicate with users. Also, be sure that the site referenced by the CommentURL doesn't hand out cookies itself—users will end up negotiating a maze of dialog boxes to reach your explanation.

Discard

If the Discard attribute is present, the browser will discard the cookie when the program exits, no matter what the Max-Age of the cookie may be. This is very useful for creating cookies that could last for hours in certain cases (a user working on a project through a browser for a long time) without accidentally leaving the cookie behind when the work is complete. In this version of cookies, the expiration time is supposed to be enforced, and browsers are expected to clean up their cookies as the cookies expire. Most browsers using Version 0 only discarded expired cookies when the browser exited—discard simply *mandates* that they discard the cookie at browser exit. The Discard attribute, in combination with Max-Age, defines the lifespan of a cookie more precisely, giving programmers more control over the life of their data.

Domain

The Domain attribute works the same way it did in Version 0. The default domain is the domain name from which the cookie came, though the script setting the cookie may specify a subsection of that domain name—**www.foozball.tablesport.com** could specify a cookie for **.tablesport.com**. As in Version 0, the domain is stored with a period placed at the front, if the period wasn't specified to make it more difficult to create generic cookies that can be accessed by multiple domains.

Max-Age

Max-Age performs a function similar to that of Expires in the old standard, but with a clearer, stronger set of rules. Instead of providing an expiration date, Max-Age gives the browser a lifespan for the cookie measured in seconds. If Max-Age is set to 60, the cookie will last for one minute. At 3,600 it gets to live for an hour, at 86,400 it lasts a day, and so on. If Max-Age is set to zero, the cookie is deleted as soon as it is received. Max-Age must be set to a positive integer or zero; negative lifetimes are not permitted. Browsers are supposed to discard cookies as soon as their Max-Age has been reached, instead of waiting until the program is exiting. This means that you cannot count on a cookie you create in a session to last the duration of a transaction. To avoid temporary cookies that disappear too soon, give Max-Age a high value and use the Discard attribute to make sure they get deleted when your transaction is complete. Of course, if you really do want the cookie to stay around for a few months, just set Max-Age accordingly.

Path

Path works as it did in Version 0. If a path is specified, only URLs that contain that complete path are eligible to read or modify the cookie. Cookies for use site-wide should always explicitly have a path of **/**.

Port

Port is an additional feature of the new cookie standard. A single Web server could host a site with several levels of security, enforced by Web servers operating on different ports. Ports allow a single machine with a single IP address to have multiple TCP/IP applications running simultaneously. All traffic for an IP address goes to that machine; the IP stack on that machine examines the incoming packets and routes them to their proper application based on the port number assigned to the packet. Port numbers can range from 0-65,535, but 0-255 are generally reserved for specific system applications that need to have a standardized location. FTP is usually on port 21, Telnet is usually on port 23, and Web servers are on port 80. You can reconfigure these any way you like or even create new services on other ports, but most people stick to the standards.

Web servers can and do float among ports fairly frequently. The default port is 80, but many servers also use port 8080 or port 81. A single machine could have a Microsoft Internet Information Server on port 80, a Netscape Communications Server on port 81, and a Lotus Domino server on port 8080, each of which has its own set of pages and even its own administrator. While it is extremely unlikely that a hacker could break into a site, set up a parallel server on the same machine, and use that server to gather cookies, it might be possible for a rogue administrator or someone else with internal access to breach security that way. If you have data that need to be kept private, setting the port attribute is probably worthwhile. Just remember that cookies are usually stored in plain text on user machines, and a secret server could easily be brought to light by someone rooting through a cookie file on a client machine if cookies are left behind.

Secure

Secure behaves as it did in Version 0, demanding that the cookies be sent securely when transmitted between client and server. It does not require encryption of the cookie on the client, nor does it do anything to hide cookie values from the user.

Version

The Version attribute is required. For this version of the cookie standard, you should always specify `Version=1`. The Version attribute will dramatically simplify the process of updating the cookie standard in the future. As we will see, the standards developers had to come up with some intricate tricks to make the new and old cookies coexist without creating serious errors for the older servers and browsers.

For more information about RFC 2109, visit the IETF at **http://www.ietf.org** or the RFC 2109 versions site at **http://portal. research.bell-labs.com/~dmk/cookie-ver.html**.

The Future of Cookies

Although the proposals surrounding RFC 2109 are still very much a work in progress, there are always calls on the Internet for more features and more disclosure. While the Comment and CommentURL attributes give developers a space to explain themselves, some privacy advocates have asked for a classification system for cookies. Cookies for tracking banner advertisements could then be sorted out from cookies for shopping carts, without requiring the browser constantly to pester the user about whether or not to accept a particular cookie. More complex schemes that use encrypted keys and certification to provide a guarantee of proper cookie use (and automatic acceptance of "certified cookies") are also in the works. Others have suggested that the software tool which creates a cookie be specified as an attribute; as we will see later, Netscape's LiveWire already includes its identification in the names of the cookies it creates.

Several other proposals, including some examined below, create cookie-like data objects that are open to multiple readers—sparing users the need to enter their address at 30 different sites. Other cookie-like proposals provide for key exchanges to make encryption simpler and more automatic. At this point, however, it looks like cookies may stay simple, focusing on what they do best and allowing other structures to carry the burdens of identification and authentication.

## CHAPTER 3

Cookie Management

Even if you have never worked with cookies before, the odds are very good that there are a few on your computer. Unless you have taken strong measures to turn cookies off completely, Netscape, Microsoft, and a host of other companies have undoubtedly left a few on your hard drive. Before we move on to how to develop sites with cookies, we will take a look at how users can manage cookies in the major browsers, examine some additional privacy and cookie management tools, and consider the significant security and privacy issues that less than 4K of text can raise.

Security, Privacy, and Cookies

Cookies have been accused of all kinds of mayhem, from stealing email addresses to opening holes that unscrupulous developers use to collect enough bits about your identity to let them break in to your computer and financial accounts. The repeated claims of the browser vendors that cookies aren't capable of such dealings seem only to breed more concern among users. Unfortunately for the myths swirling around the Internet, the vendors are right—but there are still a number of issues that deserve a much closer examination. Cookies cannot spread viruses, steal your personal information, read your hard drive, or empty your bank account surreptitiously. On the other hand, cookies can allow server operators to track your movements much the way a grocery store check-cashing card or even a credit card can, and you may not appreciate being followed.

This section of the chapter details practices that many users find offensive. Defending yourself against these practices requires a fairly sophisticated understanding of what's involved, at least if you don't want to feel perpetually inconvenienced by the walls you build. If you plan to develop sites using any of these techniques, please conform to the guidelines for cookie usage that I suggest later in this chapter.

Many sites use cookies the way biologists use tags on animals. Fortunately, Web sites need not shoot their users with tranquilizer guns before clamping a tag into their ears or tatooing them. All they have to do is ask a user's browser to create a cookie. Once users have been "tagged" with cookies, it is very easy to follow their footsteps through a site. Sites often use this information to get a clearer picture of how users navigate the site, rather than sifting through page after page of log entries that provide only cryptic information like IP address, time, date, and the page received. When users are behind firewalls or proxies, the logs effectively lie; it looks like one user from a particular address is assaulting the site repeatedly and randomly. Using cookies allows developers to create sites that identify users uniquely without getting trapped in proxies or firewalls. The browser has to support cookies and the user has to accept them, but that still brings in around 80% of users. The state chart (Figure 3-1) for this scenario looks much like the border crossing scenario from the first chapter.

Many sites have adopted strategies like this, using server add-ons that collect the user's cookie every time a page is requested. Most of these tools simply assign the user an ID number that can easily be followed rather than filling the user's cookie with complex information that would require constant uploading and downloading. By analyzing a large number of the paths taken by users, sites can determine what their most (and least) popular areas are, what sections of a site work together best, and how user interests connect. Administrators can modify the site to make frequently visited pages easier to reach, and designers can get an idea of how their interface strategies have worked.

Figure 3-1
Examining a
Browser's Papers
at Every Step

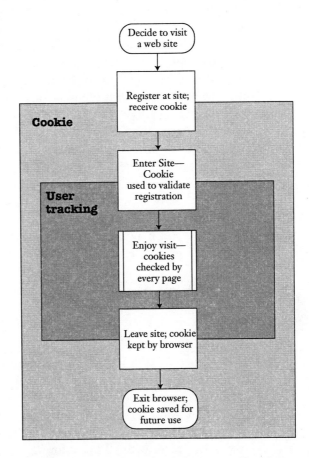

 We will examine one of these tools for tracking users, Microsoft Site Server, in Chapter 10.

This "following-around" gets more dramatic (and perhaps invasive) use from third-party banner advertisers and others with similar motives. When a page includes a banner ad from the advertiser's servers, the header information for the banner can arrive with its own request for a cookie. If

jimsdogs.com includes a banner ad that gets downloaded from **joesads.com**, you can end up with a cookie from **joesads.com**. When you visit **louisascats.com**, which also has a banner ad from **joesads.com**, **joesads** can read the cookie the previous ad left behind earlier, find out your current location, and keep track of your movements on **jimsdogs.com**, **louisascats.com**, and any other site that has a **joesads.com** banner. The operators of **joesads.com** can now put together a much more comprehensive profile than a single site operator could produce.

The official reason for using these cookies is to provide intelligent distribution of ads. Since **joesads.com** can follow you, they know which ads they have already displayed to you. This way they can adjust their mix so you do not get pummeled with identical ads at site after site. They can also use their knowledge of where you have been to target advertising to your interests, though keeping track of that would be a considerably more complex task for media buyers than figuring out who watches particular TV shows. More disturbing to many privacy advocates, these third-party sites become the sole source of a significant body of multisite information, which allows owners to sell or otherwise use these data for a significant price. While this practice may not effectively detail a particular individual, it makes it easy for people you may never have considered to study your movements and apply your preferences to their profits.

Microsoft's Site Server includes an effective way to track users across multiple sites. For more on this tool and it's implications, see Chapter 10.

Even some individual sites use this information at a higher level than just enhancing log data interpretation. Many sites offer freebies or information by mail, collecting demographic and other information about their visitors directly. A good programmer can collect the user's cookie identifier and connect the path information to the address information, to produce lists of users—complete with all the information needed for sales calls and demographic studie—sorted by interest.

If you want to protect yourself from cookie-based demographics collection, the best way to do it is not turning off cookies: it is lying about who you are, where you live, and everything else sites ask. Come up with a fake email address and name and use it wherever it seems appropriate. Only give out personal information in situations where you think it's worthwhile, and you will have a lot less to hide, though you may not feel wonderful about your new level of honesty. For a much easier and more sophisticated approach to this tactic, see the Lucent Personalized Web Assistant on page 48.

Users who spent a lot of time visiting a site are considered highly qualified targets for a stronger sales pitch. Cookies do not normally hold the sales information directly—most companies are discreet enough to keep the user's information on their server, linked to the user only by the slender thread of an ID number in a cookie (Figure 3-2):

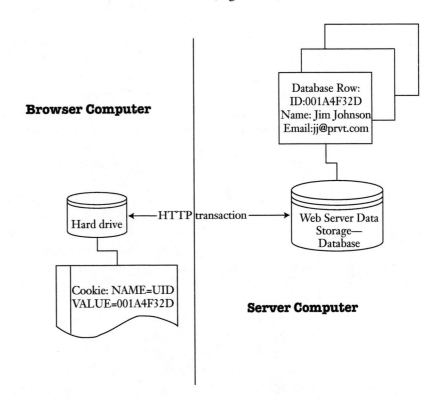

Figure 3-2
Cookie ID on the Client, User Information on the Server

In this situation, the database at the developer's site keeps all the user's information, minimizing the amount of information that has to be transferred back and forth. Privacy advocates frequently see this "hiding of information" on the server as even more of a menace than the cookies themselves, because users have no way of connecting to that server to find out what information about them is being kept. The file is private, the property of the site owner. Publicly storing all the information in the cookie at least makes it easier for users to figure out what Big Brother is thinking.

Cookies and "Spam"

If you have ever gotten one of those email messages with a subject line of "GET RICH QUICK—LIGHT WORK AT HOME FOR THOUSANDS OF $$$$$" or "BE THIN TOMORROW—THINK YOUR WAY TO FITNESS," or even something more reasonable but completely unsolicited, you have been "spammed." There are several accounts of how this Hormel meat product came to be associated with junk email, most of which cite a famous Monty Python routine about a restaurant that serves Spam with a wide variety of other foods—but every dish includes Spam. After you have been getting junk email on an account for a while, you will have many flavors of strange offers, all of which have less appeal than genuine Spam. My primary account on one of the major online services gets about five messages a day of junk at this point, and I have begun to keep my accounts in motion, never staying at a particular account for very long because of the spamstorm that inevitably pours down.

Many cookie opponents have tried to forge a link between "spam" and cookies. The powerful tracking abilities of cookies, they claim, combine with a marketer's email list to provide "validated" leads that can produce tons of unsolicited email. Adding to that the possibilities of third-party advertisers' building significant databases of user activity could lead to a "spam" free-for-all, where email accounts are overwhelmed by messages tangentially related to the site a user visited six months earlier in a strange display of slightly "targeted marketing."

Fortunately, the link is not nearly that simple. While some companies may use cookies to determine which of their visitors are worth contacting directly, few companies have come nearly that far and most are not even capable of creating a true targeted marketing solution at this point. For this scenario to happen, direct marketers would need to combine their data, building a Big Brother central database that combines demographic and address information with user Web visits. While this may sound like advertising's fabled golden bullet, the kinds of data that different developers have collected are quite randomly structured and only rarely interchangeable. Any organization willing to act as the clearinghouse for this activity would have to cope with the withering blasts from privacy advocates and likely legislation abolishing it. It would be an interesting court battle, but hardly an encouraging scenario for entrepreneurs and investors.

The real problem with email "spam" is not that it is commercial or even that it is semi-solicited at best. The "spam" problem arises because "spam" can be completely untargeted since there is virtually no cost to the sender. Why would a spammer want a targeted list of 100 users that costs the same as an untargeted list of two million? The cost of mailing for the two lists is not appreciably different, and the spammer only needs a tiny return rate on the larger list to make a greater profit. As a result, I get three get-rich-quick schemes a day in my email. While unsolicited email may develop new forms as Web sites collect more information, "spam" has very little to do with cookies.

   For more information on privacy and the net, and a considerably more hard-line approach to privacy, explore **http://www.junkbusters.com**. They have constantly updated news and commentary on cookies, junk mail, telemarketing, and other hassles of the postmodern age.

Controlling Your Cookies

If you are worried about Big Brother and want to keep advertisers and Web site marketers off your hard drive, there are a number of things you can do. If you are a Web developer who plans to be using cookies, you can use many of these same techniques to inspect and debug your cookies and to find out what happens when users refuse your cookies. Netscape and Microsoft browsers include a variety of options that let you refuse and inspect cookies. If those tools aren't enough, several third-party developers also offer cookie management tools. Finally, sometimes you can also open, edit, and delete the cookie files by hand—to satisfy your own curiosity, experiment, or help debug cookies.

By default, your browser will accept all cookies and keep them around until they expire. Recent versions of Lynx will normally accept all cookies, but "gobble" them when the program exits. Most browsers that accept cookies don't actually write to the cookie storage files until they exit.

Cookie Management Options in Netscape Browsers

Netscape created the cookie and now also provides options for rejecting cookies' creation. Netscape Navigator 2.0 and 3.0 browsers have allowed users to reject cookies individually, with a separate alert for each cookie. Netscape Communicator 4.0 and Navigator 4.0 offer additional options, which let you turn off cookies completely and also allow you to turn off cookies that come from third parties, usually advertisers. Navigator 3.0 has an option for requiring warnings for cookies on the Protocols tab under Options/Network Preferences, as shown in Figure 3-3.

Figure 3-3
Cookie
Management
Options
in Netscape
Navigator 3.0

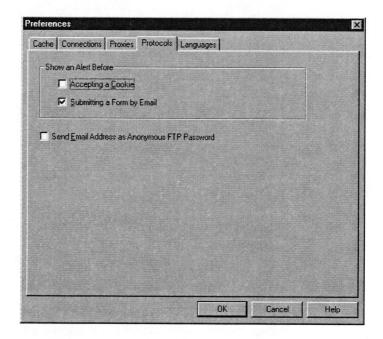

While this option allows you to accept and reject cookies, it also means that you must accept or reject every single cookie that comes your way, as shown in Figure 3-4.

Figure 3-4
Cookie Alert
Box in Netscape
Navigator 3.0

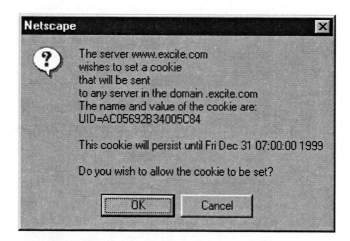

This alert box is slightly confusing—if you wish to accept the cookie, you click **OK**; to reject, click **Cancel**. Fortunately you do not have to go through this if the cookie is already set on your computer, because cookies that are already set don't bring up the alert box. Unfortunately, every time you visit a new site that uses cookies (or even revisit a site that has been polite and used cookies that expire quickly), you'll be deluged with these dialog boxes.

Turning off cookies completely in Netscape Navigator 3 and earlier browsers requires more dramatic action in the file system—see "Cookie Files" on page 50 for more details

Netscape Communicator and Navigator 4 offer a greater range of options, allowing you to reject all cookies, accept them individually, or accept all cookies. They also provide an option that prohibits cookies from third-party sites (usually banner advertisers). Netscape moved all of these options to the Advanced item under Edit/Preferences, as shown in Figure 3-5.

Figure 3-5
Cookie
Management
Options
in Netscape
Navigator and
Communicator 4

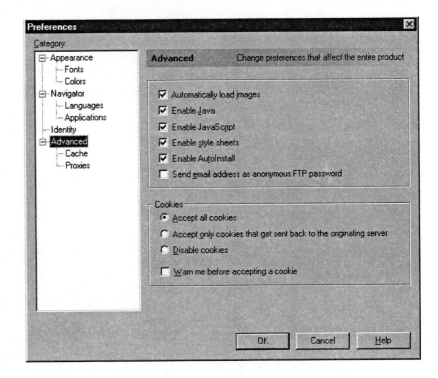

Cookie-haters are spared the trouble of rejecting cookies individually, those who are a little nervous about third-party cookies can turn them off, and people who just want convenience can accept all the cookies they get. Those who are more particular still have the option of choosing whether to accept each cookie individually, though the dialog box is still confusing, continuing to use **OK** and **Cancel** for Accept and Reject, as shown in Figure 3-6.

Figure 3-6
Cookie Alert
Box in Netscape
Navigator 4

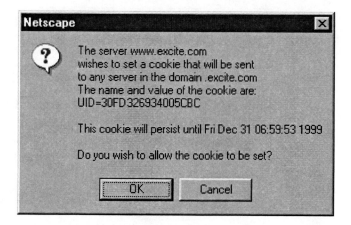

While this provides a wider selection of cookie options, it still fails to meet the demands of the cookie opponents. First, Netscape ships its browsers with a default setting of accepting all cookies without a warning. The privacy advocates would like to see this changed to requiring at least a warning, and preferably even disabling cookies entirely. Second, the choices are still weak. It might be nice to have options that always accept cookies from certain specified domains while excluding others, or accept cookies that expire quickly while prohibiting those that last more than a specified period of time. Third, once you've accepted a cookie, there is no easy way to jettison it.

The final and perhaps most significant problem is that Netscape's option for "accepting only cookies that get sent back to the originating server" doesn't always work. If **joesads.com** wants to collect the information about its ads from **jimsdogs.com** and the user has set the option to block that cookie, **joesads.com** has two choices. First, they can work with **jimsdogs.com** to move part of their cookie mechanism to the **jimsdogs.com** server. It's more effort than most banner ad companies would like to put into their work, but this option makes it more or less impossible to block these kinds of cookies. The **jimsdogs.com** server would receive a request from a user, check their **jimsdogs.com** cookie, and send it on to the **joesads.com** server. The **joesads.com** server would then reply to **jimsdogs.com** to tell it which ad to send out. It is a lot more work, but not that difficult to do. Another, simpler, option is for **jimsdogs.com** to create a domain name entry called **joesads.jimsdogs.com**, pointing directly to the same machine as **joesads.com**! The server at **joesads** would have to manipulate multiple cookies on the same user's machine and would not be able to track ads across multiple sites as easily, but could still collect a significant amount of information. Netscape could keep that from working by requiring that the cookie come from precisely the same domain (i.e. **jimsdogs.com** only, not **joesads.jimsdogs.com**) as the page it starts from, but implementing this would break many cookie-based sites and probably require a significant change in the standard. This option helps to segment site data more cleanly, but doesn't really stop the advertisers from collecting it.

Cookie Management Options in Microsoft Internet Explorer

Microsoft offers similar cookie management tools in its Internet Explorer browsers for Windows, and much more extensive tools in Internet Explorer for the Macintosh. Internet Explorer 3 and 4 for the Macintosh provide dramatically better cookie management tools than any of their competitors, beating out even many of the third parties who have entered the market with tools built specifically for cookie control. It has also been unusual in the last several years for any of the features of the Macintosh version of a Microsoft product to be significantly ahead of the Windows version.

The cookie options for all of the Windows versions are available in the Options window offered at the bottom of the View menu. In Internet Explorer 3.0, cookie management relies on a single checkbox, `Warn before accepting "cookies"` in the **Advanced** tab of the **Options** window, as shown in Figure 3-7.

If you turn off the warning, all cookies will be accepted automatically. By turning it on, you get a warning message like Figure 3-8 every time a site tries to hand you a new cookie.

This is clearer than the Netscape version, at least providing **Yes** and **No** rather than **OK** and **Cancel**, though Microsoft's warning that the page may not display correctly is a clear attempt to make you say yes. It does not tell you the name of the cookie, either. As in Netscape Navigator, rejecting cookies this way requires that you inspect every single cookie that comes your way, making a visit to a site that uses multiple cookies for a shopping cart an extremely tedious experience.

Microsoft has improved these features in Internet Explorer 4.0, providing the additional option of disabling all cookies. Cookies are in a similar location, though the cookie options are way down the list (see Figure 3-9).

Figure 3-7
Cookie Option
in Internet
Explorer 3.0
for Windows 95

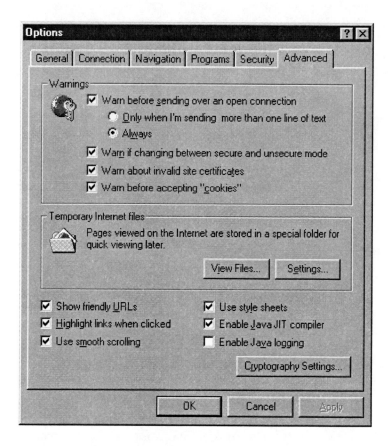

Figure 3-8
Cookie Warning
in Internet
Explorer 3.0
for Windows 95

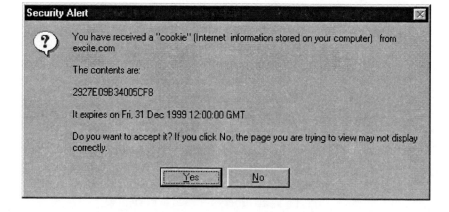

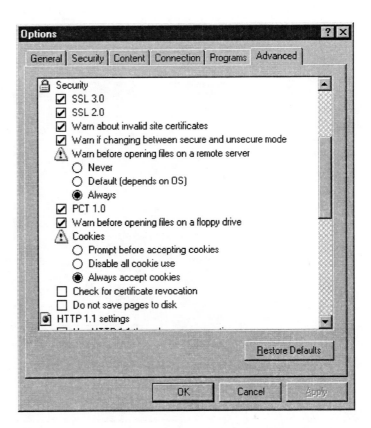

Figure 3-9
Cookie Options
in Internet
Explorer 4.0
for Windows 95

Disabling all cookies at least spares you the trouble of inspecting cookies if you don't plan to be accepting any of them. The `Prompt before accepting cookies` option gives you total control on a cookie-by-cookie basis. Internet Explorer 4 starts out by providing you even less information than the other browsers, and offers those who accept cookies "a more personalized browsing experience," as seen in Figure 3-10.

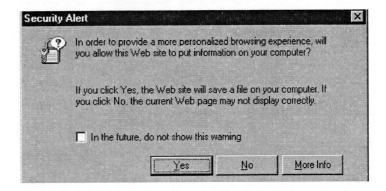

Figure 3-10
Cookie Options
in Internet
Explorer 4.0 for
Windows 95, Pt.1

Clicking the **More info** button, brings up far more detail—all of the information being stored in the cookie, in fact, as shown in (Figure 3-11).

Figure 3-11
Cookie Options
Expanded
in Internet
Explorer 4.0
for Windows 95

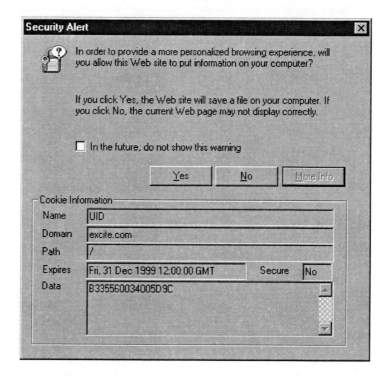

The best cookie management currently available in any major browser is definitely that of Internet Explorer 3.01 and 4.0 for the Macintosh. Microsoft has provided Macintosh users with far more control over their cookie options than any of the other contenders, providing options that allow users to accept cookies individually, or by site as well as the usual "accept all" or "never accept" options. Not only that, but Microsoft has provided a cookie management area (in the cookie area of the window revealed by **Edit/Preferences**), shown in Figure 3-12 that allows users to inspect their cookies easily and delete them as they please.

The Macintosh versions of Internet Explorer offer a better set of choices for cookie management: **Never Ask**, **Ask for Each Site**, **Ask for Each Cookie**, and **Never Accept**. The **Ask for Each Site** option is a significant improvement, making it easier to work with sites that put out multiple cookies. (Ironically, it does not always work with Microsoft's site, which uses cookies from both **microsoft.com** and **msn.com**.) When a cookie arrives, if you have asked for a warning, you will see a dialog box similar to that in the Windows versions of Internet Explorer, as shown in Figure 3-13.

Figure 3-12
Cookie
Management
in Internet
Explorer 3.01
for the Macintosh

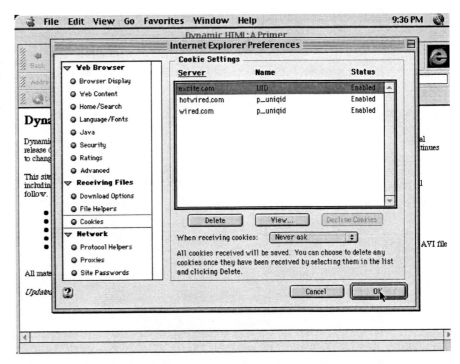

Figure 3-12
Cookie
Management
in Internet
Explorer 3.01
for the Macintosh

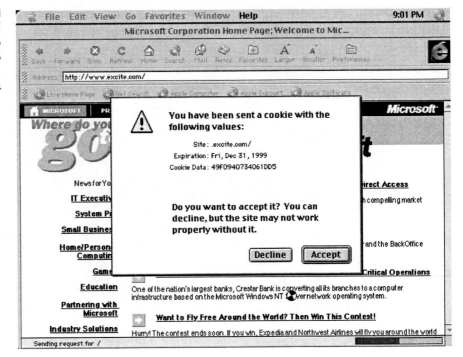

Figure 3-13
Cookie Request
in Internet
Explorer 3.01
for the Macintosh

While Internet Explorer 3 and 4 for the Mac lack the detail option of Internet Explorer 4, they go much further in allowing users to manage cookies once they have arrived. The list of cookies is open to exploration (see Figure 3-14), and users can delete cookies at will. Best of all, they can disable cookies from particular sites, locking out all further cookies from that site (with the **Disable Cookie** button) if they find the contents of the cookie too unattractive.

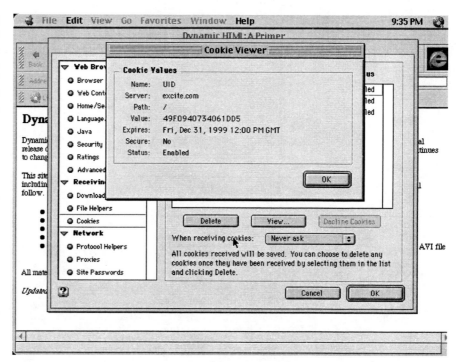

Figure 3-14
Cookie Detail
Viewing in
Internet Explorer
3.01 for the
Macintosh

Internet Explorer also lacks the option for rejecting third-party cookies. The other significant feature that is still missing in all of these browsers is the "gobbling" built into Lynx. None of the major browsers allows users to keep cookies around just for the duration of the browsing session. While most users do not mind accepting a cookie for a temporary project, like a shopping cart, none of the tools provided above makes it easy for users to keep out cookies that persist beyond the browsing session. This failing, and the lack of cookie management features in most of the browsers, has created a small market in add-ons for all the major browsers.

Third-party Programs

Since none of the browsers does a superb job of managing cookies, other companies have stepped in with their own solutions. Some of these products offer cookie management tools, while others simply wipe out your cookies on a regular basis. The most intriguing are "anonymizing" proxy servers, which let you surf the Web without ever encountering problems caused by cookies.

The listing of cookie management tools that follows is by no means complete, nor do I endorse any of these products. This section is here to encourage readers to look beyond the browsers for cookie management tools, not to recommend any particular management tool.

Luckman Interactive's Anonymous Cookie is available as a free download from **http://www.luckman.com** for Windows 95, Windows NT, and the Macintosh. The Macintosh version has a few more features, allowing you to specify which browsers you want to prevent from receiving cookies, but otherwise both versions work about the same way. When you activate Anonymous Cookie (by running the program on the Mac or by double-clicking the star icon in the bottom right of the Windows Taskbar or right-clicking it and checking **Anonymous**), you can surf as usual. Netscape and Internet Explorer behave as they usually do, with one significant difference: they can't read the cookie files that may have existed previously, and they can't write any new cookies to disk. Sites that use cookies will still work, but all cookies will disappear when you quit the browser. Luckman recommends that you turn off all cookie management in the browser, since none of the cookies will be remaining with you for long. When you come out of anonymous mode (which requires quitting the browser), you will be able to use cookies as usual.

The Windows version only works with the latest version of the browser you have installed. If you have Netscape Navigator 2.0, 3.0, and 4.0 all installed on the same machine, Anonymous Cookie only works with 4.0. This is not a problem with Internet Explorer for Windows, because Microsoft only allows you to have one version installed at a time.

WebEraser, for Windows 95 and NT, is available at **http://www.weberaser. com** for a small fee. It takes a more comprehensive approach to Web privacy, obliterating all of the files kept by browsers that contain personal information. It does not keep cookies from operating, but it incinerates all persistent cookies. In addition, it gives you considerable control over other parts of your browsing environment, include history files, cache, and registry entries, as seen in Figure 3-15.

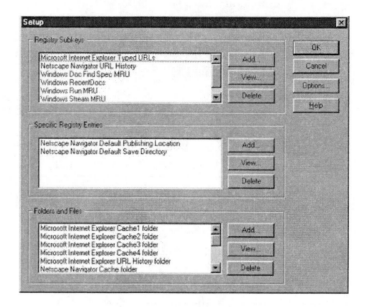

Privacy Software Corporation (**http://www.nsclean.com/**) offers a similar product in versions for Netscape and Internet Explorer browsers. (Windows 95 and NT versions were available at this writing; a Macintosh version is in development.) NSClean and IEClean give users similar control over their browsers (see Figure 3-16), and include a feature that allows you to specify which cookies are obliterated, allowing you to keep cookies you find genuinely useful. NSClean and IEClean vary in price depending on the version of browser with which you wish to use it.

Cookie Monster 1.51 for the Macintosh is a simple program that deletes the cookie files for both Netscape and Microsoft browsers every time you start your computer. (Cookie Monster's name may be changing shortly, because of a trademark conflict with Children's Television Workshop.) The program is available at **http://www.geocities.com/Paris/1778**.

Cookie Magic, a free program from Ziff-Davis, doesn't take any steps to block cookies, but it does allow you to inspect and delete cookies and also maintains a log of all cookie activity. Cookie Magic is not as useful for establishing a cookie blockade, but provides the best tools I've seen yet for monitoring cookie transactions (see Figure 3-17). Developers who need a debugging tool will find Cookie Magic a very useful management option. Cookie Magic is available from **http://www5.zdnet.com/anchordesk/story/story_579.html**.

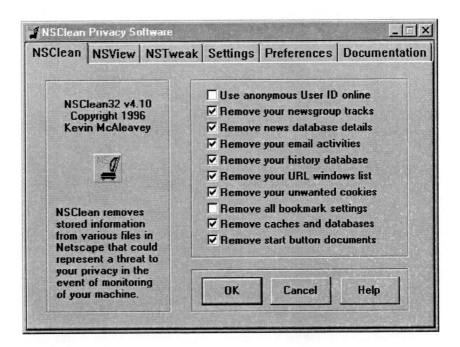

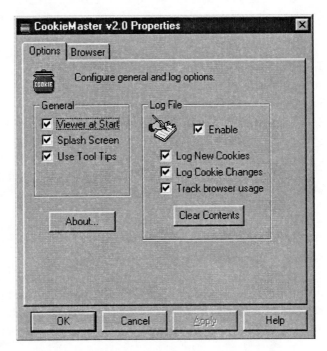

Proxies for Privacy—A Different Approach

All of the other tools discussed in this chapter work on the client. Individual users make decisions about whether to accept cookies and which cookies to accept, and what personal information to divulge. Each browser offers slightly different options, and must be configured individually. If a company decides to set a policy of not accepting cookies, it means that the computing staff have to visit every workstation and change the options on each browser installed. Because of the relatively weak options available on some browsers, even this dramatic effort may not be enough to stop the influx of cookies. Centralizing privacy management on a server can address these problems, making it easier for companies and individuals to manage privacy policies. A few companies have started to consider totally different techniques for hiding user identities with server-based technologies.

Lucent Technologies has introduced the Lucent Personalized Web Assistant (LPWA), a proxy server that lives on Lucent's own servers. A technology demonstration (use at your own risk), the LPWA is provided as a public service and as a technology testbed. The LPWA doesn't stamp out cookies; instead it takes the alternate route mentioned above of hiding identities. The LPWA uses a sophisticated set of encryption techniques and some basic proxying technology to create an anonymous browsing environment. Using as a basis the popular but basic Apache server, the researchers at Lucent's Bell Labs have made it possible for users to have one identity that connects them to the proxy, which then provides identity management. The proxy fragments that identity by encoding the username and password information users need to have to access sites using an algorithm that includes both the identity of the user and the name of the site. It sounds complicated, but it is not that messy in practice. It even allows users to receive email from the sites at which they've "registered" without having to provide their real email addresses.

Users need to set their browsers to use **http://lpwa.com**, port 8000 as their proxy server. When they start browsing, they'll have to enter an email address and a password, which the LPWA will use as keys for the rest of the browsing. The LPWA can spare users the trouble of maintaining a list of usernames and passwords for multiple sites. When users register at a site, they can enter /u for a username, /p for a password, and /@ for an email address. The LPWA intercepts these characters on their way back to the registration site and creates a unique (and indecipherable) username and password from the user's email address, password, and the domain name of the site. If email arrives from a site, the LPWA can decipher the email address and forward the email to the appropriate recipient.

The proxy authentication process provides the LPWA with enough information to maintain a session. Username and password get sent to the proxy from the browser with every request, performing a very similar service to that provided by cookies. Once the request goes past the LPWA, however, the HTTP request has been stripped of all identifying information, including the proxy authorization, browser IP address, machine type, and referring page. The information is quite sterile, made useless to most demographic and many tracking tools.

The LPWA does not filter cookies, depending instead on its tools for protecting your identity in the first place. In this scheme, cookies that relate to a non-traceable identity are reasonably harmless and provide more convenience than risk. They also make it easier for Web users to reach the kinds of sites that LPWA is designed to allow them to use privately. This system offers users who want privacy an easy way to maintain their anonymity without having to turn off cookies, allowing them to take advantage of sites that require cookies without fear of giving away their identity.

The LPWA is not a perfectly anonymous system. Users have to trust Lucent Technologies, which keeps track of all requests and handles all encryption. The transactions between the LPWA proxy and the Web site you are visiting are stripped of all personal information, but a hacker who can intercept the deciphered communications between your browser and the LPWA could conceivably track your movements. Because traffic (except that originating from Lucent) has to cross the Internet to reach the LPWA, Internet-involved communications is still open and unencoded. The LPWA cannot do anything to SSL-encrypted secure transactions, which are designed explicitly to guard against any third-party intervention of the type the LPWA depends on. Secure transactions simply pass through. At this point, there is also not very much the LPWA can do to anonymize transactions—credit cards are traceable by their very nature. Because it cannot apply the same magic to postal mail that it can to electronic mail, the LPWA does not do anything for address, city and state fields in forms. Any information you give away will still pass through. The LPWA has one other major drawback at this time: if your machine cannot reach Lucent's server, you will not be able to connect to sites for which you used the server to register. The LPWA's features (except for its ability to cloak IP address of the user) could be built into Web browsers, making this a non-issue. There is no sign of this identity management yet in any commercial products, but it may be on the horizon.

Junkbusters Corporation, whose site is dedicated to Internet privacy issues, has introduced the Internet Junkbuster Proxy, a free proxy server that stops cookies and many banner advertisements from reaching your browser. It does not offer the identity-shielding features of the LPWA, but it does cut down drastically on the amount of advertising traffic you will receive as well as shielding your browser from cookies. The Proxy differs from the LPWA because you can download and install this proxy server on your own machines, sparing you extreme dependence on another company's servers. You can customize its blocking list, allowing you to respond to new banner ad companies and other perceived nuisances directly. Unfortunately, this solution cuts users off from the potential benefits of cookies, but those who want nothing to do with cookies may find this attractive. Installing the proxy server requires a UNIX machine, which puts it out of the reach of the average user. Still, UNIX hackers, system administrators, and Internet service providers may want to take a look at this innovative piece of software, which ships complete with source code. Companies that want to let their employees browse the Web without wasting network bandwidth will definitely like its customizable demolition of banner advertisements. The Internet Junkbuster is available for download at **http://www.junkbusters.com/ht/en/ijb.html**.

Cookie Files: Examining and Blockading Cookies Directly

Cookies work the same way in both Microsoft Internet Explorer and the Netscape Communicator and Navigator browsers, but the two companies store them differently. Internet Explorer devotes a directory to cookies, while Navigator and Communicator both keep cookies in a single text file. Reading the cookies directly can be helpful, though recent programming techniques have tended to make cookie contents less revealing.

Netscape Navigator stores all of its cookies in one large file—`cookies.txt` on Windows machines, "Cookies" on UNIX machines, and MagicCookie on Macintoshes. While earlier versions of Netscape allowed users to edit the cookie files directly, more recent versions seem to detect changes and incinerate the file. While you can experiment, don't be surprised when Netscape eats your cookie file after an editing session. Version 3 of Netscape for Windows stores its `cookies.txt` file in the Navigator folder, usually `C:\Program Files\Netscape\Navigator`, unless you installed the program elsewhere. Version 4 uses a separate directory for its cookie files, allowing it to keep track of cookies separately for multiple logins on the same machine. Usually the `cookies.txt` file will be in the `C:\Program Files\Netscape\Users\`*username*`\` directory. If you work on a single-user machine that isn't normally on a network, the file may be at `C:\Program Files\Netscape\Users\`. To find it easily, just use the **Find Files** or **Folders** option on the **Start** button and look for "cookies." If you have a cookie file, it should turn up.

The files for all versions of Netscape, whatever the name and location, use the same format. One of my own cookie files appears as Figure 3-18.

```
# Netscape HTTP Cookie File
# http://www.netscape.com/newsref/std/cookie_spec.html
# This is a generated file! Do not edit.

.msn.com                TRUE   /   FALSE   899560947     MSN2.0Splash   2
.microsoft.com          TRUE   /   FALSE   937422000     MC1
        GUID=BD9A45B3BD8A45B3BD9A44B3BD9A45B3
.msn.com                TRUE   /   FALSE   937422000     MC1
        GUID=9fc039f2f81911d088a408002bb74f65
.doubleclick.net        TRUE   /   FALSE   1920499140    id
        8378abe
.wired.com              TRUE   /   FALSE   946684799     p_uniqid
        zkuw8P4N6FGU+A/2GC
.hotwired.com           TRUE   /   FALSE   946684799     p_uniqid
        zkevsO4AzF8wir4t1C
.netscape.com           TRUE   /   FALSE   946684799     NETSCAPE_ID
        10010408,110381fd
.barnesandnoble.com TRUE   /   FALSE   883612800     userid
        C795413440
.focalink.com           TRUE   /   FALSE   946641600     SB_ID
        0873072056000040615391431541052
```

As you can see, most of these cookies are simply identification numbers, various sites use to track my movements. None of them, except the MSN2.0Splash cookie that Microsoft Network uses so it knows that I have installed a plugin, has any meaningful content. I have no way of knowing what information the cookie keepers have collected from me, or how they use this tracking information. Some of the cookies are from sites I have visited, while other cookies are from advertising banners—**doubleclick.net** and **focalink.com**, for instance. The first entry going across is the domain for the cookie. The second entry, TRUE indicates whether the cookie was set by an HTTP header (TRUE) or by a JavaScript call (FALSE). The next entry, / is the path variable. All of these cookies have used / for the path, allowing any page on their site to access this cooke. The next entry, FALSE in all of these examples, indicates whether or not this is a secure cookie; secure cookies are not encrypted in this file, but they would be encrypted if sent across the Internet. The next value, a giant number, is the expiration date for the cookie, expressed in seconds since midnight GMT, January 1, 1970. The last two values are the critical name and value pair. As you might expect, few of these cookies give much meaning to either their name or their value.

Microsoft's Internet Explorer takes a different approach to cookie management. All Internet Explorer cookies are kept in a cookies directory under the Windows directory, with a few mysterious .dat files. Every cookie gets its own text file, named with the username (taken from the login name for Windows) followed by an @ sign, the domain name of the cookie, and a number indicating the sequence in which cookies from that domain arrived. Opening these files is close to useless; while you can read the name and value, Internet Explorer has encoded the rest of the values, filling the text file with numbers that have no apparent relationship to the cookie values as originally set. When you have been surfing for a while, the files in this directory can begin to pile up, as shown in Figure 3-19.

Figure 3-19
Internet Explorer
Cookies Directory

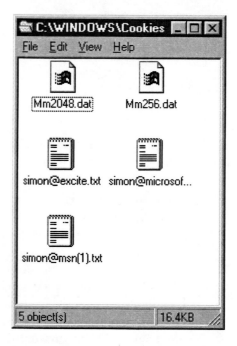

One significant advantage of this approach is that it is very easy to find particular cookies and delete them. It is even possible to destroy cookies from particular sites, because the domain name is part of the file name.

If you are a Windows 95 or NT user and get tired of deleting cookies by hand, you can automate the process with batch files that run every time you start your machine. (Macintosh users can use Cookie Monster or AppleScript to achieve similar results.) Batch files may feel like a step backward to the days of DOS, but they remain very good at handling a list of tasks on a regular basis without much user intervention. Writing batch files that delete cookie files is not a very difficult task, requiring only a few simple commands.

You can create similar files in Windows 3.1; but the techniques covered here are written for Windows 95 and NT 4.0 users.

If you have never written or edited a batch file, don't be afraid. A batch file is simply a list of commands that are executed in sequence. It is like a little program that you write using the commands that you would normally use at the DOS prompt. We will use a few extra command structures that you might not encounter in your average DOS session, but for the most part batch files are not complex programming demanding the skills of experts.

Obliterating Netscape cookies is easy, though it is pretty blunt—your batch file will delete all the cookies at one swipe. The first step in building this file is finding your `cookies.txt` file. If you're using Windows 95, click the **Start** button on the Taskbar, move the pointer up to **Find...**, and pick **Files** or **Folders...** off the submenu that appears. In the **Named** box, enter cookies.txt. Click on **Find Now**, and eventually your computer will dredge up your Netscape cookie file (as seen in Figure 3-20). Write down the path that it brings up—you may have to resize the columns by dragging the title bars to see the whole path. If you have Netscape Navigator 3, it will normally be `C:\Program Files\Netscape\Navigator`; if you have Navigator or Communicator 4 it will be `C:\Program Files\Netscape\Users\`*username*, where *username* is your Windows login name. This path may vary depending on where you installed the browser—make sure to write down the exact path.

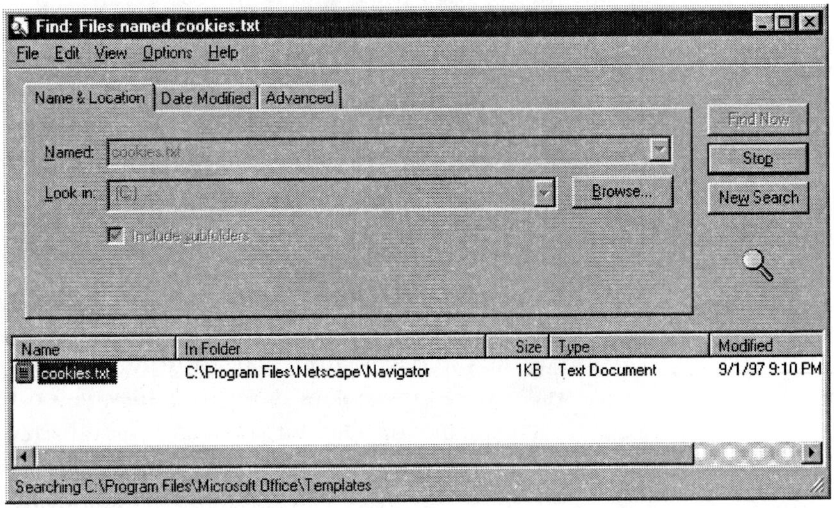

Figure 3-20
Find Dredging for
Cookie Files

Now that we've found the cookie, we can write a small program to incinerate it. Start Notepad (available on the **Start** menu under **Programs/Acces-
sories/Notepad**) and type in the following, substituting the path to your
cookie file for *NSCookiePath*:

```
@ECHO OFF
IF NOT EXIST "NSCookiePath\cookies.txt" GOTO END
DEL "NSCookiePath\cookies.txt"
:END
```

Save this file with a .bat extension—ncookdel.bat, for instance. If you
want to watch your batch file in action, you can leave off the first line. (You
will want to include it eventually, unless you enjoy closing DOS windows
by hand.) This little program checks to make sure there is a
cookies.txt file to delete, to avoid getting an error, then deletes it if it is
present. If it is not present, the program just jumps to the END label at the
end of the file. (The colon makes it a label and allows you write batch files
with more meaningful IF statements.) To make it run every time you start
the computer, put it in the C:\Windows\StartMenu\Programs\
Startup\ directory, or add a line that calls the batch file you have just
created to your C:\AUTOEXEC.BAT file. If you prefer, you can also just
add the contents of the batch file directly to the end of your
AUTOEXEC.BAT file.

Deleting the cookie files for Internet Explorer is a bit easier, because
Internet Explorer always puts the files in the same place no matter where
the program is installed. The Cookies folder lives in the main directory that
holds the Windows system files, normally C:\Windows directory in Windows 95 machines. (On Windows NT machines, it will be in the main
Windows NT directory, usually C:\WINNT.) Check to make sure the
Cookies folder is in the right place, then enter this code into Notepad or a
similar text editor:

```
@ECHO OFF
IF NOT EXIST " C:\Windows\Cookies\*.txt " GOTO END
DEL C:\Windows\Cookies\*.txt
:END
```

It works the same way, only it deletes all the separate cookie files that Internet Explorer has created in your directory instead of just deleting one large
cookies.txt file. To make this run every time you start your computer,
follow the directions given above for the Netscape version. Because Windows 95 stores its cookies in separate files, you can also single out cookies
you actually like or need for survival. Just add a few RENAME commands to
the file. For instance, if you wanted to spare a cookie named
simon@msn(1).txt you could use the following batch program:

```
@ECHO OFF
RENAME "simon@msn(1).txt" "simon@msn(1).txy"
IF NOT EXIST " C:\Windows\Cookies\*.txt " GOTO END
DEL C:\Windows\Cookies\*.txt
:END
RENAME "simon@msn(1).txy" "simon@msn(1).txt"
```

This will probably get tedious if you have a list of 20 cookies to protect. When it gets too complicated, you will probably want to turn to one of the programs mentioned above.

You can also combine the two versions to create a super cookie-killer:

```
@ECHO OFF
IF NOT EXIST " C:\Windows\Cookies\*.txt "GOTO NS
DEL C:\Windows\Cookies\*.txt
:NS
IF NOT EXIST "NSCookiePath\cookies.txt" GOTO END
DEL " NSCookiePath \cookies.txt"
:END
```

A few other direct techniques for are also available for cookie blocking. Rather than deleting the Netscape `cookies.txt` file, you can just mark it read-only. If you want to delete the cookies you have first, delete the file and create a new blank text file named `cookies.txt`. Find your `cookies.txt` file in the file system, and right-click it. Select **Properties** from the menu that appears, and check the **Read-only** box as shown in Figure 3-21.

Figure 3-21
Making the
`cookies.txt` File
Read-only

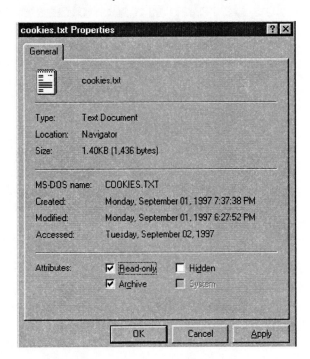

Netscape will continue to function normally; it just won't be able to save persistent cookies between sessions. You can do the same thing to the `C:\Windows\Cookies` directory, but Internet Explorer seems capable of figuring it out and turns off the write protection in some versions. Stopping Internet Explorer effectively requires a visit to the Windows Registry.

Several techniques for blocking cookies by deleting Registry entries are available on the Internet, but they change fairly regularly with browser versions. If you choose to explore the Registry and delete browser configuration information, you are definitely working at your own risk. Making mistakes in the Registry can break your browser or even lobotomize the operating system. Because of this risk and the ever-changing nature of Registry entries, this chapter will not cover that technique. The batch files and the third-party programs presented above should give even the most ardent privacy advocates the tools they need to protect themselves against invasion.

For the latest developments in cookie and cookie blocking techniques, you may want to explore **http://www.cookiecentral.com**, a good source of up-to-date cookie resources.

Should You Develop with Cookies?

After an entire chapter filled with techniques for stopping cookies, you may be wondering why it might still be worthwhile to use them. Cookies are loved and loathed. Programmers who need a way to preserve information between web pages love them, while privacy advocates loathe them. The battles over cookies are only beginning, and most likely will grow hotter before they finally cool. Webmasters of sites that use cookies are often deluged with email protesting the use of this tiny intruder, and some developers refuse to work on sites that make use of them. Companies who use cookies have had a difficult time coping with the vitriolic blasts of certain users, and apologetic explanations of cookie usage are starting to appear on a number of sites.

The remainder of this book explores the use of cookies in a wide variety of situations. I obviously feel that cookies are a useful tool, not an evil that should be banned as quickly as possible. Still, cookies are open to some level of abuse, and developers who attempt to abuse them can give the entire field a bad name. While most of their attempts will likely fail (since cookies are not very good at stealing secrets), they increase the level of concern and drive more users to turn off their cookies entirely. This leaves in the lurch programmers who need to apply cookies to real problems, since users who have disabled cookies won't be able to make those sites work.

At the moment, cookies are most useful for the kinds of applications deployed on intranets. Intranets have been touted as the solution to all of corporate computing's problems, and intranet applications undertake far more ambitious tasks than their Internet counterparts. Intranet applications are often complex, many-headed creatures that try to do work in a browser that was previously performed on a terminal or even on a PC. Many intranet applications are used to connect to legacy applications that may not be able to cope with the statelessness of the Web protocols. In this situation, cookies can be a critical tool for applying new interfaces to old applications without spending a fortune to rewrite the old application from the ground up. Even newer applications have had to deal with state issues, as developers who are used to the older client-server development tools adjust to the strange new world of the Web, which offers far fewer tools for creating the extended sessions necessary to accomplish more complex tasks. While corporate users may be as suspicious of their employer's motives for using cookies, it is generally easier to explain the business reasons for using a cookie to a fellow employee than to an irate user thousands of miles away who has no reason to trust you.

Because the Internet is a far wilder place than a corporate network, and because Internet developers have far less contact (and opportunities to build trust) with end users than do in-house intranet developers, a few guidelines for using cookies responsibly seem to be in order. These suggestions are also useful to intranet developers, who will probably have an easier time meeting them. My first suggestion is that developers use cookies only where they provide a real convenience to the user—and I don't mean junk email. While every salesperson in the world likes to think the world needs a product, the average person on the street is probably not interested. Cookies are not a great tool for generating leads, and making people into leads is not usually doing them a favor. Use cookies where they spare the user effort in navigating a site, or where state information is critical to making a site work. Otherwise, leave them alone and use other tools—cookie substitutes —that can do the same job.

My second suggestion is simply full disclosure. Be ready when users complain that you're wasting 1K on their hard drive, and that they don't feel like giving you that real estate for free. Have an explanation of how your site works and why you need cookies. It does not have to give away all the programming details or encourage hackers to blast away your site. The explanation should cover the processes involved in navigating the site and the contribution made by cookies as state maintenance tools. If you use cookies only in situations where a complex application genuinely needs state maintenance, you will have an easier time making your case. Not every user will be willing to listen, but some may calm down and a few may even prove sympathetic.

Make your cookies as small and short-lived as possible. If a cookie does not need to last beyond the browser session, don't tell it to expire two years from its arrival. Only a few cookies really need extended lifespans, and none of them should ever need to occupy more than a tiny patch of real estate. Use as few cookies as possible to accomplish a task, because users who have asked for the cookie warning are likely to become hostile after handling multiple requests for creating cookies. Users who are willing to accept one cookie may not be likely to accept four. If your application requires all the cookies it creates, you may find it crashing mysteriously after users have accepted five cookies but rejected the other three. Bombarding users with cookies is never a good idea.

Finally, never put confidential information in your cookies, including usernames and passwords. If you must include some potentially compromising information, encrypt it. Cookies are not secure containers. Anyone with a text editor can read them, and users who find that someone took the information and used it against them are bound to be angry. Make your cookies as safe as possible.

With those important caveats, we'll move on to cookie creation and development.

4

Client-side Cookie Scripting

While most cookie applications are created with server-side programming, client-side scripting is a powerful tool for certain applications and a useful supplement in others. Setting and reading cookies on the client—the browser—provides a lightweight tool for many cookie applications. JavaScript and VBScript offer similar tools for cookie management, and give developers access to all cookie properties. As we will see, there are some limitations, and the examples in this chapter will be fairly different from the examples in later chapters. Still, the tools you acquire in this chapter will help you manage, debug, and monitor your server-side applications, while filling some critical gaps in the cookie toolbox. Learning client-side scripting will also give you a significant advantage with Active Server Page and LiveWire development (Chapters 8 and 7 respectively), where the same languages and many of the same tools are applied on the server.

Why Client-side?

Most of the applications described in this book use cookies to maintain state between successive calls to a server. Netscape originally created the cookie as a sort of placeholder to allow the browser and server to keep up with each other. The cookie has proven useful even when all the cookie handling is within the browser, however, giving developers a friendly way to exchange information between successive pages and even between multiple windows and frames. Although cookie opponents are rarely any fonder of client-side cookies, the scripts that create them are readily available to the ordinary browser user, instead of being hidden away on a server. Client-side cookie code is much more public, allowing concerned users to inspect the code instead of decipher-ing odd values and trying to guess why a server keeps sending them cookies.

Client-side cookies work well in a number of situations. They're very use-ful for personalizing sites based on a limited amount of information. The amount of information scripting languages are capable of managing is getting a big boost from the latest developments in browser technology. Client-side cookies can keep track of the results of client-side processing, allowing users to save results locally without an extra trip to a server. They can provide handy reminders for sites, alerting users of further steps they need to take or a task they need to do at a site they've visited previously. Finally, they make it much easier to examine and debug complex cookie operations, even those that take place on the server side. Adding a small form to the debugging ver-sion of a site allows testers and developers to change the cookie to anything needed in the middle of testing. Client-side cookies add a whole new dimen-sion to development with cookies, one that has often been neglected.

Because there are no dependable alternatives to cookies in client-side scripting, this chapter will not cover the alternatives (like URL encoding) explored later chapters.

JavaScript and VBScript

When JavaScript appeared in Netscape Navigator 2.0, it was mostly intend-ed as a way for developers to validate form data before sending it up to the server, sparing users a lot of waiting and developers a lot of hassle caused by users entering random data into their forms. When Netscape originally created this scripting language, they called it LiveScript. LiveScript was part of the toolset for LiveWire, a Netscape product for connecting Web servers and databases covered in Chapter 7. When Netscape announced it was adding Java to its browser, it renamed LiveScript to JavaScript and changed some of its syntax to more closely resemble Java syntax. (As a result, many older JavaScript files use the extension `.ls` instead of `.js`.) JavaScript is not Java or even a cousin of Java, but looks somewhat similar. JavaScript has grown from its fairly primitive origins into a much more powerful tool, allowing developers to manipulate page properties as well as form values and browser and window properties. When the browser wars between Netscape and Microsoft began, Netscape refused to give Microsoft information on JavaScript syntax and properties, and kept the language a step ahead of Microsoft's efforts to reverse engineer their own version of JavaScript, known as JScript. After several years of squabbling, Netscape and Microsoft have finally ironed out most of their differences over JavaScript. Netscape submitted the specifications for JavaScript to the ECMA, a European standards body, and representatives from both companies had a hand in creating the "official" version specified in ECMA-262.

In the meantime, Microsoft released its own scripting language, VBScript, officially known as "Visual Basic, Scripting Edition." Based on its popular Visual Basic language, Microsoft's VBScript is a "light" version of Basic, including simple programming structures and a subset of commands. Programmers familiar with the full version of Visual Basic or Microsoft's Visual Basic for Applications can use the scripting edition quickly, applying familiar syntax and tools to new problems. Microsoft has pushed VBScript in its drive to make ActiveX controls a standard part of the Web development toolbox, making its structure mesh tightly with these compiled components. Unfortunately, VBScript works only on Internet Explorer for the Windows platform—even Internet Explorer for the Macintosh only supports JavaScript at this point.

The good news about these two languages is that they handle cookies very similarly, and that JavaScript cookie management is identical in both Netscape and Microsoft browsers. If you are developing for the Internet, you can use JavaScript and expect your code to work in both browsers without difficulties. If you are developing for an intranet aimed solely at Internet Explorer for Windows users, you can use VBScript code and not have to reconsider all of your favorite coding techniques. All examples in this chapter will be written in both JavaScript and VBScript. This book is not a complete guide to either language, but will explore all the cookie management and string-handling functions available in both. None of the programming techniques will be especially complicated, so even developers with minimal programming experience can probably figure out and modify the techniques used in this chapter.

Browsers have some strange problems with cookies in pages opened directly as files rather than via HTTP. Internet Explorer 3 has a bug that only affects developers of client-side cookies. Web pages that are opened directly as files are not permitted to create cookies at all, not even temporarily. While this has little effect on most users, because Web pages are normally downloaded via HTTP, it can make developers crazy when they try to test their pages and get mysterious errors. The easiest way to get around this bug is to test all pages from a server, rather than locally. The server can be on the same machine—it just needs to host a local Web server. Small personal Web servers available free from Apple and Microsoft can handle this light duty. Netscape browsers do not have this drastic a problem, but will not save persistent cookies to disk from pages opened as local files.

Working with Strings and Dates

The details of managing cookies in JavaScript and VBScript do not have much to do with state management. Instead, developers frequently find themselves tied down by the strange set of tools they have to work with to massage information into and out of cookies. Because the name and value items are not allowed to contain whitespace or a variety of other characters, and because you will frequently want to cram multiple pieces of information into a single cookie (so the user is not bombarded with alert boxes) you will need a strong set of tools for encoding text information and breaking strings into a variety of different parts. The string management tools in JavaScript are very different from the tools available in VBScript, so each language will receive coverage in a separate section. Both languages have strengths and weaknesses, and each section will include some specially-developed code to help you get around these differences.

Strings and Dates in JavaScript

Despite its origins as a tool for validating form data, JavaScript still does not offer a lot of functions for managing text strings or dates. The basics are all available: finding substrings in a string, slicing and dicing strings, and encoding strings and dates for proper storage in cookies. (JavaScript also includes a variety of string functions for formatting text with HTML; since they are not applicable to cookies, they will not be covered here.) Making JavaScript do more sophisticated tasks is possible, but sometimes requires developers to spend time hand-coding functions that are built into VBScript. This section will explore JavaScript's native capabilities as well as several ways to extend them.

Although all figures in this section of the chapter are from Netscape, all code samples have been tested in Internet Explorer for compatibility. Except as noted, all code here is for versions 3.0 or higher of both browsers.

JavaScript is very flexible, allowing developers to mix and match numeric variables with string variables and string variables with string objects. JavaScript will generally do its best to understand any strange combination you develop, and will convert between different types as necessary. This makes it much easier to write compact code, though you may find it more difficult to debug. If you need to figure out what kind of variable you're dealing with, the typeof() operator (available in Netscape and Microsoft browsers version 3.0 and later) can help. JavaScript includes a string datatype, which developers use for most applications without pondering the string object. The string datatype is easy to use; just assign a string value to a variable name:

```
<HTML><HEAD><TITLE>String Tester</TITLE></HEAD><BODY>
<SCRIPT>
function stringAssign(){
myString="This is a simple string value.";
alert("The value of myString is: " + myString + " and its type is:"
+typeof(myString)+".");}
stringAssign();
</SCRIPT></BODY></HTML>
```

When you load this document, you'll see the alert box presented in Figure 4-1.

Figure 4-1
String Datatype
Information

The string object affords a lot more functionality. While it provides a container for textual data, exactly like the string datatype, it also furnishes a set of methods (and a property, length) that developers can use to manipulate string values. While you can create variables that are explicitly string objects, there should not be any need to do so, because JavaScript will automatically convert string datatypes into string objects as required. If you find that a particular version of JavaScript has mysterious glitches in this conversion or suspect that there may be a performance advantage to using string objects, you can create them as follows:

```
<HTML><HEAD><TITLE>String Object Tester</TITLE></HEAD><BODY>
<SCRIPT>
function stringObjectAssign(){
myStringObject= new String("This is a string object.");
alert("The value of myStringObject is: " + myStringObject + " and its
   type is:" +typeof(myStringObject)+".");
}
stringObjectAssign();
</SCRIPT></BODY></HTML>
```

Loading this document brings up a slightly different dialog box, shown in Figure 4-2. The contents of the string and the way they are presented are the same, but this time the string is an object, not merely a string.

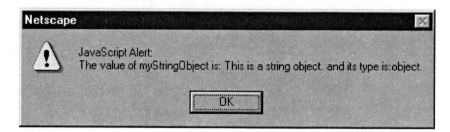

Despite this difference, you can treat both kinds of strings the same way, because JavaScript will handle any conversions needed to apply the string object functions to a plain old string.

One other complication of strings in JavaScript is the way the language uses quotes. Typically, a string is defined in a program (as in the two above) as a set of characters between two double-quote marks. This works wonderfully until the first time you need to display a string that includes double-quote marks. To get around this problem, JavaScript offers two solutions. The first one allows you to use single quotes to define the string, which frees you to use double quotes as part of the content. For instance, `quoteString='"I hate scripting!" he said.';` is an acceptable string declaration. This quote switching technique also works in HTML calls to JavaScript code, as in:

```
<A HREF="javascript:alert('Help!')"><IMG SRC="help.gif"></A>
```

Because HTML expects the quotes around the HREF attribute value, you can't use the double quotes you would normally use for the alert message. Single quotes break through the problem with a minimum of complication.

The quote situation gets more complicated when the quoted content includes both single and double quotes. Making sure that appropriate quotes appear requires the use of "escaping," which allows developers to escape from the normal restrictions on the use of particular characters in string declarations. Escaping a character requires using a backslash (\) in front of the character to be escaped, or using special escape codes to represent characters that would not normally be allowed. Inserting quotes this way allows you to include any number of quotes of any kind in any sequence. For instance,

```
<HTML><HEAD><TITLE>Quotes Tester</TITLE></HEAD><BODY>
<SCRIPT>
function stringAssign(){
myString="This \"is\" a 'lot' of \"quotes.\"";
alert("The value of myString is: " + myString);}
stringAssign();
</SCRIPT></BODY></HTML>
```

This strange little program will produce an alert box with many quotes, as seen in Figure 4-3.

Figure 4-3
Escaped Quotes in
an Alert Box

Quotes are not the only kind of character that can be escaped in this way. Backslashes also need to be escaped (\\), and newlines can be escaped as \n.

Newlines only work as line breaks in alert boxes, because HTML ignores them. Use <BR> instead for situations where your string will appear as HTML.

JavaScript offers more complete functions for "escaping" strings in ways that let you pass them as URLs or store them in cookies. Two functions built into JavaScript let you encode and decode strings to hide whitespace while keeping content. The `escape()` function does the encoding, while `unescape()` does the decoding. We'll take our quotes example and apply the `escape()` function to the string:

```
<HTML><HEAD><TITLE>String Escape Tester</TITLE></HEAD><BODY>
<SCRIPT>
function stringAssign(){
myString="This \"is\" a 'lot' of \"quotes.\"";
escapeString=escape(myString);
alert("The value of escapeString is: " + escapeString);}
stringAssign();
</SCRIPT></BODY></HTML>
```

This slightly modified code produces wildly different results, shown in Figure 4-4. All of the spaces have been replaced with `%20`, all of the double quotes with `%22`, and all of the single quotes with `%27`.

Figure 4-4
Escaped
Character
Sequence

The `escape()` function transforms all characters that are not ASCII letters or numbers and replaces them with percent signs followed by their position in the ISO 8859-1 Latin-1 character encoding. The Latin-1 set is not the same as the ASCII set to which most American developers are accustomed, so do not try to match up these characters with the ASCII set manually. The only easy way to convert the string back is with the `unescape()` function, which takes an escaped string and converts it back to normal text Using the code below returns the escaped text to something more readable, as shown in Figure 4-5.

```
<HTML><HEAD><TITLE>String Escape Tester</TITLE></HEAD><BODY>
<SCRIPT>
function stringAssign(){
myString="This \"is\" a 'lot' of \"quotes.\"";
escapeString=escape(myString);
alert("The value of escapeString is: " + escapeString);
newString=unescape(escapeString);
alert("The value of the unescaped newString is: " + newString);}
```

```
stringAssign();
</SCRIPT></BODY></HTML>
```

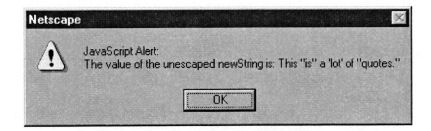

Using cookies efficiently requires a bit more knowledge of how to manipulate strings. Combining multiple variables into a single value for the cookie to store requires some coding, and extracting that information, even from multiple cookies, is considerably more complicated.

Combining strings (also known as concatenation) is simple—just use the familiar + operator. When JavaScript encounters a + operation, it checks to see if either of the operands is a string. If both values are mathematical, JavaScript adds the two numbers and returns the result. If one or more values are strings, it concatenates them, creating a combined string that starts with the first operand and ends with the second. The strange nature of the + operator can produce some unexpected results that require developers to pay close attention to the order of operations when combining string and numeric data. For example the following code produces two different results for very similar operations:

```
<HTML><HEAD><TITLE>String Concatenation Tester</TITLE></HEAD><BODY>
<SCRIPT>
document.write('8+8+"String"+8+8<BR>');
document.write(8+8+"String"+8+8+"<BR>");
document.write('8+(8+"String"+8+8)<BR>');
document.write(8+(8+"String"+8+8));
</SCRIPT></BODY></HTML>
```

As shown in Figure 4-6, the order in which the operands are processed makes a significant difference. If no parentheses are used, as in the first case, the browser processes the operation from left to right. When it encounters the "8+8", it sees that both values are numbers and therefore adds them, making 16. When it goes to add that value to "String", it sees that it has one numeric value and one string value, and therefore concatenates them, producing "16String". Because the left value from here on will always be a string, the browser will continue to concatenate additional values to the string rather than adding them. In the second case, using parentheses forces the browser to handle the parenthetical section first before moving left to right. It therefore concatenates the second eight to the "String" and the following eights before going back to the first eight. Since at this point it has a number, the first eight, and a string, "8String88", it just concatenates the first eight to the front of the string, producing "88String88". This case is reasonably clear, but can produce subtle bugs when cookies are produced from multiple variables. If some of the variables are numeric and some are strings, the + operator may add the variables rather than concatenating them, producing strange and useless results that are often hard to track down. Always double-check variables to make sure they will combine as expected, or JavaScript's loose variable typing will produce strange results.

Figure 4-6
Concatenation
vs. Addition

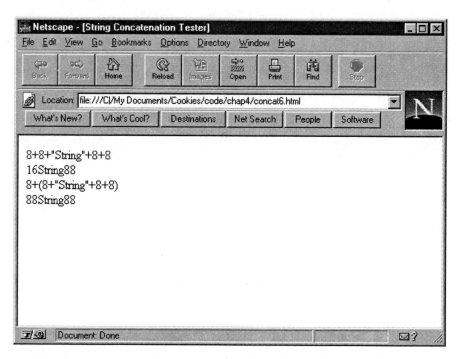

Handling the more complicated task of extracting information from strings requires applying the string object's methods. While they are not extraordinarily powerful tools, they meet the basic needs, allowing developers to parse the long and sometimes complicated strings returned by the cookie object. The string object contains one property and several methods we'll use to extract information.

Property	Value
length	Length of string in characters

Method	Return Value
charAt(*position*)	Returns the character at *position* in string.
indexOf(*substring*, *startChar*)	Returns the character position of the first occurrence of *substring* in a larger string. *startChar* is optional, and specifies a starting position for the search. Returns −1 if *substring* not found.
lastIndexOf(*substring*, *startChar*)	Returns the character position of *substring* in a larger string, but searches backward from the end of the string, or from *startChar* if specified. Returns −1 if *substring* not found.
split(*delimiter*)	Returns an array of strings, broken at the *delimiter* character.
substring(*from*, *to*)	Returns a substring, containing the portion of the original string from character *from* to character *to*.

These tools make it possible to extract meaningful portions from the strings used for cookies, allowing multiple values to be condensed into single cookies, and also allow developers to extract values from the long sequences the browser returns when more than one cookie is available.

There are two reasonably workable ways to configure strings that contain more than a single piece of information in JavaScript. The first way to make strings contain more than one piece of information is to create fixed-length strings in which the characters at a particular position are really a code containing information. In the string 147ABCD, the 1 could be relevant to one piece of code for the page, the 4 relevant to another, the 7A to another, and the BCD to yet another. As long as the location of the information in the string is fixed, it is easy to pull out the pieces. The second way is to use delimiters which indicate the beginning or end of a section of a string. Delimiters can be any character or even a set of characters, though commas, semicolons, and equals signs are the delimiters most frequently used in cookie work. The same information stored using delimiters might read 1,4,7A,BCD. Delimiters are very flexible, but require more string management on the programmer's part.

Using fixed positions makes development much easier, though cookie management will still require delimiter manipulation. The hardest part of using fixed positions is creating a scheme for encoding information and sticking to it. Fixed-position development is less flexible than delimiter development. Information left out at the beginning is often difficult to include later, and may require reshuffling considerable amounts of code. Still, for developers who can stand its restrictions, fixed positions require noticeably less programming effort for many situations and allow single cookies to act as repositories of considerable amounts of coded data.

Remember that all JavaScript strings begin with the first character at position zero. The numbers don't refer to actual characters, but rather to spaces between them. Using charAt(0) returns the first character in a string, and charAt(1) returns the second. The behavior of substring() is even stranger. Using substring(2,3) only returns the third character, which is between positions two and three. Retrieving the third and fourth characters requires substring(2,4).

The string object's charAt() and substring() methods are a complete toolkit for this kind of work. Using charAt() allows developers to pick a single character out of a string by its position, while substring returns a larger group of characters. The following example demonstrates the capabilities of both functions:

```
<HTML><HEAD><TITLE>String Chopper</TITLE></HEAD><BODY>
<SCRIPT>
function stringChop(){
stringMain=document.entry.userString.value;
alert("The first character is "+ stringMain.charAt(0)+",\n and the
third and fourth characters are " + stringMain.substring(2,4)+".");
}
</SCRIPT>
<FORM NAME="entry">
<INPUT TYPE="TEXT" SIZE=6 NAME="userString"> <A
HREF="javascript:stringChop()">Click to process</A>
</FORM></BODY></HTML>
```

Users who type in the word **MAIN** and click on the processing link will be rewarded with the alert box in Figure 4-7.

If a project uses a fixed-position method of managing cookie information, charAt() will be the normal function for reading single characters, while substring() will handle multiple characters. The substring() function will also receive constant use for writing the strings. Because all of the data in a string is sequential, and the tools JavaScript provides are fairly primitive, changing a part of a string requires separating the parts of the string being kept and combining them with the replacement parts. The following function takes an initial string, a replacement value, and the character position at which the replacement value belongs and returns the new string:

```
<HTML><HEAD><TITLE>String Chopper</TITLE></HEAD><BODY>
<SCRIPT>
function stringInsert(initial, replace, position){
start=parseInt(position);
end=start+replace.length;
newVal=initial.substring(0,start)+replace+initial.
   substring(end,initial.length);
return newVal;
}
function callInsert(){
result=stringInsert(document.entry.initialString.value,
   document.entry.replaceString.value, document.entry.replacePosi-
   tion.value);
alert(result);
}
</SCRIPT>
<FORM NAME="entry">Initial String:
<INPUT TYPE="TEXT" SIZE=30 NAME="initialString"> Replacement String:
<INPUT TYPE="TEXT" SIZE=20 NAME="replaceString"> Position:
<INPUT TYPE="TEXT" SIZE=2 NAME="replacePosition"><BR>
 <A HREF="javascript:callInsert()">Click to process</A>
</FORM></BODY></HTML>
```

Figure 4-7
Text Box Input
Broken Down by
Character Position
in JavaScript

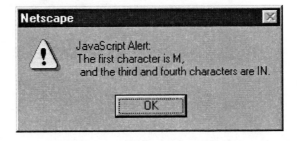

This utility function replaces one section of a string without affecting the rest, as seen in Figure 4-8. Its use is limited to character replacement, but as we will see, single characters can represent a considerable amount of data.

This code provides no error checking. When using this kind of function, developers must keep track of the length of their strings and be sure to send proper string information to avoid runtime errors.

JavaScript provides three tools for managing delimiters: the `indexOf`, `lastIndexOf`, and `split` methods. These three methods allow developers to find substrings within a string and divide delimited strings into their component parts. The next example provides a demonstration of the `indexOf()` functions, showing how to find a particular character in a string:

Figure 4-8
Replacement
Utility Function

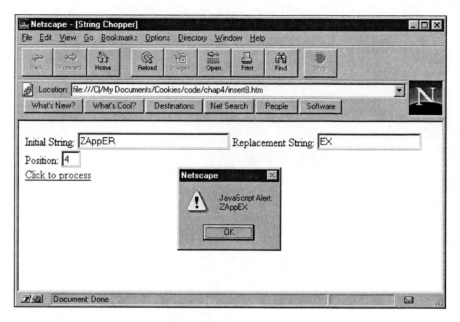

```
<HTML><HEAD><TITLE>String Search</TITLE></HEAD><BODY>
<SCRIPT>
function find(){
place=0;
result="Found at: ";
inString=document.entry.largeString.value;
findString=document.entry.findString.value;
while (place>-1) {
place=parseInt(place);
place=inString.indexOf(findString,place+1);
if (place =="") {place=-1;} //fixes a Netscape bug
if (place != -1) {result=result+place+", ";}
}
alert(result.substring(0,result.length-2)+".");
}
</SCRIPT>
<FORM NAME="entry">Initial String:
<INPUT TYPE="TEXT" SIZE=30 NAME="largeString"> Search String:
<INPUT TYPE="TEXT" SIZE=20 NAME="findString"><BR>
<A HREF="javascript:find()">Click to process</A>
</FORM></BODY></HTML>
```

This returns all of the positions of the search string, as shown in Figure
4-9, starting from the beginning of the string. (Replacing the indexOf call
with lastIndexOf would return the same sequence in reverse order.)

Figure 4-9
`indexOf`
Returning
Delimiter Values

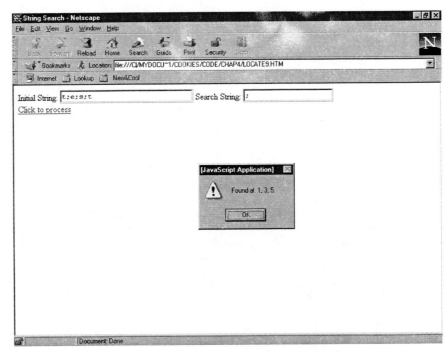

Figure 4-9
`indexOf`
Returning
Delimiter Values

Please notice the line in the code that checks for the null string in the value returned by `indexOf`. Netscape browsers will return a null string instead of −1 if the start value is greater than or equal to the length of the string, putting programs that don't check for a null value into an endless loop. Netscape Navigator 2.0 will also effectively subtract one from the start value for `lastIndexOf`, creating possible missed values.

The `split()` method, available in Netscape browser versions 3.0 and higher and Internet Explorer 4.0, goes beyond either of these search methods and breaks the string into an array of strings, using the delimiters as breaking points. This is very useful when a single cookie contains a series of values separated by semicolons, for instance. The following example allows users to enter a string containing delimiters, the delimiter they want to use, and presents a complete list of the array of strings returned.

```
<HTML><HEAD><TITLE>String Split</TITLE></HEAD><BODY>
<SCRIPT>
function breakIt(){
count=0
result="Strings:\n";
inString=document.entry.largeString.value;
delimit=document.entry.delimiter.value;
broken=inString.split(delimit);
```

```
while (count<broken.length) {
result=result+"Value "+count+" is "+broken[count]+"\n";
count++;}
alert(result);
}
</SCRIPT>
<FORM NAME="entry">Initial String:
<INPUT TYPE="TEXT" SIZE=30 NAME="largeString"> Delimiter:
<INPUT TYPE="TEXT" SIZE=2 NAME="delimiter"><BR>
<A HREF="javascript:breakIt()">Click to process</A>
</FORM></BODY></HTML>
```

When the user enters a delimited string and delimiters, the script returns a list of the pieces, as shown in Figure 4-10.

Figure 4-10
Splitting Strings
with Delimiters

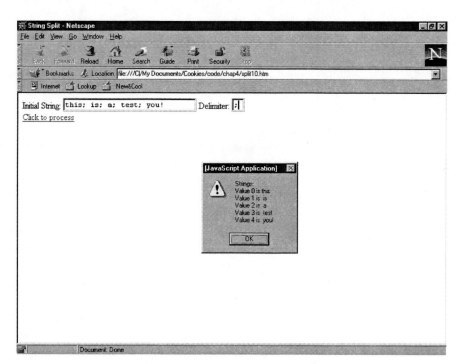

The `split()` method (and its opposite, the `join()` method of the array object) will prove extremely useful later for complex state-maintenance situations where multiple variables need to be kept. While the `indexOf()` and `lastIndexOf()` methods provide basic tools for finding substrings, the `split()` method provides a more powerful tool for storing and manipulating data sets.

The last JavaScript tool we will need to manage cookie data is the `Date()` object. Dates in JavaScript are stored as enormous integers, representing the number of milliseconds that have passed since midnight GMT,

January 1, 1970. The Date object has been plagued with bugs, but is usually close enough to accurate to be workable with cookies. (Netscape Navigator 2.0, for instance, would usually miscalculate all times on Macintosh computers by an hour, and could lose track of its time zone on all computers.) Newly created Date objects contain the date and time of their creation by default, but dates can be initialized to contain any date after 1970. JavaScript numbers months differently from most conventions—January is 0, and December is 11. As a result, subtract one from the conventional number for the month. Developers who want to create a date object can use any of five different syntaxes, all of which are useful for slightly different circumstances.

	Syntax	Results
Table 4-2 Setting a Date Value in JavaScript	`myDate=new Date()`	creates `myDate` as a new Date object containing the time at which the object was created.
	`myDate=new Date(milliseconds)`	creates `myDate` as a new Date object, set to the time of `milliseconds` after midnight, January 1, 1970 GMT.
	`myDate=new Date(datestring)`	creates `myDate` as a new Date object based on the value of `datestring`. The `datestring` must be in the format "`Month Day, Year Hours:Minutes:Seconds`", where `Month` is the English name of a month, `Day` and `Year` are valid, and `Hours:Minutes:Seconds` is a valid time expressed in 24-hour time. For instance, 3/5/78, 4:45 pm would be "`March 5, 1978 16:45:00`".
	`myDate=new Date(year, month, day)`	Creates `myDate` as a new Date object set to the date specified. To set the Date object to 4/10/99, use (1999, 3, 10) as the arguments.
	`myDate=new Date(year, month, day, hours, minutes, seconds)`	As above, except with extra arguments that fix the time more precisely. To set the date to 7/13/2021, 7:28pm, use (2021, 6, 13, 19, 28, 0) as the arguments. (*Hours* must be expressed in 24-hour time.)

The Date object also includes a large number of methods for reading and modifying its value once it has been set:

Table 4-3	getDate()	getDay()	getHours()	getMinutes()
Additional Date	getMonth()	getSeconds()	getTime()	getYear()
Methods in	setDate()	setHours()	setMinutes()	setMonth()
JavaScript	setSeconds()	setTime()	setYear()	getTimezoneOffset()

These methods may prove useful at some point in cookie manipulation, but since the Document.cookie object doesn't include any way to determine the expiration date of an already existing cookie, 90% of JavaScript date manipulation for cookies involves creating a Date object with the desired expiration date and time, and converting it to the required GMT with the toGMTString() method. The routine below is a very simple example of how to create a date and convert it to GMT.

```
<HTML><HEAD><TITLE>GMT Dates</TITLE></HEAD><BODY>
<SCRIPT>
function makeGMT(){
myMonth=parseInt(document.entry.myMonth.value)-1;//January is zero
myDate=parseInt(document.entry.myDate.value);
myYear=parseInt(document.entry.myYear.value);
myHour=parseInt(document.entry.myHour.value);
myMinutes=parseInt(document.entry.myMinutes.value);
mySeconds=parseInt(document.entry.mySeconds.value);
realDate=new Date(myYear,myMonth,myDate,myHour,myMinutes,mySeconds);
dateString=realDate.toGMTString();
alert(dateString);
}
</SCRIPT>
<FORM NAME="entry">
Month: <INPUT TYPE="TEXT" SIZE=2 NAME="myMonth">
Date: <INPUT TYPE="TEXT" SIZE=2 NAME="myDate">
Year: <INPUT TYPE="TEXT" SIZE=4 NAME="myYear"><BR>
Hour: <INPUT TYPE="TEXT" SIZE=2 NAME="myHour">
Minutes: <INPUT TYPE="TEXT" SIZE=2 NAME="myMinutes">
Seconds: <INPUT TYPE="TEXT" SIZE=2 NAME="mySeconds"><BR>
 <A HREF="javascript:makeGMT()">Click to process</A>
</FORM></BODY></HTML>
```

Note that the makeGMT() function reduces the month by one, bridging the normal (1–12) numbering of months and the JavaScript (0–11) numbering. A sample date conversion appears in Figure 4-11. Note the time change; Netscape has converted my Eastern Daylight Time to its Greenwich Mean Time equivalent.

After a detour through VBScript's equivalent (but very different) functions for handling strings and dates, we'll explore how to apply these tools to cookies.

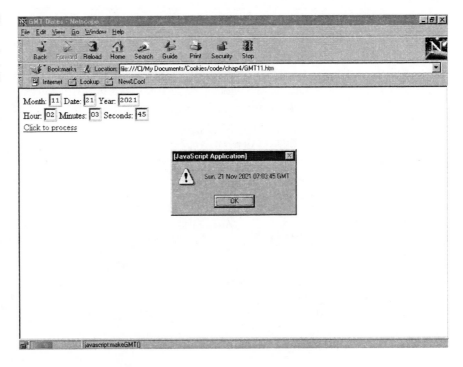

Figure 4-11
Greenwich Mean
Time Conversion
with JavaScript

Strings and Dates in VBScript

VBScript includes some powerful string functions as part of its inheritance from Visual Basic, as well as some tools for managing dates. While many of the individual tools are more powerful than their JavaScript equivalents, VBScript lacks some critical functions needed for cookie management. This section explores VBScript's powerful functions and addresses its weaknesses, even patching them with JavaScript occasionally when necessary.

> Remember: although you cannot count on VBScript to be available to patch holes in JavaScript, you can almost always count on JavaScript to be available to patch VBScript. There may be occasional users who have chopped JavaScript out of their Internet Explorer browsers, but there aren't many.

Like JavaScript, VBScript is a loosely typed language, allowing variables to be strings one moment, numeric values the next, and dates a bit later. VBScript differs from JavaScript, in that all of these variables are plain variables, without the complexity of objects. The tools for manipulating strings and dates are part of the language itself, not methods of data objects. This reduced dependence on objects produces leaner code and lessens complexity, making it easier for beginners to get started.

VBScript offers a much more general-purpose set of string manipulation functions than does JavaScript, making it easy to rearrange and modify text. It lacks a function for escaping text and the `split()` function that is so useful for managing multiple values or multiple cookies. Still, its coverage is fairly comprehensive, as shown in Table 4-4.

Table 4-4
String Manipulation Functions in VBScript

Name	Return Value
Asc(*string*)	Returns the ASCII value of the first character in the string
Chr(*value*)	Converts a number to the character that is its ASCII equivalent. Returns the ASCII character as a string
InStr(*start, string1, string2, type*)	Returns the start position of the first occurrence of *string1* within *string2*. The search begins at position **start**. The optional *type* indicates the kind of search: 0 is case-sensitive (binary); 1 is not case-sensitive.
Left(*string,length*)	Returns the first *length* characters of the *string*
LTrim(*string*)	Returns a copy of the *string* with all preceding spaces removed
Mid(*string, start, length*)	Returns a string composed of *length* characters starting at position *start* from *string*
Right(*string, length*)	Returns the last *length* characters of the *string*
RTrim(*string*)	Returns a copy of the *string* with all following spaces removed
Str(*number*)	Returns a string representation of *number*
StrComp(*string1, string2, type*)0	Compares *string1* and *string2*. The optional *type* indicates the kind of comparison: 0 is case-sensitive (binary); 1 is not case-sensitive. Returns −1 if *string1* is less than *string2*, 0 if both strings are equal, and 1 if *string1* is greater than *string2*. If either string is a null, returns NULL.
String(*value, repeat*)	Like Chr(), but returns *repeat* number of copies of the ASCII representaion of *value*
Trim(*string*)	Returns a copy of the *string* with all preceding and following spaces removed

continued

Name	Return Value
Val(*string*)	Returns a number from a *string*; reads the *string* from left to right, and stops including numbers as soon as the first non-numeric character is reached.

VBScript allows developers to concatenate strings with the plus sign, but this can have results as disastrous as those we explored in JavaScript. Fortunately, VBScript offers an alternative, the ampersand. The ampersand is evaluated last, so any mathematical additions will take place before the string concatenation. Although VBScript doesn't include any way to escape characters as JavaScript does, it is still possible to include quotes, backslashes, and other strange characters in strings by using the Chr() function as shown below.

```
<HTML><HEAD><TITLE>String Tester</TITLE></HEAD><BODY>
<SCRIPT LANGUAGE="VBScript">
function stringAssign
     myString="This "& Chr(34)&"is" & Chr(34)&"a lot"& Chr(39)&" of "&
Chr(39)&"quotes."
     MsgBox("The value of myString is: " & myString)
end function
stringAssign
</SCRIPT></BODY></HTML>
```

This script produces the ungrammatical results shown in Figure 4-12.

Figure 4-12
VBScript String
Including
Many Quotes

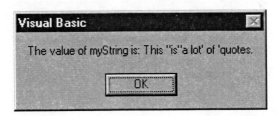

Chr() allows developers to create strings without breaking the syntax rules of VBScript. Line breaks can be created as (Chr(13)&Chr(10)), for instance. (Of course, HTML will still demand a <BR>.) While Chr() and its counterpart Asc() aren't the answer to every strange character, they extend VBScript's range much the way backslash escapes (like \ and \n) extend JavaScript.

VBScript doesn't have any equivalent to the escape() and unescape() functions of JavaScript, which receive frequent use in reading and writing cookies. Rather than reinventing the wheel, it is easier to use the JavaScript functions, suitably wrapped so that VBScript can reach them:

```
<HTML><HEAD><TITLE>String Escape Tester</TITLE></HEAD><BODY>
<SCRIPT LANGUAGE="JavaScript">
function stringEscape(escapeString){
return escape(escapeString);}
function stringUnescape(unescapeString){
return unescape(unescapeString);}
</SCRIPT>
<SCRIPT LANGUAGE="VBScript">
sub window_onLoad()
myString="This is a test string"
escapee=stringEscape(myString)
unescapee=stringUnescape(myString)
MsgBox("The value of the escaped String is: " & escapee)
MsgBox("The value of the unescaped String is: " & unescapee)
end sub
</SCRIPT></BODY></HTML>
```

This combination code produces the two dialog boxes shown in Figures 4-13 and 4-14.

Figure 4-13
The escaped String, in a VBScript Message Box

Figure 4-14
The unescaped String, in a VBScript Message Box

Combing code like this can be quite useful for a number of reasons. First, it maintains compatibility. While it would be possible to write a VBScript function that performs the same duty as escape, the changeover from ASCII to Latin-1 encoding is not always perfectly smooth, and most developers would probably create VBScript-only cookies that couldn't be read easily by JavaScript. Internet Explorer's ability to combine code from both languages fluidly also means that VBScript developers can use library code that JavaScript developers have already created. While Microsoft likes to trumpet VBScript as taking advantage of libraries of previously written code, the reality on the Web remains the reverse: many more libraries are available in JavaScript than in VBScript. Finally, code combining simply allows developers to make use of the best tool for a given situation. If some sections of code will be cleaner in JavaScript, developers can write those sections in JavaScript and other sections in VBScript. Undoubtedly they will stumble over a few syntax errors along the way, but their overall efficiency should improve.

VBScript offers a greater variety of functions for finding and returning substrings, though they don't map very well to their JavaScript equivalents. There is no `CharAt()` function, though the `Mid()` function and its siblings `Left()` and `Right()` can perform `CharAt()` duties and many more, as shown below:

```
<HTML><HEAD><TITLE>String Chopper</TITLE></HEAD><BODY>
<SCRIPT LANGUAGE="VBScript">
sub bttn1_onClick
stringMain=document.entry.userString.value
first=Left(stringMain,1)
thirdfour=Mid(stringMain,2,2)
announcement="The first character is "& first &"," & (Chr(13) &
Chr(10))&" and the third and fourth characters are " & thirdfour &"."
MsgBox(announcement)
end sub
</SCRIPT>
<FORM NAME="entry">
<INPUT TYPE="TEXT" SIZE=6 NAME="userString"><INPUT TYPE="BUTTON"
VALUE="Click to process" NAME="Bttn1">
</SCRIPT></BODY></HTML>
```

If users type **MAIN** into the input box and click on the button, they will be rewarded with the familiar dialog box in Figure 4-15.

Figure 4-15
Text Box Input
Broken Down by
Character Position
in VBScript

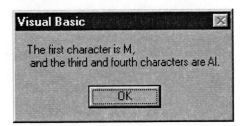

The `Left()`, `Right()`, and `Mid()` functions can also be useful for creating the kind of replacement code demonstrated in Figure 4-8. A routine like the string chopper below can be used to manage fixed-position cookie information, making it easy to change a particular value quickly.

```
<HTML><HEAD><TITLE>String Chopper</TITLE></HEAD><BODY>
<SCRIPT LANGUAGE="VBScript">
function stringInsert(initial, replace, start)
repLen=len(replace)
rightLen=(len(initial))-start-repLen
newVal=Left(initial,start) & replace & Right(initial,rightLen)
stringInsert=newVal
```

```
end function
sub bttn1_onClick
result=stringInsert(document.entry.initialString.value,
document.entry.replaceString.value,
document.entry.replacePosition.value)
MsgBox(result)
end sub
</SCRIPT>
<FORM NAME="entry">Initial String:
<INPUT TYPE="TEXT" SIZE=30 NAME="initialString"> Replacement String:
<INPUT TYPE="TEXT" SIZE=20 NAME="replaceString"> Position:
<INPUT TYPE="TEXT" SIZE=2 NAME="replacePosition"><BR>
<INPUT TYPE="BUTTON" VALUE="Click to process" NAME="Bttn1">
</FORM></BODY></HTML>
```

This code works very much like its JavaScript equivalent, as shown in Figure 4-16.

Figure 4-16
Replacement
Utility Code
in VBScript

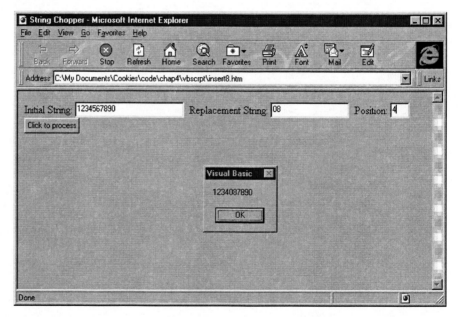

This code provides no error checking. When using this kind of function, developers must keep track of the length of their strings and be sure to send proper string information to avoid runtime errors. The types of error checking needed will vary with the source and type of the data.

VBScript's InStr() function works very much like JavaScript's indexOf() function. Both find a substring within a larger string and return the starting position of the first copy they encounter. The positions are treated differently—the first character is position 1, and positions are actual characters, not the cursor positions between them. The `InStr` function returns a 0 if the substring is not found or if the string being searched is of zero length. It returns a null if either string is null, which can produce endless loops if not checked for. The program following is a simple delimiter locator, taking a main string and a substring and returning all positions at which the substring was found:

```
<HTML><HEAD><TITLE>String Search</TITLE></HEAD><BODY>
<SCRIPT LANGUAGE="VBScript">
sub bttn1_onClick
place=0
quit=1
result="Found at: "
inString=document.entry.largeString.value
findString=document.entry.findString.value
while (quit>0)
  place=InStr(place+1,inString,findString,1)
  quit=place
  if IsNull(place) Then
     quit=0
     place=0
  end if
  if place<>0 then
     result=result & place & ", "
  end if
wend
MsgBox(Left(result,(len(result)-2))&".")
end sub
</SCRIPT>
<FORM NAME="entry">
Initial String:<INPUT TYPE="TEXT" SIZE=30 NAME="largeString">
Search String:<INPUT TYPE="TEXT" SIZE=20 NAME="findString"><BR>
<INPUT TYPE="BUTTON" VALUE="Click to process" NAME="Bttn1">
</FORM></BODY></HTML>
```

The `InStr()` function is very useful for breaking down cookie values that include delimiters, especially since VBScript 1.0 lacks the `split()` function of JavaScript. The following code provides some of the same functionality with a function that takes a string, a delimiter, and a position as its argument, and returns the appropriate piece of a delimited string, as shown in Figure 4-17.

```
<HTML><HEAD><TITLE>String Split</TITLE></HEAD><BODY>
<SCRIPT LANGUAGE="VBScript">
function breakIt(inString, delimiter, position)
place=0
if inString="" or delimiter="" or position="" then
  result="bad value"
else
  For count=1 to position-1
    if place+1<len(instring) then
      place=InStr(place+1,inString,delimiter,1)
    else
      place=null
      count=position
```

```
      end if
    Next
    if IsNull(place) or place=len(inString) then
      result= "not found"
    else
      endPoint=InStr(place+1,inString,delimiter,1)
      length=endPoint-place-1
      if endPoint=0 then length=1
      inString=inString & " "
      result=Mid(inString,place+1,length)
    end if
  end if
breakIt=result
end function

sub bttn1_onClick
found=breakIt(document.entry.initialString.value,
document.entry.delimiter.value, document.entry.position.value)
result="Piece "& document.entry.position.value & ":" & found
MsgBox(found)
end sub
</SCRIPT>
<FORM NAME="entry">Initial String:
<INPUT TYPE="TEXT" SIZE=30 NAME="initialString"> Delimiter:
<INPUT TYPE="TEXT" SIZE=2 NAME="delimiter">
Position: <INPUT TYPE="TEXT" SIZE=2 NAME="position">
<INPUT TYPE="BUTTON" VALUE="Click to process" NAME="Bttn1">
</FORM></BODY></HTML>
```

Figure 4-17
InStr Returning
Delimiter
Locations

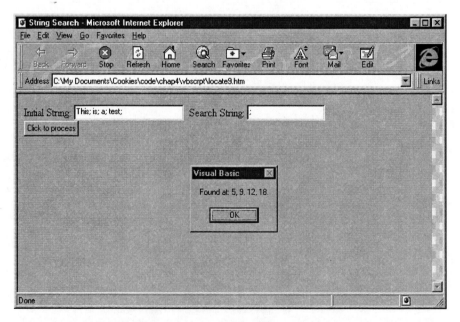

The breakIt() function allows developers to create VBScript code that can pull out multiple pieces from the same cookie or break apart the long strings that appear when multiple cookies for the same site are present. The testbed example shown in Figure 4-18 uses a simple list of numbers and letters, a scenario useful for checking that the code finds the right value.

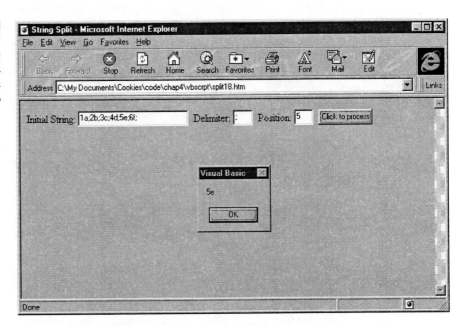

This code does a minimal amount of error checking, but relies on the developers to make sure it is passed appropriate data. Always make certain that the argument passed as position is a number, or runtime errors will result.

VBScript also offers a friendly set of date functions, which are generally more tolerant of data formats than their JavaScript equivalents. `DateValue()`, for instance, interprets date information in a variety of formats and converts it to a standard VBScript date variant. Table 4-5 lists relevant VBScript date functions and the kind of information they return.

Unfortunately for developers, VBScript includes no built-in function for converting date objects to the kind of date string the cookie object needs to set an expiration date. The date object in VBScript is also completely incompatible with the date object in JavaScript, so it takes a little more work than just passing a date from one language to another. There are three programming choices, however. The first is simply to use a handwritten time code, hard-coded into a string. Developers who want to create semi-permanent cookies (with an expiration several years away) may want to use this option. Developers who want to create persistent cookies with shorter lifespans have two more-complicated options. The first still uses JavaScript. The VBScript code passes a JavaScript function the necessary pieces of a date, and the properly formatted string is returned. The second option is to recreate the `Date.toGMTString` method in VBScript. This is not difficult, but does take a significant amount of code.

Table 4-5
VBScript Date
Functions

Function	Return Value
Date()	Returns the current date as a date sub-type of variant
DateSerial(*year*, *month*, *day*)	Returns the date specified by year, month, day as a date subtype of variant
DateValue(*string*)	Returns a date subtype of variant based on the date value included in the string. Allows for greater flexibility in date entry
Day(*date*)	Returns the day of the month as a numeric value
Hour(*date*)	Returns the hour as a numeric value
Minute(*date*)	Returns the minutes as a numeric value
Month(*date*)	Returns the month, as a numeric value from —12
Now()	Returns the current date and time as a date subtype of variant
Second(*date*)	Returns the seconds as a numeric value
Weekday(*date*, *firstDay*)	Returns the weekday as a number 1-7. The *firstDay* is optional and allows developers to specify on which day the week starts. 0 indicates that the computer should use its default; a number indicates which day (1=Sunday, 7=Saturday, etc.) the week should begin.
Year(*date*)	Returns the year as a numeric value

The code for using the JavaScript functions (called by a VBScript function that handles the necessary translations) looks like the following:

```
<HTML><HEAD><TITLE>GMT Dates - VBScript and JavaScript</TITLE></HEAD>
  <BODY>
<SCRIPT LANGUAGE="JavaScript">
function convGMT(VBday,VBmonth,VByear){
VBmonth=VBmonth-1;
realDate=new Date(VByear,VBmonth,VBday);
dateString=realDate.toGMTString();
return(dateString);
}
```

```
</SCRIPT>
<SCRIPT LANGUAGE="VBScript">
sub Bttn1_onclick
myDate=DateValue(document.entry.myDate.value)
myDay=Day(myDate)
myMonth=Month(myDate)
myYear=Year(myDate)
myGMT=convGMT(myDay,myMonth,myYear)
MsgBox(myGMT)
end sub
</SCRIPT>
<FORM NAME="entry">
Date: <INPUT TYPE="TEXT" SIZE=10 NAME="myDate">
<BR>
<INPUT TYPE="BUTTON" VALUE="Click to process" NAME="Bttn1">
</FORM></BODY></HTML>
```

These two bits of script take a string from the text entry box on the page. VBScript's `DateValue()` function converts that to a date, using whatever formats are available to the user on this machine. (`DateValue()` uses the preferences specified in the **Regional Settings** control panel.) The VBScript function then extracts the day, month, and year, and passes them to the JavaScript `convGMT` function, which combines them back into a date and returns that date as a GMT string, suitable for use in a cookie. The results appear in Figure 4-19.

Figure 4-19
JavaScript GMT
Conversion Called
from VBScript

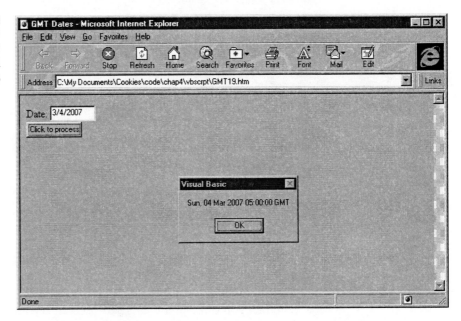

The second option is to recreate JavaScript's `Date.toGMTString` function entirely in VBScript. This is not especially difficult, except for the

need to convert some numeric values back into the short strings required
by the format; as shown in Figure 4-20.

```
<HTML><HEAD><TITLE>GMT Dates - VBScript only</TITLE></HEAD><BODY>
<SCRIPT LANGUAGE="VBScript">
function convGMT(convDate)
Dim weekdays(6)
weekdays(0)="Sun"
weekdays(1)="Mon"
weekdays(2)="Tue"
weekdays(3)="Wed"
weekdays(4)="Thu"
weekdays(5)="Fri"
weekdays(6)="Sat"
Dim months(11)
months(0)="Jan"
months(1)="Feb"
months(2)="Mar"
months(3)="Apr"
months(4)="May"
months(5)="Jun"
months(6)="Jul"
months(7)="Aug"
months(8)="Sep"
months(9)="Oct"
months(10)="Nov"
months(11)="Dec"

myWeekday=Weekday(convDate)-1
myDay=Day(convDate)
if myDay<10 then myDay="0" & myDay
myMonth=Month(convDate)-1
myYear=Year(convDate)
convGMT=weekdays(myWeekday) & ", " & myDay & " " & months(myMonth) & "
" & myYear & " 00:00:00 GMT"
end function

sub Bttn1_onclick
myDate=DateValue(document.entry.myDate.value)
myGMT=convGMT(myDate)
MsgBox(myGMT)
end sub
</SCRIPT>
<FORM NAME="entry">
Date: <INPUT TYPE="TEXT" SIZE=10 NAME="myDate">
<BR>
<INPUT TYPE="BUTTON" VALUE="Click to process" NAME="Bttn1">
</FORM></BODY></HTML>
```

VBScript purists may prefer this version, as it is easier to debug scripts that
remain in one language. Because VBScript offers no time-zone conversion
utilities, the script ignores the time, posting midnight for the date. If this is
unacceptable, you can either change the default setting by editing the string
returned by convGMT or develop your own set of routines.

Figure 4-20
Date Conversion
in VBScript

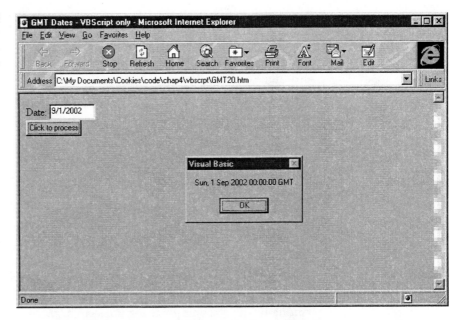

VBScript 2, and 3—A Briefing

Microsoft has released VBScript 2.0, which ships with IIS 3.0 and Internet Explorer 4.0, and a beta of VBScript 3, which is (so far) identical to 2 but has additional hooks for debugging scripts. These VBScripts offer several new functions, many of which can be applied to cookies. All of these features are covered in greater detail in Chapter 8 on Active Server Pages, but are noted here so that client-side developers aren't left behind.

VBScript 2.0 offers an `Array()` function, which can condense the long declarations of month and weekday abbreviations used in the date function above. Declaring the weekdays array would only require:

```
weekdays=Array("Sun", "Mon", "Tue", "Wed", "Thu", "Fri", "Sat")
```

VBScript 2.0 also offers a `split()` function much like JavaScript's. This function accepts a string to be split, the parameter at which to split it, and optionally the number of strings to return and the type of comparison (case-sensitive is 0, non-case-sensitive is 1). For instance,

```
splitString=split("0;1;2;3;4")
```

will return a array with five members. The value of `splitString(0)` will be 0, that of `splitString(1)` will be 1, and so forth. Microsoft

continued

has also created a `join()` function that parallels the JavaScript array object's `join()` method. This function takes as arguments an array and a delimiter, and returns a string consisting of all the elements in the array separated by the delimiter character. The code

```
item[1]="hello!"
item[2]="123456789abcdef"
combo=join(item,";")
```

will return the string "`hello!;123456789abcdef`". The `join()` function is effectively the reverse of the split functions. It is worth being careful with delimiters, however, because the appearance of a delimiter in the text of an array item makes it possible to `join()` together a string that will not `split()` properly.

Developers who need to change string content will also be pleased with the `replace()` function, which seeks out a substring and replaces it with a new value. The `replace()` function takes as arguments the initial string, the string to be replaced, the replacement string, and, optionally, the starting point for the search, the number of times to perform the replacement, and the type of comparison to be made. `Replace()` is very handy for changing the delimiter in a string quickly, or for changing bits of text. For example,

```
newString=replace("I hate chocolate", "ate", "was fed")
```

will return the string "`I hwas fed chocolwas fed`". Cookie developers in need of a quick fix to a misnamed or oddly valued cookie will find plenty of use for `replace()`.

The last significant improvement to VBScript that has a direct impact on cookie management is the Dictionary object, which allows developers to create arrays with elements accessed by name instead of number. The Dictionary object is available on the client side, but because of its complexity will be used only in Chapter 8 on Active Server Pages.

Because none of this code is compatible with most of the many copies of Internet Explorer 3 still in regular use, it will not be used for the client-side libraries that follow. Of course, you may add the code at your own risk. Only use the more recent VBScript improvements in situations where you are certain what version of VBScript is available, or in code used to generate Active Server Pages. The following code snippet will let you check which version of VBScript is present in a browser environment:

```
VBver=ScriptEngineMajorVersion()
If VBver="" then VBver=1
msgBox(VBver)
```

> The kind of detection code developers normally use to determine the version and maker of the browser will not always be useful in this situation, because VBScript 2.0 can be added to Internet Explorer 3.0 as a replacement for the older version. Many sites doing extensive VBScript intranet development have already added VBScript 2.0 to their installed base. For more details, visit **http://www.microsoft.com/vbscript/** or explore a recent VBScript book like *Learning VBScript* from O'Reilly and Associates, Paul Lomax, 1997.

Cookie Management on the Client

Now that we've covered the tools needed to manage the information stored inside cookies, it is time to look at how cookies are used in the client-side environment. The tools provided for reading and writing cookies in both VBScript and JavaScript are minimalist, requiring considerable work to make cookies easily useful. After an exploration of the `document.cookie` property, we will create a set of cookie management functions to help developers focus on their program logic rather than on the particulars of the `document.cookie` property.

The Strange Behavior of Document.cookie

Cookies are set and examined through one property, `document.cookie`, in both JavaScript and VBScript. Developers who have not worked extensively with Web scripting or with objects before often find it strange that cookies are read from and written to by something that seems like a variable rather than a procedure. Netscape's early decision to make cookies a part of the Document object is also bewildering, since multiple documents can read the same cookies. Unlike other properties of the Document object, the Cookie property value often remains the same between different pages, at least different pages on the same site. The Document object is a best approximation for where cookies belong, providing an adequate place to store information that could change from page to page.

`Document.cookie` is a strange container, with a set of behaviors that doesn't always seem consistent. A program that sets its value in one line and reads its value in the next will get two different answers, which can lead to confusion. The value read may include multiple cookie values and will leave out all Cookie properties except for the key name and value pairs. While it might seem more sensible to have included separate read and write methods for cookies, the original approach taken by Netscape 2.0 has remained the only approach to creating cookies, even several versions later, in both the Netscape and Microsoft browsers.

Setting cookies is done by assigning a string value to the `document.cookie` property. The string must loosely follow the format:

```
name=value; expires=date; path=path; domain=domain; secure
```

Only the initial name and value pair are required. All other settings are optional, and can follow in any order. The expiration date must, of course, be in the GMT format. The Domain and Path fields must be legitimate domain and path descriptions. The cookie will be secure if the Secure field is present.

It is easy to see how your browser handles this. The following piece of JavaScript code sets two cookies in separate calls, then pops up an alert box with the current value of `document.cookie`.

```
<HTML>
<HEAD><TITLE>document.cookie test - JavaScript</TITLE></HEAD>
<BODY>
<SCRIPT>
function setCookie(){
document.cookie="test1=tester";
document.cookie="test2=tester2";
alert(document.cookie);}
setCookie();
</SCRIPT>
<H1>Cookie Test</H1>
</BODY></HTML>
```

As shown in Figures 4-21 and 4-22, what comes out of the cookie is not exactly what went into it.

Figure 4-21
JavaScript Return Value of `document.cookie` in Netscape Communicator

Figure 4-22
JavaScript Return
Value of
document.cookie
in Microsoft
Internet Explorer

VBScript behaves identically, as the results, from the following code demonstrate (Figure 4-23).

```
<HTML>
<HEAD><TITLE>document.cookie test - VBScript</TITLE></HEAD>
<BODY>
<SCRIPT LANGUAGE="VBScript">
sub window_onload
document.cookie="test1=tester"
document.cookie="test2=tester2"
MsgBox(document.cookie)
end sub
</SCRIPT>
<H1>Cookie Test</H1>
</BODY></HTML>
```

Figure 4-23
VBScript Return
Value of
document.cookie
in Microsoft
Internet Explorer

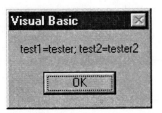

If Internet Explorer produces the results shown in Figure 4-24, the browser is failing to create the cookies because it cannot handle cookie creation from files that were opened directly. As mentioned on page 62 Internet Explorer will only create cookies for pages retrieved from a Web server; it cannot create cookies for pages that were opened from a file on a local hard drive or even from a file server. Set up a small server (like Microsoft's Personal Web Server, which runs under Windows 95) and open the page using an HTTP connection.

Figure 4-24
Failed Return
Value of
document.cookie
in Microsoft
Internet Explorer

Remember, if the server is on your own machine, the easiest way to reach files on your Web server is to use **http://127.0.0.1/filename**. As long as you have TCP/IP installed, and no matter what network you're on, 127.0.0.1 always refers to the machine on which you're working. Many of the examples pictured in this book will be called from 127.0.0.1.

Making it Sensible: Cookie Utility Functions

While it is possible to use the `document.cookie` property to manage all of your cookie needs, it is simpler in the long run to create a utility library that can manage cookies consistently. The JavaScript and VBScript string and date handling functions presented above will let you write routines that work well with `document.cookie`, but reinventing the wheel for every function that uses a cookie creates code that is hard to understand. By combining all the code needed to read and write cookies into a small set of tested functions, developers can make their debugging considerably less complicated. This section looks at two major approaches to creating a utility toolbox. The first and simpler one creates functions for reading and writing cookies and works in both JavaScript and VBScript. The second approach is considerably more complex, but has the advantage of encapsulating cookies with a Cookie object, allowing developers to manage cookies more transparently. This approach works only in JavaScript. Most of the examples in the remainder of the chapter will use the first approach, but developers who can count on their users' having the latest browsers may prefer the second.

JavaScript, Done Simply

The simplest way to handle cookies is to create two functions: one that writes cookies, and one that reads them. The function that writes the cookie must accept arguments for all the possible parts of the cookie, and process them into a proper cookie string that gets assigned to `document.cookie`. The function reading the cookie needs to take the string returned by document.cookie and break it down, returning only the value of the cookie requested. Accomplishing these tasks requires a considerable amount of the string and date manipulation already covered.

 Developers can use the JavaScript code below in two ways: it can be included directly in every page that uses the code, or stored in a separate `.js` file and shared by multiple pages. Storing the code in a separate file requires users to have a Netscape or Microsoft browser Version 3 or higher, and may necessitate some setup on the server to make certain that it understands the JavaScript MIME type of `application/x-javascript`. To store the code in a separate file, enter the code (without the SCRIPT tags) and save it as `cooklib.js` or something similar. Then add it to HTML files with `<SCRIPT SRC="cooklib.js" LANGUAGE="JavaScript"></SCRIPT>`. The browser will download the extra JavaScript and treat it as if it were included in the file. Always remember to put this extra `<SCRIPT>` element before any other code that needs to call the functions.

```
<SCRIPT>
function ReadCookie(name){
var allCookie, CookieVal, length,start,end;
cookieVal="";
name=name+"=";   //append equals to avoid false matches.
allCookie=document.cookie;
length=allCookie.length;
if (length>0) {//no cookies - user probably incinerated.
    start=allCookie.indexOf(name,0)
    if (start!=-1) {//avoid if cookie wasn't set.
     start+=name.length;
     end=allCookie.indexOf(";",start);
     if (end==-1) {end=length;}
     cookieVal=unescape(allCookie.substring(start,end));
    }
}
return(cookieVal);
}
function WriteCookie(name,value,expires,domain,path,secure){
var CookieVal,CookError;
CookieVal=CookError="";
if (name) {
CookieVal=CookieVal+escape(name)+"=";
    if (value) {
    CookieVal=CookieVal+escape(value);
     if (expires) {
     CookieVal=CookieVal+"; expires="+expires.toGMTString();
     }
```

```
        if (domain){
        CookieVal=CookieVal+"; domain="+domain;
        }
        if (path) {
        CookieVal=CookieVal+"; path="+path;
        }
        if (secure) {
        CookieVal=CookieVal+"; secure";
        }
        }
        else {CookError=CookError+"Value failure";}//need value
}
else {CookError=CookError+"Name failure";}//need name
if (!CookError) {
    document.cookie=CookieVal;//sets cookie
    if (value != ReadCookie(name)) //checks to make sure OK
    {CookError="Write failure";}

}
return CookError;
}
</SCRIPT>
```

This code is designed to work with Netscape Navigator 2.0 as well as with more recent browsers. For maximum compatibility with older browsers, use this set of cookie functions.

The JavaScript version of the simple utility library requires only two functions: WriteCookie() and ReadCookie(). ReadCookie() has a fairly simple task—finding the name in the string of cookies returned by document.cookie and extracting the matching value. The string methods already covered (indexOf(), substring(), length(), and unescape()) provide the tools needed to extract the information.

WriteCookie() is made a bit more complex by the fact that most cookies do not use all the available parameters. As a result, the function has to check the parameter list to see which parameters were actually passed, and do some checking to make sure they are valid. JavaScript does not require that all parameters be passed. This makes working with cookies much easier since the Domain, Path, and Secure properties are only rarely used. WriteCookie() also returns error codes in English if fed bad data, allowing developers to figure out more easily where their code went wrong.

Most developers will not want to use all six parameters, but Write-Cookie() is ready to handle them. JavaScript is forgiving about calling functions with fewer parameters than required, and WriteCookie() is equipped to deal with the problem. Calling WriteCookie(testCookie, testing) will create a cookie with a name of testCookie and a value of testing, but no expiration, domain, path, or security. Most of the time, developers using persistent cookies will assign name, value, and expiration (which takes a JavaScript Date object), but not bother with the last three parameters. Occasionally a program may need to pass Domain or Path values without setting an expiration; to do that, just pass an empty string ("") for the expiration value. The function will create a cookie that includes all the other parameters but ignores expiration.

The WriteCookie() function also does some simple error checking. The name and value parameters are required for a cookie to be set, and WriteCookie() returns an error if either parameter is missing. WriteCookie() also calls ReadCookie() to make sure the cookie was written, and returns an error if it was not. There are several reasons it might not have been written—the user could have turned off all cookies, or could have rejected this particular cookie, or one of the parameters might have had an inappropriate value. An expiration date in the past, or a Domain name or path that does not match the page trying to set the cookie can keep the browser from accepting the cookie. If code depends on the successful deployment of a cookie, it is always worth checking. Unfortunately there are not many alternatives to cookies on the client side of Web development.

If all users are going to be working with Netscape 3.0 or higher, developers can also check to make sure that data types are appropriate with the typeof() operator. The following code would allow the WriteCookie() function to accept dates already converted to GMT format as well as Netscape date objects, for instance.

```
if (expires) {
GMTdate=expires;
if (typeof(expires)=="object"){ //date check Navigator 3.0+
GMTdate=expires.toGMTString();
} //Navigator 3.0+ only!
CookieVal=CookieVal+GMTdate;
```

This code makes two assumptions that may cause problems: first, that any strings passed to it are GMT format dates, and second, that any objects passed to it are Date objects. It is likely to be wrong in either of those assumptions, and there are no good ways in JavaScript to double-check those assumptions. Still, this kind of code can provide some flexibility to developers trying to coax previously written scripts that addressed cookies in assorted different ways to work through a common interface.

Utility Functions for Keeping Multiple Values in a JavaScript Cookie

Another extremely useful, though optional, tool is a routine for storing multiple values in the same cookie. The easiest way to do this is with a function that can take a variable number of arguments, looping through as many times as necessary to create a combination value. Reading back the values uses another simple loop. The only restriction developers face with this style of cookie programming is a limitation on the characters used in the values. This routine will use delimiters for maximum flexibility, and the delimiter cannot appear elsewhere in the values. To make it easier to change the delimiter, the delimiter is set as a separate variable in this code. These functions will work with Netscape Navigator 2.0 and higher, as well as with Internet Explorer 3.0 and higher.

```javascript
function combine(){
var delimiter, numArgs, combination, i;
combination="";
delimiter="|";
numArgs=combine.arguments.length;
if (numArgs>1) {
    for (i=0; i<numArgs; i++) {

combination=combination+combine.arguments[i]+delimiter;
    }
}
return combination.substring(0, combination.length-1);
}

function breakdown(combination){
var delimiter, start, end, count;
broken=new Object();
delimiter="|";
start=end=0;
count=1;
end=combination.indexOf(delimiter,end)
while ((end) && (end>-1)){
    broken[count]=combination.substring(start,end);
    count++;
    start=end+1;
    end=combination.indexOf(delimiter,start)
}
broken[count]=combination.substring(start,combination.length);
//make sure to get the last piece
broken[0]=count+1;
return broken;
}
```

Note that the values are not escaped; the cookie setting functions will take care of this. The array returned by breakdown() is not a simple

Netscape 3.0 array, but is instead an array compatible with Netscape 2.0. The length of the array is stored in position 0. To read back the array, you could use code like:

```
broken=breakdown(combinedString);
result="";
for (i=1; i<returnArray[0]; i++) {
result=result+"Value "+i+" is "+broken[i]+"\n";
}
alert(result);
```

With a suitable string, the results would look like Figure 4-25.

Figure 4-25
Returned Array
from a Delimited
String

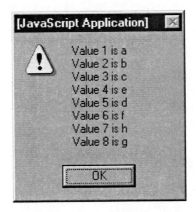

VBScript, Done Simply

Creating compatible functions in VBScript is a bit more complicated. As noted above, VBScript has no `escape()` function, leaving developers to use the JavaScript version, cook up their own version, or make certain that all of their cookie values are acceptable without any conversions. In order to maximize compatibility between the cookies created by these libraries, the VBScript functions provided here will call a pair of JavaScript functions. Developers who need to create a set of pure VBScript cookie functions can remove the function calls to `JSescape` and `JSunescape` as noted in the code comments. For dates, developers can choose to use either the call to JavaScript functions or the VBScript conversion function shown above. (In the interests of keeping the VBScript library as much in VBScript as possible, the code here will use the longer VBScript version. Using the JavaScript date conversion function will require changing the arguments in `WriteCookie()`'s call to the `convGMT()` function.)

> VBScript developers can also choose to use the entire JavaScript library. VBScript's tolerance for calling JavaScript functions may be of particular use to developers who want to centralize their cookie library code. Unlike the JavaScript code, VBScript code cannot be placed in a separate file to be shared by multiple pages. The <SCRIPT SRC="*url*"> syntax works for JavaScript, but returns odd errors for VBScript. VBScript developers should include the library code, or the parts they need, directly in their HTML files.

```
<SCRIPT LANGUAGE="JavaScript">
function JSescape(toEscape) {
return escape(toEscape);
}
function JSunescape(fromEscape) {
return unescape(fromEscape);
}
</SCRIPT>
<SCRIPT LANGUAGE="VBScript">
function convGMT(convDate)
Dim weekdays(6)
weekdays(0)="Sun"
weekdays(1)="Mon"
weekdays(2)="Tue"
weekdays(3)="Wed"
weekdays(4)="Thu"
weekdays(5)="Fri"
weekdays(6)="Sat"
Dim months(11)
months(0)="Jan"
months(1)="Feb"
months(2)="Mar"
months(3)="Apr"
months(4)="May"
months(5)="Jun"
months(6)="Jul"
months(7)="Aug"
months(8)="Sep"
months(9)="Oct"
months(10)="Nov"
months(11)="Dec"
myWeekday=Weekday(convDate)-1
myDay=Day(convDate)
if myDay<10 then myDay="0" & myDay
myMonth=Month(convDate)-1
myYear=Year(convDate)
convGMT=weekdays(myWeekday) & ", " & myDay & " " & months(myMonth) &
" " & myYear & " 00:00:00 GMT"
end function

function combine(arguments)
dim delimiter, numArgs, combination, i
combination=""
delimiter="|"
if IsArray(arguments) then
```

```
        numArgs=UBound(arguments)
        if (numArgs>1) then
         for i=1 to numArgs
            combination=combination & arguments(i) & delimiter
           next
        end if
end if
combine=Left(combination, len(combination)-1)
end function

function breakdown(combination)
dim delimiter, startPos, endPos, count
dim broken()
reDim broken(1)
delimiter="|"
startPos=1
endPos=1
count=1
endPos=InStr(endPos, combination,delimiter)
while (endPos>0)
    broken(count)=Mid(combination, startPos,endPos-startPos)
    count=count+1
    reDim Preserve broken(count)
    startPos=endPos+1
    endPos=InStr(startPos,combination, delimiter)
wend
broken(count)=Mid(combination, startPos, len(combination))
'This picks up the last entry. Returns nothing if there is none.
breakdown=broken
end function

function ReadCookie(name)
dim allCookie, CookieVal, length,startPos, endPos
cookieVal=""
name=name& "=" 'append equals to avoid false matches.
allCookie=document.cookie
length=len(allCookie)
'check for no cookies - user is probably incinerating cookies.
if (length>0) then
    startPos=InStr(1, allCookie,name)
    'if string appeared - otherwise cookie wasn't set.
    if (startPos>0) then
     startPos=startPos + len(name)
     endPos=InStr(startPos,allCookie,";")
     if (endPos<1) then endPos=length+1
     cookieVal=JSunescape(Mid(allCookie,startPos,endPos-startPos))
            'leave out JSUnescape for pure VB
    End if
End if
ReadCookie=cookieVal
End Function

function WriteCookie(name,value,expires,domain,path,secure)
dim CookieVal,CookError
CookieVal=""
CookError=""
if name <> "" then
    CookieVal=CookieVal & JSescape(name) & "=" 'leave out the JSescape
            for pure VB
    if value<>"" then
```

```
      CookieVal= CookieVal & JSescape(value) 'leave out JSescape for
              pure VB
  if expires<>"" then CookieVal=CookieVal & ";
              expires="&convGMT(expires)
  if domain<>"" then CookieVal=CookieVal & "; domain="&domain
  if path<>"" then CookieVal=CookieVal & "; path="&path
  if secure<>"" then CookieVal=CookieVal & "; secure"
      else CookError="Value failure" 'need valid value
  end if
else CookError=CookError & "Name failure" 'need valid name
end if
if (CookError="") then
    document.cookie=CookieVal 'sets cookie
    if (value <> ReadCookie(name)) then CookError="Write failure"
    ' checks to make sure it worked
end if
writeCookie=CookError
end function
</SCRIPT>
```

These functions and their JavaScript counterparts behave identically, with
one significant difference: the rules for passing arguments differ markedly.
VBScript is not as tolerant as JavaScript of functions with an indeterminate
number of arguments. As result, the `writeCookie` function needs to have
all of its arguments all of the time. Developers who do not want to set the
Expiration, Domain, Path, or Secure parameters must pass the function
empty strings. Also, the `combine()` function now takes as its argument an
array, rather than a list of strings. The `breakdown()` function returns an
array. While VBScript will not accept a variable number of parameters, it is
quite tolerant of arrays that need to increase or decrease their number of
elements, and functions can pass and return arrays as arguments. To determine the length of the array, just use the `UBound()` function on the
returned array value.

JavaScript, More Elegantly

Developers who want to be able to treat cookies as simple variables may
find lacking the procedures provided above. Using cookies still requires
extra steps: calling a function, providing it the name of the cookie, and
checking the result. While this is useful, it is not as transparent as checking
`myCookie.value` to find out what the current value of the cookie is.
JavaScript has an answer to this, allowing developers to use prototypes to
create their own classes for objects. Using prototypes enables developers to
encapsulate cookies and treat them much like other variables, rather than as
strange external entities that require extra management effort.

JavaScript is not a true object-oriented language like Java, and as a result,
its options for creating and managing objects are awkward at best. For
instance, there is no way to shield property values from intruding func-

tions—code outside the object can call all methods and directly modify all values without giving the object a chance to respond. (This means that developers who modify cookie values simultaneously in more than one window have to make a call to the `write()` method every time they change a value—JavaScript cannot do this automatically.) The code in this section requires extra processing overhead, but provides a much smoother interface. Navigator 3.0, in particular, may have difficulties with pages that instantiate too many cookie objects simultaneously because of problems in its garbage collection routines. Still, developers who work with multiple cookie values on a regular basis may find this an easier and more extensible option than tracking the names and values of many cookies.

Prototypes are available only in Netscape and Microsoft browsers Version 3.0 and higher. The code in this section does not work at all with Netscape Navigator 2.0. Developers who need to provide cookie functionality to users of Navigator 2.0 should use the library functions above.

JavaScript objects are fairly chameleon-like, appearing in a wide variety of situations that other languages would handle with more convential procedural structures. Objects and their methods can be defined and redefined during program execution, and their properties can be accessed in a number of ways. All JavaScript objects are partially arrays; all arrays are also objects. Just as elements can be added to an array on the fly, so too can properties be added to an object. Adding a property to an object is simple: just assign it a value. JavaScript will create the property. This feature makes it extremely easy to create flexible objects that keep track of multiple values in single cookies. The only difficult part (apart from the odd syntax used for creating objects in JavaScript) is keeping the user-created variables separate from the object's primary variables. Because the object stores all properties and methods as part of an array, we can check the names of the properties and methods to avoid storing them as cookie data. The code to create `CookieJar` objects follows.

```
function CookieJar(owner,name,expires,domain,path,secure){
this._owner=this._name=this._expires=this._domain=this._path=null;
this._secure=false;
if (owner) {this._owner=owner;} //document object of page calling
function
if (name) {this._name=name;}
if (expires) {this._expires=expires;}//note: should be date.
if (domain) {this._domain=domain;}
if (path) {this._path=path;}
if (secure) {this._secure=true;}
}
```

```
function CookieJar_read(){
var cookieVal, seek, start, middle, end, value, flag, error;
error="";
if (this._name!=null) {
    cookieVal=this._owner.cookie;
    if (cookieVal!=null) {
      seek=escape(this._name) + "=";
      start=cookieVal.indexOf(seek);
      if (start>-1) {
          start+=seek.length;
          end=cookieVal.indexOf(";", start);
          if (end==-1) {end=cookieVal.length;}
          value=unescape(cookieVal.substring(start,end));
          start=end=middle=flag=0; //reset start,end for use with our
                value only
          while (flag>-1){ // flag to mark not found
          //break into pieces; name/value pairs for object
          middle=value.indexOf("^",start);
          end=value.indexOf("|",middle);
          flag=end;
          if (end==-1) {end=value.length;}
          this[value.substring(start,middle)]=value.
              substring(middle+1,end);
          start=flag+1; //flag held end value safely to this point
          }
      }
      else {error="value not found"}
      }
      else {error="No cookies!";}
}
return error;
}

function CookieJar_write(){
if (this._name!=null) {
var cookieString, value, error;
cookieString=escape(this._name) + "="; //more flexible
//read object properties into value
value=error="";
for (property in this) {
  if ( (property.charAt(0)!="_") && (typeof(this[property])
      !="function") ){
    value+=property+"^"+this[property]+"|";
  }
}
cookieString+=escape(value.substring(0,value.length-1)); //chops off
final | and escapes
cookieString+=";";
checkString=value.substring(0,value.length-1); //used at end
if (this._expires) {cookieString+="expires="+this._expires.
  toGMTString();}
if (this._domain) {cookieString+="domain="+this._domain;}
if (this._path) {cookieString+="path="+this._path;}
if (this._secure) {cookieString+="secure;";}
this._owner.cookie=cookieString;
//check to make sure it worked...
cookieVal=this._owner.cookie;
seek=escape(this._name) + "=";
    start=cookieVal.indexOf(seek);
```

```
        if (start>-1) {
            start+=seek.length;
            end=cookieVal.indexOf(";", start);
            if (end==-1) {end=cookieVal.length;}
            value=unescape(cookieVal.substring(start,end));
            }
if (checkString!=value) {error="Write failure"};
}
return error;
}

function CookieJar_crunch(){
var cookieString,expire;
cookieString=escape(this._name) + "=kill;";
expire=new Date(1975,1,1);
cookieString+="expires=" + expire.toGMTString();
//that's all, folks...
this._owner.cookie=cookieString;
for (property in this) {
  if ( (property.charAt(0)!="_") && (typeof(this[property])
      !="function") ){
    this[property]=null;
  }
}}
//declaration to create "object"
new CookieJar();
CookieJar.prototype.read=CookieJar_read;
CookieJar.prototype.write=CookieJar_write;
CookieJar.prototype.crunch=CookieJar_crunch;
```

The CookieJar class has a constructor function and three methods. The constructor function takes as arguments the Document object of the page calling it and all of the usual cookie parameters except for value. The class could be simplified by leaving out the Document object, but this can create problems when the code for the CookieJar class is in a separate file from the document using it. The value argument need not be declared because the CookieJar will create its value from the properties assigned to the object. Properties internal to CookieJar objects begin with an underscore (_); all other properties will become part of the value. (Because JavaScript provides no intrinsic way to separate these properties, naming conventions are the only easy way to implement this.) For example, the following code will create a cookie whose value contains the pairs chocolate and chip and caramel and apple:

```
myCookie=new CookieJar();
myCookie.chocolate="chip";
myCookie.caramel="apple";
errValue=myCookie.write();
```

The write() method encodes all the property names and values into a single cookie value, which is then associated with the _Name property of the cookie object. This encoding uses the delimiters ^ and |, which should not appear in either the name or the value of the properties. The `write()` method verifies the cookie after writing it, and returns an error if the cookie was not written. (This can happen when users have disabled cookies or reject a cookie, because an illegal value was stored as part of the cookie, or because the cookie has grown beyond the 4K limit.) The `read()` method checks the cookie and decodes all the stored values, reassociating properties with their values. `myCookie.caramel` will be restored to `apple` and `myCookie.chocolate` will be restored to `chip` when the `read()` method is called:

```
errValue=myCookie.read();
```

If there are no cookies available, or no values in the cookie, the error value is worth reading. (It is not mandatory—`myCookie.read()` has the same effect on the object's values.) Also note that the constructor for the object does not read in the initial values. This allows developers to create new sets of values, overwriting the old, when they update the material stored in the cookie. If the contructor read in the values, all the old properties would linger along with the new one. Developers who reused the cookie but changed the property names could quickly approach the 4K limit. All cookie objects that need to read in previous values should use the `read()` method immediately after their creation.

The `crunch()` method will remove this cookie from the user's computer:

```
myCookie.crunch();
```

The `crunch()` method both deletes the cookie and sets the value of all the object's non-core properties to null. Setting the cookie again requires setting the values and calling the `write()` function again; `read()` will return only nulls.

The code below provides a simple test of the cookie object library. For best effect, set the browser to ask before accepting cookies.

```
<HTML>
<BODY>
<SCRIPT LANGUAGE="JavaScript" SRC="cookob.js">
</SCRIPT><SCRIPT>
expiration=new Date(1999,10,4);
myCookie=new CookieJar(document, "yucko",expiration);
myCookie.junk="testing junk";
myCookie.zipper="testing zippers";
myCookie.write();
myCookie.crunch();
myCookie.read();
alert (myCookie.junk +"\n" + myCookie.zipper);
</SCRIPT>
<H1>Cookie Test</H1>
</BODY></HTML>
```

This code is mildly unusual, but makes it easy to see what is happening. Running the code as is, with the warning for cookies turned on, produces the initial message shown in Figure 4-26.

Figure 4-26
Cookie Warning
Message

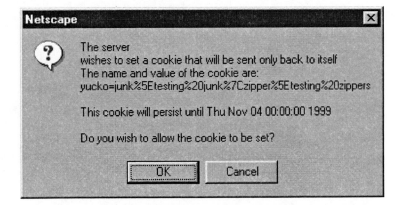

The next message is caused by the `crunch()` method. The date to be set is a little behind the times, as shown in Figure 4-27.

Figure 4-27
Cookie
Destruction
Message

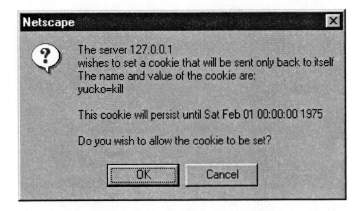

The final message, shown in Figure 4-28, displays the results of the crunched cookie: a pair of nulls.

Figure 4-28
Cookie Values
Successfully
Destroyed

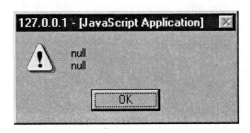

For a more positive result, comment out or delete the `myCookie.crunch()` line. The final results will read as shown in Figure 4-29.

Figure 4-29
Cookie Values
Read into
the Object

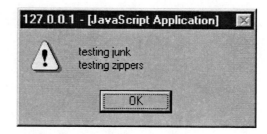

Now that the toolbox is full, it is time to march forward and start using some cookies.

Client-side Cookie Applications

Now that we have a full set of tools, we can begin creating applications that apply them. These client-side cookie applications are useful for the most part only for maintaining state on a user's computer, though later chapters will come back to them to expand them into server-side functionality as well. (Cookies created on the client side will still get passed to the server with every HTTP request, so don't pretend to be preserving privacy with this style of application.)

Client-side cookies cannot walk users through most of the applications discussed in Chapter 1. Because of the completely open nature of their code, these cookies are extremely vulnerable to tampering, so that they become useless for anything involving private information. Cookies in this situation are great for keeping small amounts of information on the user's computer, providing a low level of customization or a tiny bit of data storage, but should not be taken for more than that. Figure 4-30 shows the transactionless state management that cookies can provide.

While it is possible and even sometimes convenient to use client-side scripting to implement shopping carts, shopping carts by their very nature are intended for a transaction between a shopper and a merchant, not just a shopper and a cart. The examples that follow illustrate some of the tasks for which purely client-side cookie scripting is useful. Tasks that use both client-side and server-side scripting will be explored in Chapters 6,7, and 8.

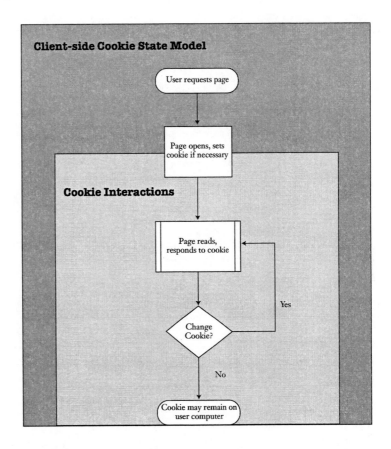

Figure 4-30
Client-side Cookie
State Diagram

CookieView

Our first application is still partially a utility package. All it does is display all the cookies that are available to the current page, and allow users to set the value of a cookie by entering a new value. CookieView is not a page that most developers want to make available to users, but it is extremely useful for debugging pages. CookieView uses a textarea box to provide reasonably convenient viewing of (escaped and unescaped) cookie contents, and a few input fields to allow for changes to cookies and cookie destruction. CookieView uses the WriteCookie() and ReadCookie() functions, as well as some additional code with functions that make it easier to display multiple cookie values simultaneously.

```
<HTML>
<HEAD><TITLE>CookieView</TITLE></HEAD>
<BODY>
<H1>CookieView</H1>
<FORM NAME="cookieView">
Active cookies for this page:<BR>
```

```
<TEXTAREA NAME="viewer" ROWS=10 COLS=80></TEXTAREA><BR>
<A HREF="javascript: unescapeView()">Unescape data</A>
    
<A HREF="javascript: escapeView()">Escape data</A>
<P>Cookie Entry Area:</P>
Name: <INPUT TYPE="TEXT" SIZE=30 NAME="cookieName"><BR>
Value: <INPUT TYPE="TEXT" SIZE=50 NAME="cookieValue"><BR>
Expiration: <INPUT TYPE="TEXT" SIZE=15 NAME="cookieExpires">
Domain: <INPUT TYPE="TEXT" SIZE=15 NAME="cookieDomain">
Path: <INPUT TYPE="TEXT" SIZE=15 NAME="cookiePath">
Secure: <INPUT TYPE="CHECKBOX" NAME="cookieSecure"><BR>
<A HREF="javascript: setCookie()">Set this cookie</A>
</FORM>
<SCRIPT LANGUAGE="JavaScript" SRC="jscooklb.js"></SCRIPT>
<SCRIPT LANGUAGE="JavaScript">
function stringInsert(initial, replace, position){
start=parseInt(position);
end=start+replace.length;
newVal=initial.substring(0,start)+replace+initial.substring(end,
        initial.length);
return newVal;
}
function cookieSplit(inString){
var findString, place;
inString=" "+inString;
findString=";";
place=0;
while (place>-1) {
place=parseInt(place);
place=inString.indexOf(findString,place+1);
if (place =="") {place=-1;} //fixes a Netscape bug
if (place != -1) {inString=stringInsert(inString,"\n",place);}
}
return inString;
}
function unescapeView(){document.cookieView.viewer.value=
        unescape(document.cookieView.viewer.value);
}
function escapeView(){
currentCook=document.cookie;
document.cookieView.viewer.value=cookieSplit(currentCook);
}
function setCookie(){
var name, value, expires, domain, path, secure;
name=document.cookieView.cookieName.value;
value=document.cookieView.cookieValue.value;
if (document.cookieView.cookieExpires.value){
expires=new Date(document.cookieView.cookieExpires.value);}
domain=document.cookieView.cookieDomain.value;
path=document.cookieView.cookiePath.value;
secure=null;
if (document.cookieView.cookieSecure.checked){
secure="TRUE";}
WriteCookie(name,value,expires,domain,path,secure);
escapeView();
}
escapeView();
</SCRIPT>
</HTML>
```

Most of the functions used directly in this page should be familiar. The `stringInsert()` function comes directly from code used earlier in this chapter. The `cookieSplit()` function is a modified version of the earlier `find()`. Instead of just reporting where it found the desired string, it calls `stringInsert()` to replace the semicolons with newlines, putting each cookie on its own line. The `unescapeView()` function just makes the current contents of the viewer window more readable by using JavaScript's `unescape()` function. The `escapeView()` function is considerably more complex. It can't just `escape()` the contents of the document window, because the equal signs would become garbled and all the line breaks would disappear. Instead, this function refreshes the `cookieView` display, running the current value of `document.cookie` through the `cookieSplit()` function and displaying the results. Names and values are still escaped, but the equal sign remains clear. The `setCookie()` function collects the data from the form fields and calls the `WriteCookie()` function from the library functions. Then it calls `escapeView()` to refresh the display, providing instant gratification to those who want to create and destroy cookies at will.

Developers who need to see their cookies exactly as the script receives them will appreciate the "escaped view" shown in Figure 4-31, while developers who prefer to read their values in something resembling normal text will prefer the unescaped version of Figure 4-32.

Figure 4-31
"Escaped
View" of the
`CookieView` Page

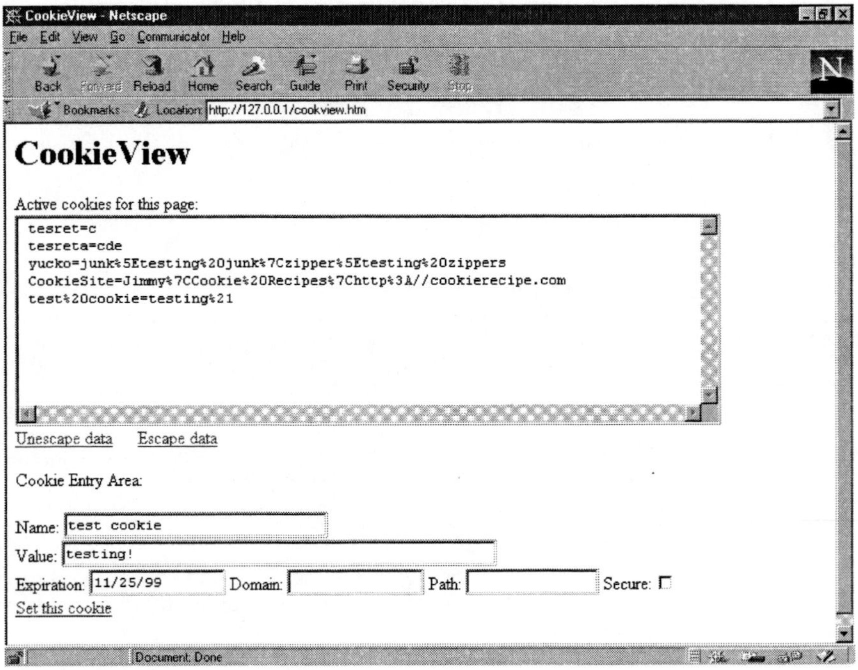

Figure 4-32
"Unescaped
View" of the
`CookieView` Page,
Delivering more
Comprehensible
Information

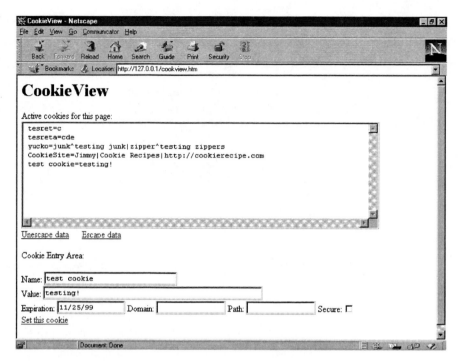

The VBScript version uses the same set of functions, though it retreats to JavaScript for some of the code handling escaping. (To keep this code short, I have also used the JavaScript date conversion function, modifying `WriteCookie()` slightly to pass parameters correctly.) As noted above, the VBScript functions must be included in the script directly to maintain compatibility with older versions of Internet Explorer.

```
<HTML>
<HEAD><TITLE>CookieView</TITLE></HEAD>
<BODY>
<H1>CookieView</H1>
<FORM NAME="cookieView">
Active cookies for this page:<BR>
<TEXTAREA NAME="viewer" ROWS=10 COLS=80></TEXTAREA><BR>
<A HREF="javascript: unescapeView()">Unescape data</A>
    
<A HREF="javascript: escapeView()">Escape data</A>
<P>Cookie Entry Area:</P>
Name: <INPUT TYPE="TEXT" SIZE=30 NAME="cookieName"><BR>
Value: <INPUT TYPE="TEXT" SIZE=50 NAME="cookieValue"><BR>
Expiration: <INPUT TYPE="TEXT" SIZE=15 NAME="cookieExpires">
Domain: <INPUT TYPE="TEXT" SIZE=15 NAME="cookieDomain">
Path: <INPUT TYPE="TEXT" SIZE=15 NAME="cookiePath">
Secure: <INPUT TYPE="CHECKBOX" NAME="cookieSecure"><BR>
<A HREF="javascript: setCookie()">Set this cookie</A>
</FORM>
<SCRIPT LANGUAGE="JavaScript">
```

```
function unescapeView(){document.cookieView.viewer.value=
          unescape(document.cookieView.viewer.value);}

function JSescape(toEscape) {
return escape(toEscape);
}
function JSunescape(fromEscape) {
return unescape(fromEscape);
}

function convGMT(VBday,VBmonth,VByear){
VBmonth=VBmonth-1;
realDate=new Date(VByear,VBmonth,VBday);
dateString=realDate.toGMTString();
return(dateString);
}
</SCRIPT>
<SCRIPT LANGUAGE="VBScript">
function ReadCookie(name)
dim allCookie, CookieVal, length,startPos, endPos
cookieVal=""
name=name& "=" 'append equals to avoid false matches.
allCookie=document.cookie
length=len(allCookie)
'check for no cookies - user is probably incinerating cookies.
if (length>0) then
    startPos=InStr(1, allCookie,name)

    'if string appeared - otherwise cookie wasn't set.
    if (startPos<>-1) then
     startPos=startPos + len(name)
     endPos=InStr(startPos,allCookie,";")
     if (endPos<1) then endPos=length+1
     cookieVal=JSunescape(Mid(allCookie,startPos,endPos-startPos))
    End if
End if
ReadCookie=cookieVal
End Function

function WriteCookie(name,value,expires,domain,path,secure)
dim CookieVal,CookError
CookieVal=""
CookError=""

if name <> "" then
    CookieVal=CookieVal & JSescape(name) & "="
if value<>"" then
    CookieVal= CookieVal & JSescape(value)
    if expires<>"" then CookieVal=CookieVal & ";
expires="&convGMT(Day(expires),Month(expires),Year(expires))
    ' note changes to convGMT parameters to allow JS convGMT
    if domain<>"" then CookieVal=CookieVal & "; domain="&domain
    if path<>"" then CookieVal=CookieVal & "; path="&path
    if secure<>"" then CookieVal=CookieVal & "; secure"
        else CookError="Value failure" 'need valid value
    end if
else CookError=CookError & "Name failure" 'need valid name
end if

if (CookError="") then
```

```
        document.cookie=CookieVal 'sets cookie
        if (value <> ReadCookie(name)) then CookError="Write failure"
        ' checks to make sure it worked
    end if
    writeCookie=CookError
    end function

    function stringInsert(initial, replace, start) repLen=len(replace)
    rightLen=(len(initial))-start-repLen
    newVal=Left(initial,start) & replace & Right(initial,rightLen)
    stringInsert=newVal
    end function

    function cookieSplit(inString)
    dim place, quit, findString
    place=0
    quit=1
    findString="; "
    while (quit>0)
      place=InStr(place+1,inString,findString,1)
      quit=place
      if IsNull(place) Then
          quit=0
          place=0
      end if
      if place<>0 then
          inString=stringInsert(inString,chr(13) & chr(10),place-1) 'note
                  use of chr(13) & chr(10) to create line break
      end if
    wend
    cookieSplit=inString
    end function

    sub escapeView
    currentCook=document.cookie
    document.cookieView.viewer.value=cookieSplit(currentCook)
    end sub

    sub setCookie
    dim name, value, expires, domain, path, secure
    name=document.cookieView.cookieName.value
    value=document.cookieView.cookieValue.value
    if (document.cookieView.cookieExpires.value<>"") then expires=DateVal-
    ue(document.cookieView.cookieExpires.value)
    domain=document.cookieView.cookieDomain.value
    path=document.cookieView.cookiePath.value
    secure=null
    if (document.cookieView.cookieSecure.checked) then secure="TRUE"
    errorVal=WriteCookie(name,value,expires,domain,path,secure)
    escapeView
    end sub

    escapeView
    </SCRIPT>
    </HTML>
```

This version of `CookieView` looks and behaves exactly like the JavaScript
version, as shown in Figures 4-33 and 4-34. The structures in this example
are remarkably similar to their JavaScript counterparts.

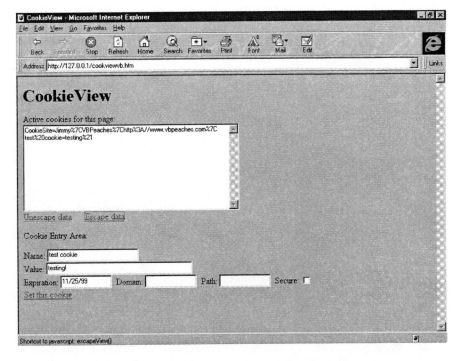

Personalizing Web Pages

Our next application is perhaps the classic use of client-side cookies. Sites have used cookies to add personalization information since cookies first appeared. Personalizing pages on the client side is a little more difficult than personalizing pages from the server, because of the limited amount of information that can be stored and because of the restrictions on what scripting languages can do to a page after it has loaded. The first example in this section employs script to write directly to a page, using a cookie to define what a page should look like when it loads.

JavaScript and VBScript both allow developers to write code that effectively writes a document into the browser. This code can only run as the page is loaded; no changes can be made after the program finishes its intial run. Both take advantage of the `document.write()` method to create their pages. To apply cookies using these tools, developers need to create two pages: one to set the value of the cookie object, and the other to write the page. The amount of information that can be transferred using this technique is fairly small, and developers will quickly hit a wall if they want to use it to encode more than a user's name, some colors, and possibly a link or two. In this example, the first page will use an entry page that collects information through dialog boxes and displays it in form fields on the page. The second page actually uses the information to create its content.

The code for both pages uses the simpler JavaScript cookie library presented above.

```
<HTML>
<HEAD><TITLE>Cookie Page Creator</TITLE></HEAD>
<BODY BGCOLOR="#FFFFFF">
<H1>Page Creation with Cookies</H1>
<P>Welcome to a demonstration of how to use cookies to store
information to be used in web pages. This page will allow you to enter
information through a short series of dialog boxes. You can see the
information you have entered in the form fields below. The cookie this
page sets will last for two days after this session is complete.</P>
<A HREF="javascript:interview()">Talk to the cookie maker</A><BR>
<A HREF="cookiepage.htm">See the page created by the cookies.</A><BR>
<FORM NAME="DisplayCookie">
<H3>Current Cookie Contents (read-only)</H3>
Your name is:
<INPUT TYPE="TEXTBOX" ID="Name" SIZE="15"><BR>
Your favorite site's name is:
<INPUT TYPE="TEXTBOX" ID="SiteName" SIZE="30"><BR>
Your favorite site's address is:
<INPUT TYPE="TEXTBOX" ID="SiteAddress" SIZE="60"><BR>
</FORM>
<SCRIPT LANGUAGE="JavaScript" SRC="jscooklb.js"></SCRIPT>
<SCRIPT LANGUAGE="JavaScript">
function setFields(){
var cookieValue, pieces;
cookieValue=ReadCookie("CookieSite");
```

```
pieces=breakdown(cookieValue);
for (i=0; i<3; i++){
document.forms[0].elements[i].value=pieces[i+1];
}
}
function interview(){
var name, sitename, address, expiry;
name=prompt("What is your first name?","");
sitename=prompt("What is your favorite site?","");
address=prompt("What is your favorite site's address?","http://");
value=combine(name,sitename,address);
expiry=new Date((new Date()).getTime()+172800000);
WriteCookie("CookieSite",value, expiry);
setFields();
}
setFields();
</SCRIPT></BODY></HTML>
```

The code for the second page (cookiepage.htm) uses the same library,
but is otherwise much simpler:

```
<HTML>
<HEAD><TITLE>This page created with Cookie Information</TITLE></HEAD>
<BODY>
<SCRIPT LANGUAGE="JavaScript" SRC="jscooklb.js"></SCRIPT>
<SCRIPT LANGUAGE="JavaScript">
cookieValue=ReadCookie("CookieSite");
pieces=breakdown(cookieValue);
document.write ("<H1>"+pieces[1]+"'s page.</H1>");
document.write ("<P>My favorite site is <A
        HREF='"+pieces[3]+"'>"+pieces[2]+"</A>.</P>");
</SCRIPT>
</HTML>
```

Although the first page can present the values stored in the cookie through
text fields on a form, they don't have the impact of direct inclusion in the
HTML, as is seen in Figures 4-35 and 4-36.

Figure 4-35
Interview Page

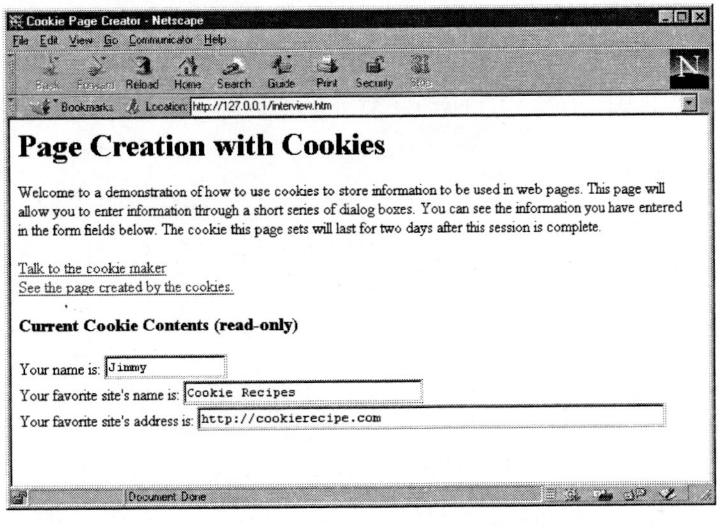

Figure 4-36
Cookie-created
Page

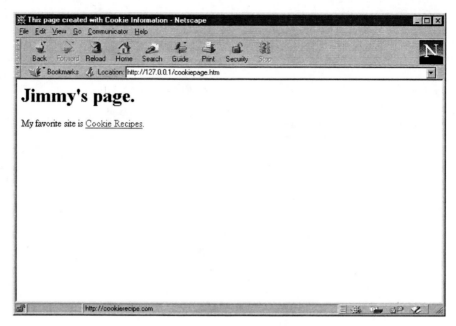

VBScript can produce the same results, using the code in the following two
listings:

```
<HTML>
<HEAD><TITLE>Cookie Page Creator</TITLE></HEAD>
<BODY BGCOLOR="#FFFFFF">
<H1>Page Creation with Cookies</H1>
<P>Welcome to a demonstration of how to use cookies to store informa-
tion to be used in web pages. This page will allow you to enter infor-
mation through a short series of dialog boxes. You can see the infor-
mation you have entered in the form fields below. The cookie this page
sets will last for two days after this session is complete.</P>
<A HREF="javascript:interview()">Talk to the cookie maker</A><BR>
<A HREF="vbokiepage.htm">See the page created by the cookies.</A><BR>
<FORM NAME="DisplayCookie">
<H3>Current Cookie Contents (read-only)</H3>
Your name is:
<INPUT TYPE="TEXTBOX" ID="Name" SIZE="15"><BR>
Your favorite site's name is:
<INPUT TYPE="TEXTBOX" ID="SiteName" SIZE="30"><BR>
Your favorite site's address is:
<INPUT TYPE="TEXTBOX" ID="SiteAddress" SIZE="60"><BR>
</FORM>
<SCRIPT LANGUAGE="JavaScript" SRC="jscooklb.js">
function JSescape(toEscape) {
return escape(toEscape);
}
function JSunescape(fromEscape) {
return unescape(fromEscape);
}
</SCRIPT>
```

```
<SCRIPT LANGUAGE="VBScript">
function convGMT(convDate)
Dim weekdays(6)
weekdays(0)="Sun"
weekdays(1)="Mon"
weekdays(2)="Tue"
weekdays(3)="Wed"
weekdays(4)="Thu"
weekdays(5)="Fri"
weekdays(6)="Sat"
Dim months(11)
months(0)="Jan"
months(1)="Feb"
months(2)="Mar"
months(3)="Apr"
months(4)="May"
months(5)="Jun"
months(6)="Jul"
months(7)="Aug"
months(8)="Sep"
months(9)="Oct"
months(10)="Nov"
months(11)="Dec"
myWeekday=Weekday(convDate)-1
myDay=Day(convDate)
if myDay<10 then myDay="0" & myDay
myMonth=Month(convDate)-1
myYear=Year(convDate)
convGMT=weekdays(myWeekday) & ", " & myDay & " " & months(myMonth) & "
        " & myYear & " 00:00:00 GMT"
end function

function combine(arguments)
dim delimiter, numArgs, combination, i
combination=""
delimiter="|"
if IsArray(arguments) then
    numArgs=UBound(arguments)
    if (numArgs>1) then
     for i=1 to numArgs
         combination=combination & arguments(i) & delimiter
       next
end if
end if
combine=Left(combination, len(combination)-1)
end function

function breakdown(combination)
dim delimiter, startPos, endPos, count
dim broken()
reDim broken(1)
delimiter="|"
startPos=1
endPos=1
count=1
endPos=InStr(endPos, combination,delimiter)
while (endPos>0)
    broken(count)=Mid(combination, startPos,endPos-startPos)
    count=count+1
    reDim Preserve broken(count)
```

```
    startPos=endPos+1
    endPos=InStr(startPos,combination, delimiter)
wend
broken(count)=Mid(combination, startPos, len(combination))
'This picks up the last entry. Returns nothing if there is none.
breakdown=broken
end function

function ReadCookie(name)
dim allCookie, CookieVal, length,startPos, endPos
cookieVal=""
name=name& "=" 'append equals to avoid false matches.
allCookie=document.cookie
length=len(allCookie)
'check for no cookies - user is probably incinerating cookies.
if (length>0) then
    startPos=InStr(1, allCookie,name)
    'if string appeared - otherwise cookie wasn't set.
    if (startPos>0) then
     startPos=startPos + len(name)
     endPos=InStr(startPos,allCookie,";")
     if (endPos<1) then endPos=length+1
     cookieVal=JSunescape(Mid(allCookie,startPos,endPos-startPos))
    End if
End if
ReadCookie=cookieVal
End Function

function WriteCookie(name,value,expires,domain,path,secure)
dim CookieVal,CookError
CookieVal=""
CookError=""

if name <> "" then
    CookieVal=CookieVal & JSescape(name) & "=" 'leave out the JSescape
            for pure VB
    if value<>"" then
     CookieVal= CookieVal & JSescape(value) 'leave out JSescape for
              pure VB
     if expires<>"" then CookieVal=CookieVal & ";
             expires="&convGMT(expires)
     if domain<>"" then CookieVal=CookieVal & "; domain="&domain
     if path<>"" then CookieVal=CookieVal & "; path="&path
     if secure<>"" then CookieVal=CookieVal & "; secure"
        else CookError="Value failure" 'need valid value
    end if
else CookError=CookError & "Name failure" 'need valid name
end if
if (CookError="") then
    document.cookie=CookieVal 'sets cookie
    if (value <> ReadCookie(name)) then CookError="Write failure"
    ' checks to make sure it worked
end if
writeCookie=CookError
end function

sub setFields
dim cookieValue, pieces
cookieValue=ReadCookie("CookieSite")'
pieces=breakdown(cookieValue)
```

```
for i=0 to 2
document.forms(0).elements(i).value=pieces(i+1)
next
end sub

sub interview
dim info(4)
dim today,expiry,errorVal
info(1)=prompt("What is your first name?","")
info(2)=prompt("What is your favorite site?","")
info(3)=prompt("What is your favorite site's address?","http://")
value=combine(info)
today=Now()
expiry=DateSerial(Year(today),month(today),day(today)+2)
errorVal=WriteCookie("CookieSite",value, expiry,"","","")

setFields
end sub
setFields
</SCRIPT></BODY></HTML>
```

The code for the receiving page (`vbokiepage.htm`) doesn't need all the functions available in the library; it only uses the `ReadCookie` and breakdown functions.

```
<HTML>
<HEAD><TITLE>This page created with Cookie Information</TITLE></HEAD>
<BODY>
<SCRIPT LANGUAGE="JavaScript">
function JSescape(toEscape) {
return escape(toEscape);
}
function JSunescape(fromEscape) {
return unescape(fromEscape);
}

</SCRIPT>
<SCRIPT LANGUAGE="VBScript">

function breakdown(combination)
dim delimiter, startPos, endPos, count
dim broken()
reDim broken(1)
delimiter="|"
startPos=1
endPos=1
count=1
endPos=InStr(endPos, combination,delimiter)
while (endPos>0)
    broken(count)=Mid(combination, startPos,endPos-startPos)
    count=count+1
    reDim Preserve broken(count)
    startPos=endPos+1
    endPos=InStr(startPos,combination, delimiter)
wend
```

```
broken(count)=Mid(combination, startPos, len(combination))
'This picks up the last entry. Returns nothing if there is none.
breakdown=broken
end function

function ReadCookie(name)
dim allCookie, CookieVal, length,startPos, endPos
cookieVal=""
name=name& "=" 'append equals to avoid false matches.
allCookie=document.cookie
length=len(allCookie)
'check for no cookies - user is probably incinerating cookies.
if (length>0) then
    startPos=InStr(1, allCookie,name)
    'if string appeared - otherwise cookie wasn't set.
    if (startPos>0) then
     startPos=startPos + len(name)
     endPos=InStr(startPos,allCookie,";")
     if (endPos<1) then endPos=length+1
     cookieVal=JSunescape(Mid(allCookie,startPos,endPos-startPos))
    End if
End if
ReadCookie=cookieVal
End Function

cookieValue=ReadCookie("CookieSite")
pieces=breakdown(cookieValue)
document.write ("<H1>"+pieces(1)+"'s page.</H1>")
document.write ("<P>My favorite site is <A
        HREF='"+pieces(3)+"'>"+pieces(2)+"</A>.</P>")
</SCRIPT>
</HTML>
```

All future VBScript code listings will omit the library to conserve space. The code listing will include <!--VBSCRIPT COOKIE LIBRARY CODE HERE--> where the VBScript library should be added.

The results for VB are similar, as shown in Figures 4-37 and 4-38. The underlying mechanisms may have changed, but the output is close to identical.

Figure 4-37
Cookie-based
Page Creator
Using VBScript

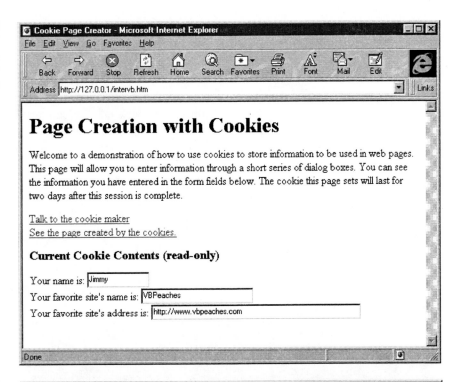

Figure 4-38
Cookie-based
Page Created
with VBScript

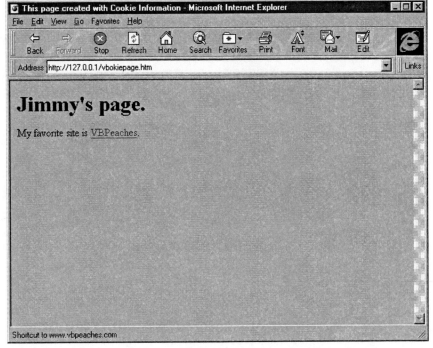

Interface Management: Cookies and Frames

Even if developers take advantage of all 20 cookies available and stuff them with the maximum amount of information, the number of pages with significant content that can be created using `document.write` is still very limited. A more common approach takes advantage of frames. Cookies and frames can be a powerful combination. Cookies provide a stable source of information, while frames provide the flexibility needed to take advantage of that information. Cookies also provide a common place where frames can share data, avoiding many of the complications created by scripts that communicate across frame boundaries.

This example will build a small site with a navigation list that allows a user to a choose home page from among the options. The user can set the cookie from the navigation bar frame, or use scripts written into the target files to set the cookie from the document.

The base document for all of these versions is the same:

```
<HTML>
<HEAD><TITLE>Frames and Cookies demo</TITLE></HEAD>
<FRAMESET COLS="150,*">
<FRAME FRAMEBORDER=0 SRC="controls.htm" NAME="controls">
<FRAME FRAMEBORDER=0 SRC="target.htm" NAME="targetFrame"></FRAMESET>
</HTML>
```

This document could also read the cookie and use `document.write()` to create the frameset if there were a good architectural reason for that, but for this example all of the action will take place in the lower frames.

The `controls.htm` file can set the cookie to the current page displayed in the `targetFrame`, or take the user "home" to the chosen page:

```
<HTML>
<HEAD><TITLE>Frames and Cookies demo</TITLE></HEAD>
<SCRIPT LANGUAGE="JavaScript" SRC="jscook1b.js"></SCRIPT>
<SCRIPT LANGUAGE="JavaScript">
function writeTarget(){
var targetFile, expires;
expires=new Date((new Date()).getTime()+172800000);
//two-day lifespan for cookie
targetFile=(parent.targetFrame.window.location);
WriteCookie("homepage",targetFile, expires);
}

function goHome(){
var targetFile;
targetFile=ReadCookie("homepage");
parent.targetFrame.window.location=targetFile;
}
</SCRIPT>
<BODY>
<H2>Controls</H2>
```

```
<A HREF="target1.htm" TARGET="targetFrame">Target 1</A><BR>
<A HREF="target2.htm" TARGET="targetFrame">Target 2</A><BR>
<A HREF="target3.htm" TARGET="targetFrame">Target 3</A><BR>
<A HREF="target4.htm" TARGET="targetFrame">Target 4</A><BR>
<A HREF="target5.htm" TARGET="targetFrame">Target 5</A><BR>
<P><A HREF="javascript:writeTarget()">Make this Home</A><BR>
<A HREF="javascript:goHome()">Go Home</A><BR></P>
</BODY></HTML>
```

This code reads and writes the URL of the document in `targetFrame`. The `writeTarget()` function reads the URL from the frame and writes it to the cookie; goHome() reads the cookie and writes the URL. (Note that both of these address the `window.location` property, not the `document.location` property. The `document.location` property is read-only in Internet Explorer.) The page also provides a simple list of other pages which the user can visit.

The next key page is `target.htm`. This file should just read the cookie and move to the page it specifies. If the cookie is not set, or if cookies are disabled, the remaining HTML content of `target.htm` should provide a generic home page document for the site.

```
<HTML>
<HEAD><TITLE>Frames and Cookies demo</TITLE>
<SCRIPT LANGUAGE="JavaScript" SRC="jscook1b.js"></SCRIPT>
<SCRIPT>
var target;
target=ReadCookie("homepage");
if ((target!="") && (target!=window.location)) {
//checks to avoid empty window or endless loop
    window.location=target;
}
</SCRIPT>
</HEAD>
<BODY>
Alternate content goes here.
</BODY></HTML>
```

The controls frame or even the top-level frameset could open this page to the proper location, but using the target window this way makes it very easy to provide alternate content, even in the event of someone's opening the file outside the frameset in a browser that does not support cookies or scripting. This style of frame programming degrades reasonably gracefully.

The `targetx.htm` files themselves can be anything. `Target5.htm` has some extra code built into it to allow the page to make itself the home page for the frameset without any intervention from the controls frame:

```
<HTML>
<HEAD><TITLE>Frames and Cookies demo</TITLE></HEAD>
<BODY>
<SCRIPT LANGUAGE="JavaScript" SRC="jscook1b.js"></SCRIPT>
```

```
<SCRIPT LANGUAGE="JavaScript">
function writeMyTarget(){
var targetFile, expires;
expires=new Date((new Date()).getTime()+172800000);
//two-day time limit - extend if desired
targetFile=(window.location);
WriteCookie("homepage",targetFile, expires);
}
</SCRIPT>
Target5!<BR>
<A HREF="javascript:writeMyTarget()">Make this your home page of
        choice!</A>
</BODY></HTML>
```

The `writeMyTarget()` function gets the URL of the page from `window.location` and writes it into the cookie. This code is portable—it can be dropped into any page in the frameset as is, and will record the correct page location without further intervention.

The first time users open this site, (assuming no cookie has yet been set) they will see a screen resembling Figure 4-39.

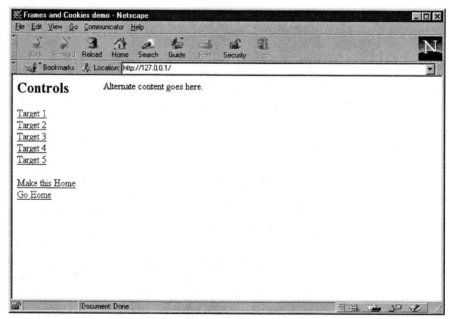

Figure 4-39
Opening the Site for the First Time, Netscape Communicator 4.0

Picking a target window from the list in the left frame leads to the page of choice, as shown in Figure 4-40.

Figure 4-40
Exploring
Target5, Netscape
Navigator 3.0

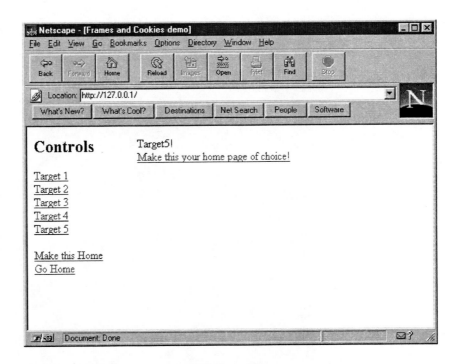

Figure 4-40
Exploring
Target5, Netscape
Navigator 3.0

If the user clicks on the **Make this your home page of choice!** text in the `Target5` page or on the **Make this Home** text in the control frame, `target5.htm` will become the default page for the `targetFrame` of this frameset. The next time a user visits (or clicks on the **Go Home** text), Figure 4-40 will appear once again. Obviously, most sites will have more exciting content than this demonstration. A Human Resources intranet site, for instance, might allow visitors consistently to open to their health benefits, dental benefits, 401K plan, or policies page by default. It is not a gigantic leap, saving a click or two, but visitors who come back to a site on a regular basis may well prefer to avoid the journey through pages and pages of unwanted material.

The VBScript versions of the files are very similar, producing the results shown in Figures 4-41 and 4-42. The top-level frameset is identical. Listings for `controls.htm`, `target.htm`, and `target5.htm` follow.

Figure 4-41
VBScript Opening
Page, Internet
Explorer 3.0

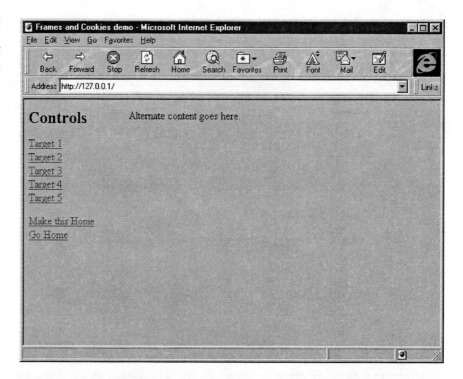

Figure 4-42
VBScript target5,
Internet
Explorer 4.0

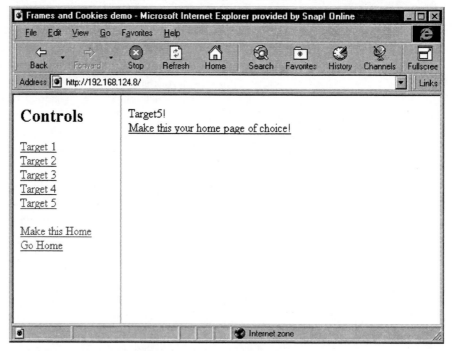

The `Controls.htm` listing is:

```
<HTML>
<HEAD><TITLE>Frames and Cookies demo</TITLE></HEAD>
<SCRIPT LANGUAGE="JavaScript">
function JSescape(toEscape) {
return escape(toEscape);}
function JSunescape(fromEscape) {
return unescape(fromEscape);}
</SCRIPT>
<SCRIPT LANGUAGE="VBScript">
<!--VBSCRIPT COOKIE LIBRARY CODE HERE -->
sub writeTarget
dim targetFile, expires, today
today=Now()
expires=DateSerial(Year(today),month(today),day(today)+2)
targetFile=(parent.targetFrame.window.location)
errorValue=WriteCookie("homepage",targetFile, expires,"","","")
end sub
sub goHome
dim targetFile
targetFile=ReadCookie("homepage")
parent.targetFrame.window.location=targetFile
end sub
</SCRIPT>
<BODY>
<H2>Controls</H2>
<A HREF="target1.htm" TARGET="targetFrame">Target 1</A><BR>
<A HREF="target2.htm" TARGET="targetFrame">Target 2</A><BR>
<A HREF="target3.htm" TARGET="targetFrame">Target 3</A><BR>
<A HREF="target4.htm" TARGET="targetFrame">Target 4</A><BR>
<A HREF="target5.htm" TARGET="targetFrame">Target 5</A><BR>
<P><A HREF="javascript:writeTarget()">Make this Home</A><BR>
<A HREF="javascript:goHome()">Go Home</A><BR></P>
</BODY></HTML>
```

The `target.htm` listing is:

```
<HTML>
<HEAD><TITLE>Frames and Cookies demo</TITLE>
<SCRIPT LANGUAGE="JavaScript">
function JSescape(toEscape) {
return escape(toEscape);
}
function JSunescape(fromEscape) {
return unescape(fromEscape);
}

</SCRIPT>
<SCRIPT LANGUAGE="VBScript">
function ReadCookie(name)
dim allCookie, CookieVal, length,startPos, endPos
cookieVal=""
name=name& "=" 'append equals to avoid false matches.
allCookie=document.cookie
length=len(allCookie)
'check for no cookies - user is probably incinerating cookies.
if (length>0) then
    startPos=InStr(1, allCookie,name)
```

```
                  'if string appeared - otherwise cookie wasn't set.
                  if (startPos>0) then
                   startPos=startPos + len(name)
                   endPos=InStr(startPos,allCookie,";")
                   if (endPos<1) then endPos=length+1
                   cookieVal=JSunescape(Mid(allCookie,startPos,endPos-startPos))
                  End if
            End if
      ReadCookie=cookieVal
      End Function

      sub window_onload
      dim target
      target=ReadCookie("homepage")
      if ((target<>"") and (target<>window.location)) then
            window.location=target
      end sub
      </SCRIPT>
      </HEAD>
      <BODY>
      Alternate content goes here.
      </BODY></HTML>
```

The `target5.htm` listing is:

```
<HTML>
<HEAD><TITLE>Frames and Cookies demo</TITLE></HEAD>
<BODY>
<SCRIPT LANGUAGE="JavaScript">
function JSescape(toEscape) {
return escape(toEscape);}
function JSunescape(fromEscape) {
return unescape(fromEscape);}
</SCRIPT>
<SCRIPT LANGUAGE="VBScript">
<!--VBSCRIPT COOKIE LIBRARY CODE HERE -->
sub writeMyTarget
dim targetFile, expires, today
today=Now()
expires=DateSerial(Year(today),month(today),day(today)+2)
targetFile=(window.location)
errorValue=WriteCookie("homepage",targetFile, expires,"","","")
end sub
</SCRIPT>
Target5!<BR>
<A HREF="javascript:writeMyTarget()">Make this your home page of
choice!</A>
</BODY></HTML>
```

In Version 3 of the Netscape and Microsoft browsers, frames were the most
advanced document-control technology available. The latest browsers from
both companies have brought significant advances, though the advances are
incompatible. Cookies can work with both companies' versions of Dynamic
HTML to provide a more consistent user interface and make users feel at
home.

Interface Management: Cookies and Layers

Netscape's main tool for creating dynamic Web pages is the Layer element. Layers are like frames in many ways, though they can be positioned anywhere on the desktop and sized to fit. Layers can use content specified within the document creating them, or accept content from outside sources. Layers make it easy to create animations and pop-up interfaces like menus and dialog boxes. Cookies can control which layers appear on a page, making it easy to customize interfaces to allow users to pick up where they left off. Layers are attached to the page that creates them; moving to another page clears all the layers and requires them to be rebuilt. Cookies can assist with this process, allowing multiple pages to present a similar interface.

This set of examples uses the JavaScript object library instead of the JavaScript function library. Because layers work only in Netscape 4, there is no point in preserving compatibility with older versions of Netscape or with VBScript. The object library also makes it easier to store multiple values and associate them with intelligible names that can easily be connected to layer information.

Like frames, layers are effectively mini-documents. This example will keep track of three layers which are used by two documents. All of the layer contents are stored in files external to the two documents that use them, simplifying content management and allowing a small amount of cookie information to have a much greater impact. Keeping the cookie objects in sync between multiple pages will require regular calls to the `read()` and `write()` methods of the cookie object. The two documents are shells, providing some content on their own and layer navigation as well. The first document provides an entryway with several menus contained in layers; as shown in Figure 4-43.

```
<HTML>
<HEAD><TITLE>Layers Entryway</TITLE></HEAD>
<BODY>
<H1>Welcome to the layers demonstration</H1>
<A HREF="page2.htm">Come on in....</A><BR>
<A HREF="javascript:toggle(1)">Menu 1</A>   
<A HREF="javascript:toggle(2)">Menu 2</A>   
<A HREF="javascript:toggle(3)">Menu 3</A>
<LAYER NAME="menu1" VISIBILITY="hide" TOP=200 LEFT=40 HEIGHT=200
   WIDTH=200 SRC="menu1.htm"></LAYER>
<LAYER NAME="menu2" VISIBILITY="hide"TOP=200 LEFT=300 HEIGHT=200
   WIDTH=200 SRC="menu2.htm"></LAYER>
```

```
<LAYER NAME="menu3" VISIBILITY="hide"TOP=200 LEFT=560 HEIGHT=200
    WIDTH=200 SRC="menu3.htm"></LAYER>
<SCRIPT LANGUAGE="JavaScript" SRC="cookob.js"></SCRIPT>
<SCRIPT LANGUAGE="JavaScript">
function setLayers(){
for (i=1; i<4; i++){
visible=status["menu"+i];
if (visible!="hide") {visible="inherit";}
document.layers["menu"+i].visibility=visible;
} }
function toggle(menuLayer){
var current
current=document.layers["menu"+menuLayer].visibility;
if (current!="hide"){
        document.layers["menu"+menuLayer].visibility="hide";
        status["menu"+menuLayer]="hide";
        }
else {
        document.layers["menu"+menuLayer].visibility="inherit";
        status["menu"+menuLayer]="inherit";
        }
status.write();
}
var expires=expires=new Date((new Date()).getTime()+1728000000); //20
    days to expire
var status=new CookieJar(document, "layers", expires);
status.read();
setLayers();
</SCRIPT>
</BODY></HTML>
```

Figure 4-43
Cookie Layers
Entryway

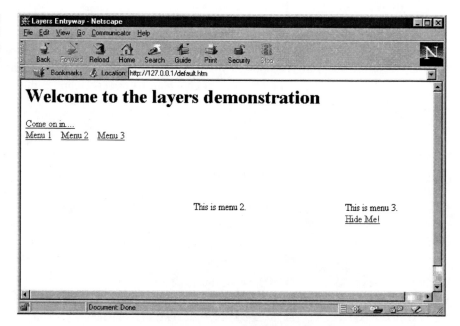

The second page (page2) contains the same code, except for the text at the top, as shown in Figure 4-44. Developers who plan to use this technique across many pages will probably want to create a layer management library that itself includes the cookie management library.

Figure 4-44
Cookie Layer
Menus at Work

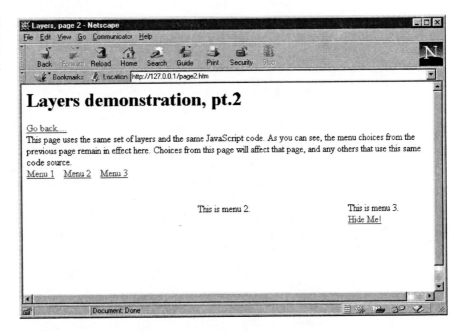

```
<HTML>
<HEAD><TITLE>Layers, page 2</TITLE></HEAD>
<BODY>
<H1>Layers demonstration, pt.2</H1>
<A HREF="default.htm">Go back....</A><BR>

This page uses the same set of layers and the same JavaScript code. As
you can see, the menu choices from the previous page remain in effect
here. Choices from this page will affect that page, and any others
that use this same code source.<BR>
<A HREF="javascript:toggle(1)">Menu 1</A>   
<A HREF="javascript:toggle(2)">Menu 2</A>   
<A HREF="javascript:toggle(3)">Menu 3</A>
<LAYER NAME="menu1" VISIBILITY="hide" TOP=200 LEFT=40 HEIGHT=200
    WIDTH=200 SRC="menu1.htm"></LAYER>
<LAYER NAME="menu2" VISIBILITY="hide"TOP=200 LEFT=300 HEIGHT=200
    WIDTH=200 SRC="menu2.htm"></LAYER>
<LAYER NAME="menu3" VISIBILITY="hide"TOP=200 LEFT=560 HEIGHT=200
    WIDTH=200 SRC="menu3.htm"></LAYER>
<SCRIPT LANGUAGE="JavaScript" SRC="cookob.js"></SCRIPT>
<SCRIPT LANGUAGE="JavaScript">
function setLayers(){
for (i=1; i<4; i++){
visible=status["menu"+i];
if (visible!="hide") {visible="inherit";}
document.layers["menu"+i].visibility=visible;
} }
```

```
function toggle(menuLayer){
var current
current=document.layers["menu"+menuLayer].visibility;
if (current!="hide"){
    document.layers["menu"+menuLayer].visibility="hide";
    status["menu"+menuLayer]="hide";
    }
else {
    document.layers["menu"+menuLayer].visibility="inherit";
    status["menu"+menuLayer]="inherit";
    }
status.write();
}
var expires=expires=new Date((new Date()).getTime()+1728000000);
var status=new CookieJar(document, "layers", expires);
status.read();
setLayers();
</SCRIPT>
</BODY></HTML>
```

The menu files themselves can contain any valid HTML that fits in the space provided. (The code above uses a name convention of `menux.htm` for the source files, where *x* is a number from 1 to 3.) One important point to remember is that layers are treated as parts of the document itself; while they have their own properties, they share scripts with the parent layer. The code for the `menu3` shown in the above example is:

```
<HTML>
<BODY>
This is menu 3.<BR>
<A HREF="javascript: toggle(3)">Hide Me!</A>
</BODY></HTML>
```

This also helps keep the cookie objects in sync, sparing developers a battle between layer functions and document functions. This code can be expanded dramatically to include any property of the Layer element. Cookies can store source file, position, and size data as well as visibility to allow the browser to create complete interfaces that remain consistent across pages.

Interface Management: Cookies and the Document Object Model

Microsoft's latest contender in the browser wars, Internet Explorer 4, takes a completely different approach to creating more interactive HTML. Instead of clustering data into layers and allowing developers to manipulate the layers, Microsoft allows developers to manipulate elements directly. This solution is considerably more flexible, though that same flexibility can swamp developers who try to do too much at once. Cookies—in concert with a good set of naming conventions—can help developers keep track of a reasonably large number of parts, enabling them to create persistent interfaces similar to the frames and Netscape's layers previously discussed.

One of the many areas in which Microsoft's Dynamic HTML excels is outlines. Using simple scripting, developers can show and hide subheads as the user needs them. Outline-based interfaces can present a vast amount of information on a single page without requiring multiple trips to a server. Cookies can enhance these outlines by acting as a kind of bookmark—the parts of a large directory that the reader needs will be the first thing they see when they return to a document.

 Although Internet Explorer 4.0 supports VBScript, this example is written using only the JavaScript cookie object library. Creating cookies that manage more than a small number of cookie values using the VBScript (or JavaScript) function library will quickly become unwieldy. Using the object library saves developers considerable hassle, allowing them to use naming conventions instead of enormous arrays.

Although this example uses a very simple outline, containing only a few items, the cookie should be able to scale to 20 or 30 items before running out of space. (Microsoft appears to allow cookies a little more room than the 4K rule, which should help.) Developers who need to scale to very large outlines should probably come up with breakdown points to allow the outline to be handled by multiple cookies.

```
<HTML>
<HEAD>
<TITLE>Outline with Naming Convention</TITLE>
</HEAD>
<BODY BGCOLOR=#FFFFFF>
<DIV ID="Main" onClick="outlineAction()">
<DIV ID="Section1" CLASS="Manager">1.0 Headline 1</DIV>
<DIV ID="Section1t" CLASS="Manager" STYLE="display:none">1.1 Headline
   1, Level 2
<DIV ID="Section1tt" STYLE="display:none">
<DIV ID="Area1" CLASS="Manager">1.1.1 Headline 1, Level 3, Part
   1</DIV>
<DIV ID="Area1t" STYLE="display:none">1.1.1.1 This could link to some-
   place</DIV>
<DIV ID="Area2" CLASS="Manager">1.1.2 Headline 1, Level 3, Part
   2</DIV>
<DIV ID="Area2t" STYLE="display:none">1.1.2.1 This could link to some-
   place</DIV>
</DIV>
</DIV>
<P> </P>
<DIV ID="Section2" CLASS="Manager">2.0 Headline 2</DIV>
<DIV ID="Section2t" STYLE="display:none">
<DIV>2.1 This could link to someplace</DIV>
<DIV>2.2 This could link to someplace</DIV>
<DIV>2.3 This could link to someplace</DIV>
<DIV>2.4 This could link to someplace</DIV></DIV>
<P> </P>
<DIV ID="Section3" CLASS="Manager">3.0 Headline 3</DIV>
<DIV ID="Section3t" STYLE="display:none">
```

```
<DIV>3.1 This could link to someplace</DIV>
<DIV>3.2 This could link to someplace</DIV>
</DIV>
</DIV>
<SCRIPT LANGUAGE="JavaScript" SRC="cookob.js"></SCRIPT>
<SCRIPT>
function setOutline(){
for (property in status) {
  if ( (property.charAt(0)!="_") && (typeof(this[property])
      !="function") ){
    if (typeof(this[property])=="object") {
    targetObject=document.all(property);
     //alert (targetObject.style.display+" "+status[property]);
    targetObject.style.display=status[property];}
  }
 }
}
function outlineAction(){
var source, targetID, targetObject; source=window.event.srcElement;
if (source.className=="Manager") {
targetID=source.id + "t";
targetObject=document.all(targetID);
if (targetObject.style.display=="none") {
        targetObject.style.display="";
        status[targetID]="";
    }
    else {
        targetObject.style.display="none";
        status[targetID]="none";
    }
}
status.write();
}
var expires=new Date((new Date()).getTime()+1728000000);
var status=new CookieJar(document, "layers", expires);
status.read();
setOutline();
</SCRIPT>
</BODY>
</HTML>
```

Note that the scripts are all kept at the bottom of the document. If the scripts were up at the top, the sections would not yet be available when setOutline() began running and would produce errors all over. The setOutline() function itself is a slightly modified version of the engine that drives WriteCookie(), using the *for property* in *object* syntax to loop through all the available properties of an object. In this case, the property names correspond to the ID attributes of the outline elements and the values are those of the elements' style.display properties. If there isn't any cookie, the document loads as specified in the HTML—an unopened outline. Every time a user opens or closes the outline, the changes are saved. Asking to be alerted about every cookie will cause hassles with this one, as every change sets off a cookie alert. If necessary, the status.write() call could be removed from the outlineAction() function and placed somewere else for those who really need to use it and don't want to be pestered with loads of cookies.

Figures 4-45 and 4-46 show the outline in action.

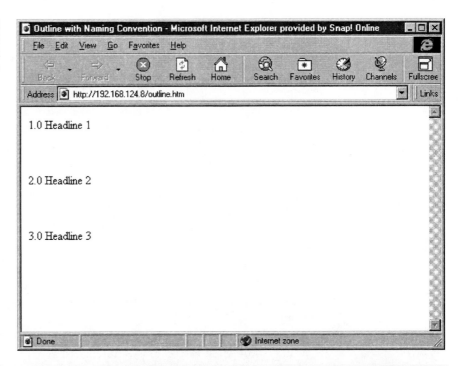

Figure 4-45
The Original
Outline

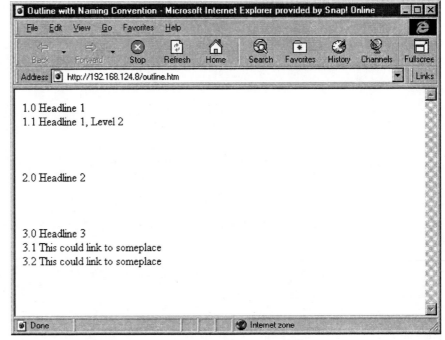

Figure 4-46
The Outline, a
Few Clicks (and
Cookies) Later

Taking Notes

Our last example will provide a somewhat unusual service for a web site: a notepad. Most cookies hold information created by a program rather than by the user. While this notepad is not terribly sophisticated (remember—its contents can be read by the server that provides the service), it provides an example of something different that could prove useful in certain situations. While its lack of security precludes its use for sensitive situations, like transactions and human resources, it does provide a useful tool for situations like Web site design reviews. This cookie makes it possible for any readers to take notes for themselves, and can be connected to server-side software (which will be considered later) to produce an instant record of reader responses.

This cookie will be created in a pop-up window, separate from the main document. This gives the notepad its own space, allowing it to persist while the user flips from page to page. The cookie is used to keep the information available between user sessions, so the user can see the notes taken on a previous visit. Unlike our previous cookie applications, this one waits for the user to specify that information should be saved, instead of saving it constantly.

The only change that must be made to the Web site hosting the notepad is adding some code to create the notepad space; the notepad is otherwise autonomous. The code (for once) is short and simple:

```
<HTML>
<HEAD>
<TITLE>Outline with Naming Convention</TITLE>
</HEAD>
<BODY BGCOLOR=#FFFFFF>
<SCRIPT LANGUAGE="JavaScript">
function popNotepad(){
window.open("notepad.htm","NotePad",'toolbar=0,location=0,
directories=0,status=0,menubar=0,scrollbars=1,resizable=0,
copyhistory=0,width=450,height=250');}
</SCRIPT>
<A HREF="javascript: popNotepad()">Click here to take notes</A>
<!--The real content of the page goes here -->
</BODY>
</HTML>
```

or, using VBScript,

```
<HTML>
<HEAD>
<TITLE>Outline with Naming Convention</TITLE>
</HEAD>
<BODY BGCOLOR="#FFFFFF">
<SCRIPT LANGUAGE="VBScript">
sub popNotepad
window.open "notepad.htm", "NotePad",
```

```
         "toolbar=no,status=0,menubar=0,width=450,height=250"
end sub
</SCRIPT>
<A HREF="javascript: popNotepad">Click here to take notes</A>
<!--The real content of the page goes here -->
</BODY>
</HTML>
```

Most of the action in the notepad takes place in the notepad.htm. When it
loads, it reads any previously stored information. The user can type into the
text area as desired, and save changes. The user can also opt to incinerate the
cookie. The code for this only requires the ReadCookie() and Write-
Cookie() methods of the function libraries created above. The JavaScript
version of notepad.htm is little more than wrapper code for those functions:

```
<HTML>
<HEAD><TITLE>Note Pad</TITLE></HEAD>
<BODY BGCOLOR="#FFFFFF">
<H2>Notepad</H2>
<P>The text box below is available for your comments. Please note that
these comments cannot be counted on to be private.</P>
<FORM NAME="noteSpace">
<TEXTAREA NAME="viewer" ROWS=5 COLS=45></TEXTAREA><BR>
<A HREF="javascript:saveNote()">Save</A>    <A
      HREF="javascript:revertNote()">Revert to
      previous</A>     <A
      HREF="javascript:deleteNote()">Delete Completely</A>
</FORM>
<SCRIPT LANGUAGE="JavaScript" SRC="jscooklb.js"></SCRIPT>
<SCRIPT LANGUAGE="JavaScript">
function saveNote(){
var noteValue, expires;
noteValue=document.noteSpace.viewer.value;
expires=new Date((new Date()).getTime()+1728000000);
WriteCookie("NotePad",noteValue,expires);
}

function revertNote(){
var noteValue;
noteValue=ReadCookie("NotePad");
document.noteSpace.viewer.value=noteValue;
}

function deleteNote(){
WriteCookie("NotePad"," ",new Date(1));
//sets date to one millisecond aft midnight, 1/1/70
document.noteSpace.viewer.value="";
}
revertNote();
</SCRIPT>
</BODY></HTML>
```

The results are promising, as shown in Figure 4-47.

Figure 4-47
The JavaScript
Notepad
Application in
Internet
Explorer 4.0

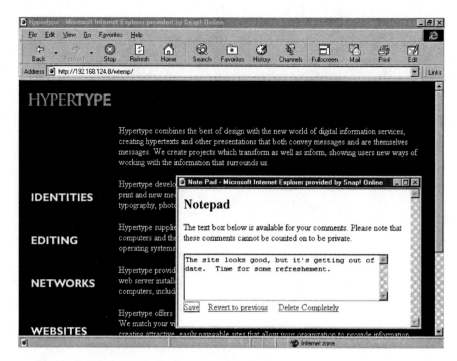

The VBScript version is just as simple:

```
<HTML>
<HEAD><TITLE>Note Pad</TITLE></HEAD>
<BODY BGCOLOR="#FFFFFF">
<H2>Notepad</H2>
<P>The text box below is available for your comments. Please note that
these comments cannot be counted on to be private.</P>
<FORM NAME="noteSpace">
<TEXTAREA NAME="viewer" ROWS=5 COLS=45></TEXTAREA><BR>
<A HREF="javascript:saveNote()">Save</A>    <A
      HREF="javascript:revertNote()">Revert to
      previous</A>     <A
      HREF="javascript:deleteNote()">Delete Completely</A>
</FORM>
<!--VBSCRIPT COOKIE LIBRARY CODE HERE -->
sub saveNote
dim noteValue, expires, today
noteValue=document.noteSpace.viewer.value
today=Now()
expires=DateSerial(Year(today),month(today),day(today)+2)
errorVal=WriteCookie("NotePad",noteValue,expires,"","","")
end sub

sub revertNote
dim noteValue
noteValue=ReadCookie("NotePad")
document.noteSpace.viewer.value=noteValue
end sub
```

```
sub deleteNote
dim today, expires
today=Now()
expires=DateSerial(Year(today),month(today),day(today)-100)
errorVal=WriteCookie("NotePad"," ",expires,"","","")
document.noteSpace.viewer.value=""
end sub
revertNote
</SCRIPT>
</BODY></HTML>
```

The only thing trickier about VBScript is the date handling, but otherwise most of the code is identical. It works well in Internet Explorer 3.0, as shown in Figure 4-48.

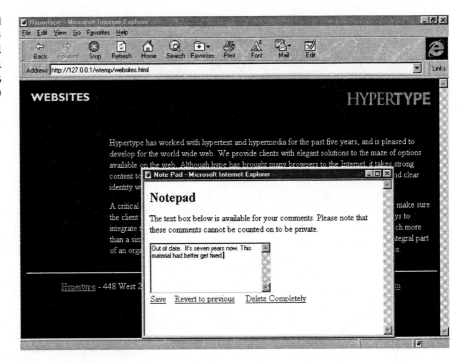

Figure 4-48
VBScript Notepad Cookie Application in Internet Explorer 3.0

Client Interactions with the Server

Although all of these examples use cookies created by a browser, servers still have full access to these cookies. As later chapters explore the world of server-side cookies, a wide variety of new uses for client-side cookies will appear. Even though the examples presented in this chapter are not capable of much on their own, they provide a strong foundation for richer applications that take advantage of both the browser,s and the Web server's abilities to manage cookies. Many shopping cart applications, for example, use client-side programming to implement the cart and keep track of the user's selection. This takes advantage of the spare processing cycles on the user's machine and avoids tying up the server any more than is absolutely necessary. When the user is ready to check out, all of the information stored in that cookie is available to the server.

## CHAPTER 5

Server-side Cookie Applications

Before the march into server-side cookie application development begins, we need to look at what client-side cookies did and how server-side cookies will differ. Although both styles of cookie programming use the same basic tools, their approaches are quite different. Client-side cookies are useful for certain situations involving limited amounts of data, while server-side cookies are good for larger projects that need to connect to larger quantities of information. Some applications may even be able to make use of both kinds of cookies. Neither approach is a complete solution to state management by itself, though many sites choose one kind of cookie or the other (usually the server flavor) and stick with it throughout a site. In this chapter we explore the implications of cookies for working with data stored at a central location—the server—as opposed to distributed information scattered among browsers.

A Question of Resources

While some pundits have proclaimed the browser the icon of distributed computing, the reality seems more and more the reverse. While people are buying personal computers at a greater pace than ever, the way they are using them is changing dramatically once again. As browsers have spread, the resources needed to feed them have been centralized, cycling back to models from earlier days of computing.

Before the Web, most personal computers were their own microcosms, each with its own applications and files. While many offices had file servers, not everyone used these enormous shared resources, and many administrators were just as happy to see users keep their own personal set of files on their own hard drive, reducing the strain on the network. While it might not have been as convenient for individuals in times of disaster (hard drive failure with no backup, for instance), it was less likely to fray the nerves of large groups stuck waiting for a network request or cursing because the network gave way under the strain and froze. After years of centralized mainframe computers, it seemed like a convenient and even perhaps economical idea to give users computing power at their desks, reducing the strain on the MIS department's overloaded databases.

When the Web appeared, the model changed again. Web browsers provided a friendly, easy way to publish information. Unlike file servers, they came with an interface that made it easy to connect files together and provide navigational hierarchies. Unlike databases, they could store just about any kind of information, including the multimedia that added sparkle to millions of Web sites. Best of all, learning how to create these documents was extremely easy. When the Web first arrived, a thorough explanation of HTML took only a few pages or a few minutes. Even without the tools that have since appeared to build pages for users, assembling a basic site could take a few hours or days, not the weeks or months involved in more complex projects. The Web was best, of course, for static documents, but there was enough interesting content which could be presented in that format to get the Web started. HTML made it possible to share documents on a whole new level, easily and conveniently.

If the Web had stopped at this point in its development, it seems likely that sooner or later every computer would have had its own Web server, and the Web would have been an incredibly intricate do-it-yourself project distributed over millions of computers. To a certain extent this has happened; many intranets, even enormous corporate intranets, began life in a small server on the desk of an employee who felt like doing something new. Software vendors have distributed millions of personal Web servers along with Web development tools, operating systems, and other staples of Web software. (A few have even successfully charged for them.) The Web has grown like kudzu, throwing down roots even in hostile soils and growing at a fantastic pace.

While the kudzu has sprawled, however, trees have put down roots. Though users' first experiences with browsers may have been exciting, their experiences with servers were, until recently, fairly unpleasant. Administering a Web server was more of a task than the average browser user was willing to handle. As a result, more large servers cared for by people with the resources to manage them soon appeared. While the personal Web servers continue to sprout, any site that is genuinely popular will sooner or later move to a server (if it didn't begin on one) because of the performance toll that large numbers of Web hits can impose on a machine doing other processing. Even responding to requests for static documents can impose a performance toll on someone trying to use a spreadsheet on the same machine; serving dynamic documents often stall or crash an overburdened personal computer. Centralized servers, with dedicated resources, make more sense even in a distributed publishing environment.

Centralized servers provide other significant advantages besides relief for overburdened desktops. It's much easier to connect a large database server or even a mainframe to a single large Web server than to hundreds of smaller servers distributed throughout a company. Security issues can be managed from the center, making it easier for administrators to provide appropriate data to different sets of users. Multiple users can be hosted on the same machine, making it easy for a single team of administrators to support thousands of users if necessary. Of course, if that one server goes down, many people will be angry, but it is still easier than coping with decentralized servers that don't get turned on if their owner does not show up for work that day. The power of a centralized Web server, properly connected to other services, makes it possible to use even the simplest Web browser for business applications.

At the same time that servers are becoming more powerful, processing power on the Web is becoming more spread out. The latest browsers provide considerably more programmability than their predecessors, allowing both sides to participate in the conversation as something approaching full partners. The cookie processing demonstrated in Chapter 4 may seem relatively tiny compared to some of the database queries and other tasks that server-side processing is called upon to do constantly, but the impact of thousands of browsers supplementing the tools available on the server can be a tremendous boon for efficiency.

Building for these two worlds requires a clear vision of the strengths of each. Servers are excellent tools because of their ability to connect to a variety of data sources and the wide variety of supporting software that is available to create those connections. Browsers are excellent tools because they are easy to use and have a relatively simple presentation interface. Both sides are becoming more and more programmable, making it easier to build applications on both sides of the HTTP connection. Until browsers gain the necessary tools for more direct connections to a wider variety of data sources, servers are going to remain their intermediaries. Given the costs that direct, large-scale connectivity between browsers and business data sources would impose in software development, administration, and especially security, it seems likely that centralized Web servers will remain a key part of any Web-based solution for a long time. Cookies can provide the glue that connects these two worlds of development.

State and the Server

While cookies aren't an integral part of establishing a connection to non-HTML data sources, they provide the key to making those connections work over multiple transactions. Moving the Web past a one-form, one-processing application model requires building structures good for more than one transaction. Cookies provide a tool that can link particular users to the right set of server resources, making it much simpler for developers to create Web sites that adjust to user needs and keep up with users throughout their work.

When cookies first arrived in Netscape 1.1, all the processing apart from presentation was taking place on the server. CGI (Common Gateway Interface, which connects Web requests to other programs running on the Web server) was the only tool commonly available that let developers create dynamic Web sites. Since then, clients have taken over a significant share of processing, but the server remains a key gateway. Server-side applications can use cookies to take advantage of an enormous number of background resources for making more sophisticated use of tiny bits of information than is possible in the field with a client-side cookie script. Client-side cookie scripting can do many things more efficiently and more effectively than server-side code, but still lacks the direct connections needed to make many applications work.

Border Crossings, Server-side

Our examination of these interactions starts by looking at the border-crossing scenario first discussed in Chapter 1. Border-crossing scenarios are a field in which the dominance of server-side processing is largely unquestioned. This basic model of establishing identity and traveling based on that identity (supplemented with appropriate additional documents) will serve well for most of our server-side transactions. A server can do an excellent job as a border guard, quietly controlling access and tracking user movements. In combination with a relational database or other data provider, a server can maintain lists of visitors, noting their passage and barring entry when needed. Best of all, the server needs only to keep a stub—effectively a passport—in a cookie on the client, while keeping track of all permissions—the visas—in a secure vault on a server far away from the user.

Remember, cookies themselves are not secure. Users can edit their cookies (or use telnet, as we will see below) to hack their way into systems that are not well-enough protected. Although we will discuss several methods for improving cookie security, cookies should always be combined with other forms of security if they are used to protect sensitive information. In the following chapters, we will explore how to combine cookies with traditional user authentication to build a more flexible but secure system.

The state requirements for implementing a passport and visa model appear in Figure 5-1. Recreating this on a server will not be too difficult. When a user requests a page, the server checks to see if the user has a passport—a cookie providing a user ID for this site. If there is no passport cookie, the server generates a new user ID, assigns it basic privileges, and places a passport cookie on the user's browser. (This process could require visiting additional pages to fill out an application, or it might just be an automatic assignment.) After the user ID has been determined (from the cookie or by creating a new one), the server can check the user's visa for different areas of the site, by comparing the user ID to a list of pages and areas that the user is either permitted to visit or prohibited from visiting. If the visa is acceptable, the server sends back the page requested. If the visa is not acceptable, the user gets a rejection message.

Figure 5-1
Border Crossings
Revisited

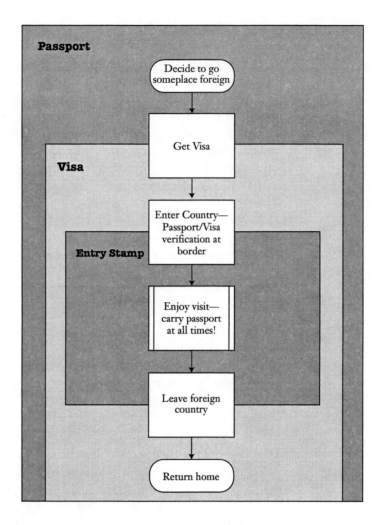

There are many different ways to implement this simple ID verification; several of them may be appropriate under particular circumstances. For simple sites that are more interested in tracking users than in restricting their movements, it may be acceptable to have the server create user ID cookies automatically, without any connection to an authentication database. All that these cookies would do is provide tracking information to servers following user movements. A more-sophisticated approach would combine this cookie with an authentication database that could limit the areas into a which a user was allowed. A simple version of this authentication might rudely announce to users that they were not welcome at particular URLs, while a more advanced version might restructure the site around a user's identity, removing links to areas they could not visit anyway. Of course, the advanced version would still need some kind of warning page to alert users who strayed into forbidden zones (perhaps by typing in a URL directly) that they were not welcome.

We will diagram a fairly complex version of this authentication process and implement parts of it as appropriate (and feasible, given the rough tools available) in later chapters. Figure 5-2 shows a version of the process shown in Figure 5-1, as it might appear in a Web application. Using this breakdown, we will be able to analyze our situation and figure out how best to apply cookies (or alternative strategies, if appropriate) to our situation.

Figure 5-2
Modularized
Border Crossing

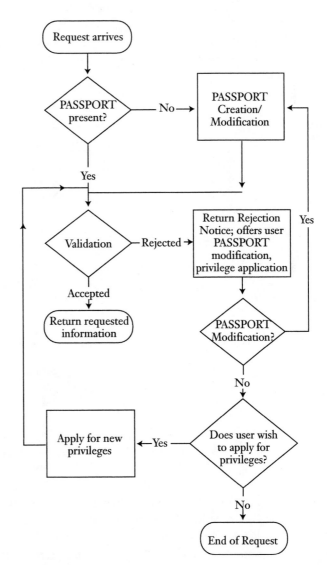

We will call the program checking these identities the border guard. Its first problem is that many of these visitors have no passports. Every site has to create its own cookies, so first-time visitors (and visitors who have destroyed their cookies) will not have a passport. Our first task is a fairly simple one—checking the Cookie headers of the request for a Passport cookie. If there is a Passport cookie, the processing can shift to validation; if not, the user has to apply for a passport.

Applying for a Passport cookie could happen several different ways. The border guard could immediately issue a unique Passport cookie that just identifies the user, without bothering to store that ID value in a central directory (in this case, a simple database). This would permit the site to track the user, and possibly even assign some privileges later. This simple method for issuing Passport cookies is shown in Figure 5-3.

Figure 5-3
Issuing a
Simple Passport

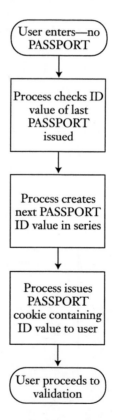

A more sophisticated process might send the user to a registration site, collecting information and assigning privileges based on the information collected. To keep that information connected to the passport value, the value and the information would be stored in a database, as shown in Figure 5-4.

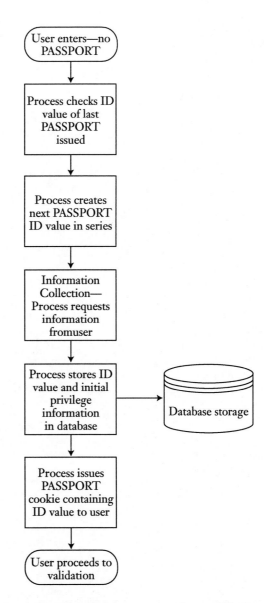

Once users have passports, they can proceed to validation. The validation process could be trivial, a check to make sure that the Passport value is meaningful and not random text, as shown in Figure 5-5.

More sophisticated site managers using more detailed permissions strategies will prefer to use some kind of database system for storing permissions, as shown in Figure 5-6. As we will see in later chapters, there are several techniques for storing these permissions and applying them to user requests.

Figure 5-5
Trivial
Validation Check

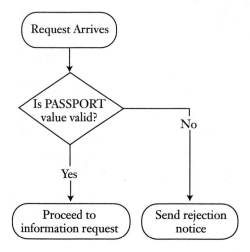

Figure 5-6
More
Sophisticated
Validation Check

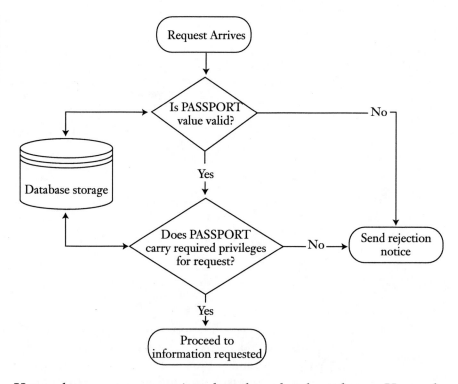

Users whose requests are rejected are bound to be unhappy. Users who have the right privileges, but no cookie, will probably want to modify their passports. Sites that have collected information about users, including a username and password, can allow the users to return to the passport creation area to create a new cookie that accurately reflects their identity.

Alternatively, users may be rejected because they lack not only a passport, but the proper permissions to visit an area. To keep these users happy, developers who implement permissions should also implement a process that allows users to apply for new permissions. Applying for permissions does not necessarily mean receiving them, but site developers should at least provide an outlet for requests.

How Secure are These Borders Anyway?

Cookie-based border-crossing techniques provide users with convenience; they never provide significant security. Although there are ways to strengthen the security of the ID value itself with checksums and other tools, preventing hackers from choosing random values to take advantage of other users' privileges, cookies by their very nature present an enormous security hole. Anyone with physical access to a user's computer has access to all of its cookies. The cookie files themselves are open to anyone with a text editor, making it easy to cut and paste cookies. While most users spend all their time on the same computer, very few users have security set up to keep out the average passerby who needs to use a computer. There are some operating systems (Windows NT and UNIX, for example) that can lessen this risk, but most browsers, and most cookies, are stored on very insecure Windows 95 and Macintosh clients.

The kinds of cookie-based security described above are most useful for sites providing information that comes at very low cost, which can be visited in exchange for some (not necessarily true) demographic information or a membership fee. The security might also be useful for sites that want to present selected portions of their content to users, before opening up the entire site to unprepared users. These methods will not withstand a dedicated hacker, especially if cookie information is transmitted insecurely (as it almost always is) or if the hacker can get access to a computer that already has a Passport cookie on it.

These cookies can, however, strengthen other forms of authentication. Cookies can provide a limited form of security, requiring users to log in from the same computer every time. (This would require some modifications to the registration process, but is not very difficult.) Even if someone has stolen the CEO's username and password, it still will not work unless the login is done from the computer on the CEO's desk, or the value of that cookie, as well as the username and password are known. Authentication information is provided to server-side scripts along with the cookie information, and may be used along with the cookie information during the validation process.

Shopping Carts and Servers

Shopping carts are one of the most popular applications of cookies, and one of the easiest to explain to users. Cookies and shopping carts seem like a reasonable match, each storing a particular set of goods until such time as the buyer reaches the cash register. The kind of information involved in a shopping cart (typically item and quantity) is small enough to fit in the 4K of space provided by a cookie, and the shopping cart can be made to disappear quite easily between browser sessions or when an order is complete. Our model will follow the real-world model described in Chapter 1 and shown in Figure 5-7.

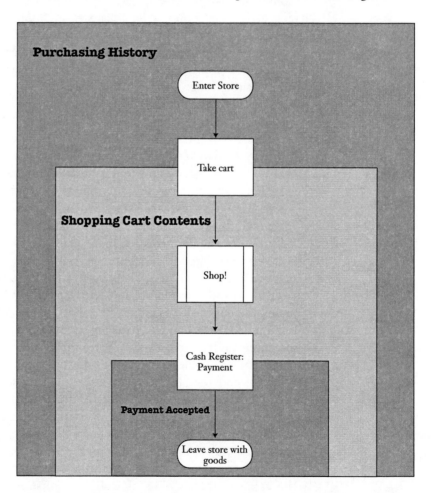

Figure 5-7
Shopping Carts in
the Real World

A shopping cart application generally consists of several parts. The cart itself is a cookie maintained by scripts that are available from all the pages of the catalog being presented. The scripts for adding and removing items may be hosted on the server, or included within the catalog pages themselves for execution on the browser. The cash register, normally run on the server, will read those cookies, check with the user that the goods are actually wanted, and transform the chosen items into an order. After the order has been built, other e-commerce mechanisms (not cookies) will handle the financial transactions and the task of getting the goods to the customer.

Our shopping-cart processing applications will follow the model shown in Figure 5-8. The user will browse a page or pages, making selections which are stored in a cookie. When an order is ready to be placed, a different script will double-check the order, allowing the user to change quantities and remove selections. When the processing is complete, the script will pass off the finished order to an e-commerce system for final processing.

Figure 5-8
An Electronic
Shopping Cart

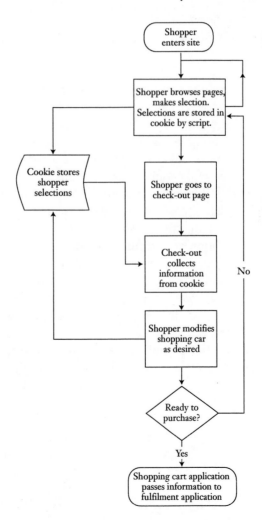

This part of the process is much easier to implement than the fulfillment part, which requires interfaces to other systems, like credit-card billing and shipping. The shopping-cart application only needs to keep track of which items, and how many, the user wants. This can be stored as a quantity and part number in the client cookie, and the cookie can hold many entries—up to its 4K limit. The developer can choose whether to maintain the shopping cart on the client or the server; in the examples in the following chapters, we will use several different strategies for handling this, each of which fits best with a particular tool or situation. A shopping-cart application must have a server component to connect to the fulfillment processes, but the actual handling of the contents of the cart can be done with client-side browser scripting or with a server-side application.

Partitioning Applications

When cookies first arrived, they were very clearly a technology that server-side applications could use to keep track of browser users. With the rise of browser-side scripting, cookies are no longer merely a server-side technology. Client-side cookies certainly have their limitations, but finding their strengths and combining them with those of server-side cookies promises a more efficient environment for data processing as well as a simplified way to build complex applications.

The main strength of client-side cookie scripts is that they can manipulate their cookies without requiring an extra trip to the server. While a user might initially find it acceptable for all additions and modifications to a shopping cart full of goods to require a trip to the server and back, repeated trips can cause extended delays. The server will also be burdened with additional processing, slowing down other users. Client-side cookie scripts can only work with a limited set of resources (usually, the page in which they reside), but they can do their work with less overhead and less hassle than server-side cookies.

Server-side cookies bring far more depth to a project, though they also inflict the overhead of an HTTP transaction every time a change to a cookie is needed. Cookies can be considerably smaller, however, as relevant information is stored on the server rather than on the client, and is linked to the user by a simple ID number. The information stored on the server can be as simple as a text file listing users or as complex as an object-relational database or a mainframe computer still churning away in a specially built cold room. Server-side transactions tend to require more development, including often-difficult links to databases and complex systems for maintaining user information.

Although there are many situations where it is clear that either server-side or client-side cookie scripting is a better choice, projects where both kinds of scripting are appropriate have begun to appear more often as browsers and scripting languages have grown more powerful. Deciding where to split a project—and how to keep the two parts communicating—is often difficult. Leaning too far in the direction of client-side cookie scripting may produce enormous scripts that process their large chunks of information slowly and inefficiently. On the other hand, leaning too far in the direction of server-side cookie scripting can greatly increase the load on a server without providing much tangible benefit to users, apart from giving them a good opportunity to get take a coffee break.

Although many developers will disagree about particular instances (and many situations can, of course, be resolved either way), there are some general guidelines worth following for partitioning cookie-based applications between the browser and the server. The parts of a cookie application that belong on the client include:

- Processes that may take place more than once on a given page—choosing items for a shopping cart, for instance
- Information that only gets used to personalize a page and will not be needed in any server-side processing
- Processes that can draw their information directly from an HTML page are eligible for client-side handling; processes that draw their information from the particular condition of a page (such as the results of Dynamic HTML scripting) generally must use client-side scripting anyway.

The parts that need to take place on the server include:

- Processes related to proprietary or sensitive information that can't be trusted to client-side data storage
- Information drawn from databases or other non-HTML forms of data, or that connect to other backend processing
- Processes that collect information for centralized storage.

Several of the examples used in the following chapters will take advantage of the strengths of both sides, demonstrating these issues of partition and presenting concrete solutions. Programmer preference or the needs of a particular situation may determine partitioning tactics more than any general principles, however. An already-overburdened server may not be able to handle the additional load of keeping track of simple cookies, or an odd mix of older browsers may leave client-side cookie scripting an unreliable tool. Real-world problems often overshadow the apparent technical "needs" of a state-management application. Fortunately, shifting from one strategy to the other may not always be exceptionally difficult—a cookie is a cookie, providing the same information to tools on either side of the HTTP transaction.

Cookie Communications

Using cookies with servers is made easier by a set of additions to the standards used to transfer information on the Web. As we have seen, cookies are just simple text files, storing a small set of data on the browser computer. Cookie-enabled browsers do more than just store that information (as we have done with our client-side cookies)—they transfer appropriate cookie information with every HTTP request. All the cookies with the domain value **.microsoft.com** and a path of / get transferred with every request made to a site at **microsoft.com**. The server doesn't have to repeat all the cookie values; it just lists cookie values that it wants set.

This cookie uploading can add significant overhead to the transaction times users experience, especially on slow connections. This transfer overhead is the primary reason cookies are limited to 4K and each site can only have 20 cookies on a user's computer. 80K of extra uploading every time a user needs to connect to a site is already more than enough for the average user. (In addition, cookies are sent with requests for graphics, potentially multiplying the delays.) There may be times that multiple cookies containing large amounts of data are appropriate, but try to keep them to a minimum. As we shall see throughout the book, cookies for the client side are the only ones especially prone to this overgrown state; there are better ways of handling large amounts of data available to servers.

Cookies are an unofficial addition to the specifications for the HTTP as well as a browser feature. To see how they work, we'll take a look at some HTTP requests and analyze their contents. Fortunately, HTTP, is not a very complicated protocol, at least at the level we need to examine. Most Web browsers are available at port 80 on the server. HTTP requests use a simple vocabulary of plain-text commands to initiate transfers. Most people never see these commands, because the Web browser handles them automatically, but they can be a useful debugging tool. Developers working with CGI scripts in particular may want to know the internals of HTTP. Our brief examination focuses on a few possibilities made available by HTTP, those most likely to be used in contexts involving cookies.

The Do-it-yourself Browser

While most people prefer to use browser software, it is not so difficult, and can even be useful occasionally, to talk directly to a Web server. Communicating directly requires only a network connection and a telnet program. Connecting to Web servers this way can be a little frustrating, because the connection cuts off as soon as the server has finished downloading the file. Addressing a server through telnet will quickly teach you a lesson about how stateless HTTP really is. Telnetting to the Web server is easy: just tell your telnet program to connect to the server you want, on port 80. From the command line, this will probably look like:

```
telnet www.webtype.com:80
```

Once you are connected, you can type in requests directly. (The Web server will not echo your keystrokes, which can make life difficult. The easiest way to handle these connections is to type up the request in a separate file, and paste it into the telnet session.)

HTTP Transactions

Creating these requests requires a little knowledge about HTTP. HTTP has gone through a few versions, from the original 0.9 to the still-common 1.0 to the most recent 1.1. We will focus on 1.0, since it has the parts we need. 1.1 adds to that collection, but none of its changes have a direct impact on cookies in particular. When a Web browser needs to request a file from a Web server, it composes a request. A client request is generally quite simple, containing:

- A method and a URI target for that method
- The version of HTTP the browser is using
- General headers containing further information about the request and its status
- Request headers containing information about the request and the browser
- Entity headers containing information about the entity body that follows
- An entity body, which may be form data or a file to be posted.

A URI is a Uniform Resource Identifier, which in this case will behave as an URL, a Uniform Resource Locator. URIs include both absolute links (URLs) and relative links (partial addresses).

A request begins with a client request method, a simple command telling the server what kind of transaction is taking place. A listing of client request methods is shown in Table 5-1.

Table 5-1
Client Request
Methods

Method	Description	HTTP version
GET	Retrieves a document from the server	0.9, 1.0, 1.1
HEAD	Retrieves only the headers for a document from the server	1.0, 1.1
POST	Sends information, usually from a form, to the server	1.0, 1.1
PUT	Asks that the server store the entity-body of the request on the server at the specified URL	1.0, 1.1
DELETE	Asks that the server delete the file at the specified URL from the server	1.1
TRACE	Follows the request in detail through a chain of proxy servers	1.1
OPTIONS	Requests a list of the options (usually request methods) available	1.1

The requests we will be using throughout this book are GET and POST. The HEAD method is occasionally useful for diagnostics as well as the caching functions it normally assists, but GET and POST together support about 95% of Web requests. In this chapter, we will explore GET; the POST method exhibits similar behavior with regard to cookies.

Using GET is very simple, and can be done without any additional header information. GET just retrieves a file from the server. The version of HTTP being used has to be on the same line as the GET request; otherwise the server assumes that this is a request made using HTTP 0.9 and just returns the file without examining any additional headers. Version 1.0 is indicated by HTTP/1.0, while version 1.1 is indicated by HTTP/1.1. To request the test.htm file using GET and version 1.0 of HTTP, type the following into your connected telnet session:

```
GET /test.htm HTTP/1.0
```

If you leave off the HTTP/1.0, the server will process the GET request immediately when you hit the enter key. If you include the version, the server will wait to accept more request headers. When you're finished entering the header information, just enter a blank line and the server will process the request. A sample session is shown below:

```
GET /test.htm HTTP/1.0

HTTP/1.0 200 OK
Server: Microsoft-IIS/3.0
Date: Sat, 08 Nov 1997 20:17:33 GMT
Content-Type: text/html
Accept-Ranges: bytes
Last-Modified: Sat, 08 Nov 1997 20:12:58 GMT
Content-Length: 90

<HTML>
<HEAD><TITLE>Testing...</TITLE></HEAD>
<BODY>This is just a test!</BODY>
```

The response the server gives provides some basic information about the request (that it was HTTP version 1.0, and that the URL was retrieved well), as well as information about the date of the request, the content-type of the file, the last-modified date of the file (useful for caching strategies), and the length of the file. (Accept-Ranges indicates that IIS will accept requests for portions of the file smaller than the entire file.) After a blank line, which signals the end of headers just like the blank line signaling the end of the request, the entity-content, the requested file, appears.

Cookie information always appears in the header. A more complicated request follows in the telnet session (to **www.jaundicedeye.com**) below:

```
GET /cgi-bin/knocker.cgi HTTP/1.0

HTTP/1.1 302 Moved Temporarily
Date: Sat, 08 Nov 1997 20:01:02 GMT
Server: Stronghold/2.0 Apache/1.2b10
Set-Cookie: firstvisit=081197; expires=Fri 31-Dec-1999 23:59:00 GMT;
path=/; domain=www.jaundicedeye.com;
Location: http://www.jaundicedeye.com/toc_new.html
Connection: close
Content-Type: text/html

<HTML><HEAD><TITLE>302 Moved Temporarily</TITLE>
</HEAD><BODY><H1>Moved Temporarily</H1>
The document has moved <A
HREF="http://www.jaundicedeye.com/toc_new.html"
>here</A>.<P></BODY></HTML>
```

This session has called a simple CGI script, which sets a cookie for the site to use and then redirects the user's browser to its "real" destination, a regular HTML file. Users of older browsers, which may not be capable of keeping up with this redirection, will see the HTML at the bottom of the server's response.

We will examine the key parts of this interaction for their relevance to our cookie work. First, this server identifies itself as using HTTP Version 1.1. Some of the information provided here (like `Connection: close`) isn't relevant to an HTTP 1.0 browser—but the browser will ignore the extra information, just as browsers with cookies turned off will ignore all cookies sent their way. The next important piece of information is the `302 Moved Temporarily` response. An HTTP 1.0 or 1.1-enabled browser will redirect the browser to the location designated later in the response after it has parsed all the intermediate headers. Browsers unable to handle the redirect will parse all the way through to the end, displaying the HTML code that serves as a manual redirect. The date and server details are informational, but following them is the reason for this CGI script's existence: the Set-Cookie header:

```
Set-Cookie: firstvisit=081197; expires=Fri 31-Dec-1999 23:59:00 GMT;
            path=/; domain=www.jaundicedeye.com;
```

This line will set a cookie named `firstvisit` that has a value of `081197`. The cookie will be persistent, lasting until December 31, 1999. The path is explicitly set to `/`, which allows all parts of the site to see this cookie. The domain is set to **www.jaundicedeye.com**, which would have been the default anyway.

Setting multiple cookies is easy; just include as many Set-Cookie headers as you need cookies.

All this script does is set a cookie and redirect the user to another page. Users who do not have their browsers set to alert them about cookies will not even notice the script passing by, unless their connection is slow or the script breaks for some reason. We will create a simple script that does just this in Chapter 6. Once the cookie is at the browser, it will be sent along with the HTTP request to every URL that matches its domain and path variables. The only parts of a cookie sent back to the browser are the name and value pairs—domain, path, expires, and secure are all omitted. The Cookie header is added to a request to carry these:

```
GET /file.htm HTTP/1.0
Cookie: name=value
```

Multiple cookies can be specified by separating the name-value pairs with semicolons. We will see how the server can process these cookies in the chapters that follow, because the details change with every tool.

Putting the Parts Together

Now that we have a roadmap for a few applications, and a basic understanding of how cookies are communicated between Web browsers and Web servers, it is time to begin implementing. In the chapters that follow, we will examine how to build server-side applications that use cookies with CGI and Perl (Chapter 6), Netscape LiveWire (Chapter 7), and Microsoft Active Server Pages (Chapter 8). We will create similar applications in each of the chapters, highlighting the strengths and weaknesses of each of the tools. We will also take a look at a newcomer to cookies, Java, and explore some techniques for using cookies with Java on both the client (with applets) and the server (with servlets). After we have seen how to build cookie applications by hand, we will examine a prepackaged site management package that makes extensive use of cookies, Microsoft Site Server.

## CHAPTER 6

Cookies and CGI

The Common Gateway Interface (CGI) was one of the earliest tools for connecting HTTP requests to programs, and it remains extremely popular despite the appearance of new tools. CGI is available on nearly every Web server, and provides basic services that developers can use to read in Web requests and send back appropriate responses. For our purposes, the cookie information is the most critical part of those requests and responses. CGI development demands more from the programmer than many of the other tools explored in this book, but can provide rewards in compatibility across server platforms and the considerable number of libraries available to simplify the task. This chapter will explore CGI applications that take advantage of cookies, demonstrating how to set, collect, and process cookies using the most popular language for CGI development, Perl.

Introduction to the Common Gateway Interface

The CGI provides a set of standards that allow Web servers and programs to communicate with each other. CGI has been available since the earliest days of the NCSA and CERN servers, and continues to be available on Web servers from Netscape, Microsoft, Apache, Sun, IBM, Lotus, O'Reilly, and nearly every other server vendor. There may occasionally be extra information made available or a slightly different standard for communicating it (the WinCGI standard, for example), but all of these systems allow developers to use a common set of tools for passing information between Web servers and programs.

The CGI takes the information from the HTTP requests (shown in the previous chapter) and passes it to the program as a set of variables. When the server receives an HTTP request directed at a script, it parses the request headers and transforms them into a list of variables which is sent to the CGI program as standard input when the program first begins. Table 6-1 shows a standard list of CGI variables as well as the equivalents in the Perl CGI.pm module; more variables may appear on particular servers.

Table 6-1
Standard List of CGI Variables

Variable	CGI.pm method	Contents
AUTH_TYPE	auth_type()	Authentication type, if the user had to log in with a user name and password
CONTENT_LENGTH	none	The length in bytes of the request (Used with POST requests only)
CONTENT_TYPE	none	The MIME type of data sent in the request; generally application/x-www-form-urlencoded (Used with POST requests only)
GATEWAY_INTERFACE	none	Provides the name and revision number of the CGI interface used; CGI/1.1 would indicate Version 1.1 of the CGI interface
HTTP_ACCEPT	accept()	Provides a list of the MIME types the browser will accept as a response
HTTP_COOKIE	raw_cookie()	Provides the cookies available to the requested URL as a list of URL-encoded name value pairs separated by semicolons
HTTP_REFERER	referer()	Provides the URL of the page from which the user reached the requested URL

continued

Variable	CGI.pm method	Contents
HTTP_USER_AGENT	user_agent()	Provides information about the user's browser
PATH_INFO	path_info()	Extra path information provided in the URL (Often used for CGI redirection programs)
PATH_TRANSLATED	path_translated()	The absolute path on the server used to reach the script; useful for accessing files in directories on the server
QUERY_STRING	query_string()	Information sent to the server as part of the URL after a question mark (Frequently used with GET requests)
REMOTE_ADDR	remote_addr()	The IP address of the machine making the request
REMOTE_HOST	remote_host()	The domain name of the machine making the request, if available
REMOTE_USER	remote_user()	The name used to authenticate with the Web server; present only if the user had to authenticate at some point during the current browser session with this server
REQUEST_METHOD	request_method()	The request method used to make this request, generally GET or POST, though some scripts may want to check for HEAD
SCRIPT_NAME	script_name()	The name of the script; useful for reconstructing URL references to the script
SERVER_NAME	server_name()	The server name (domain name if available, IP address if not) of the server that received the request; like SCRIPT_NAME, useful for reconstructing URL references.
SERVER_PORT	server_port()	The port number on the server that received the request
SERVER_PROTOCOL	none	The protocol used to make the request; usually HTTP/1.0 or HTTP/1.1.
SERVER_SOFTWARE	server_software()	Provides information about the HTTP server that received the request in the format name/version

Creating a CGI program is mostly a matter of matching up appropriate outputs to particular inputs. When a request arrives, the CGI program parses the information it receives from the Web server, extracting information like the query string, the form information sent by a POST request, and any cookies that came with the request. Based on this information, the CGI application will interact with server-side resources like files and databases (if necessary) and generate a response for the user, usually a set of headers followed by some HTML. This response is passed back to the server when the program concludes, and the server then passes the response to the user.

CGI programs are not limited to producing HTML output, but most return only HTML.

CGI programs can be written in nearly any language, from Visual Basic to assembly to C to Tcl to Python to Perl, but Perl still retains the lion's share of CGI development. CGI only specifies what the Web server sends to the program and what it expects back; the CGI standard by itself places no limits or expectations on the behavior of that program. Unlike the other tools covered in later chapters, CGI provides no built-in mechanisms for accessing databases, maintaining state, or even writing programs. CGI is the ultimate do-it-yourself environment for Web programming, which gives it enormous flexibility. Still, many programmers prefer to avoid reinventing the wheel, which has led to the development of some powerful libraries for CGI programming. They do not offer all the features of the server development environments that will be covered in the next chapters, but they can certainly spare developers a lot of hassle.

CGI does have some drawbacks. Every time a user makes a call to a CGI program, the server builds the CGI request and runs that program—usually as a separate application. Other tools, like Active Server Pages and servlets, can run dynamic requests in the same program space as the server, reducing the overhead needed to create dynamic pages. The implementation varies from server to server and platform to platform; most UNIX machines run CGI applications as separate processes, while Windows and Macintosh programs run CGI as applications or services. Using a server company's proprietary systems (Netscape's NSAPI or LiveWire or Microsoft's ISAPI or Active Server Pages, for instance) often demands less overhead and is therefore quicker, but comes at a cost: those dynamic pages must always be hosted on the particular server for which they were developed. Using CGI may be more complicated, but it allows developers to choose their own tools and keep their Web applications much more portable. Perl applications can usually move from platform to platform, and even C and C++ programs can often be recompiled.

When using Perl with IIS, there is an application called Perl for ISAPI that allows the server to work with one copy of the Perl application, avoiding the constant relaunching of the interpreter. Perl for ISAPI is availabe from **http://www.activestate.com**.

CGI and Perl

Perl remains the language of choice for many CGI developers, and will be the only language used in this chapter. There are several reasons for Perl's popularity. Perl is available for nearly every kind of UNIX, for Windows 95 and NT, and for the Macintosh, as well as for a variety of other platforms. Developers can use their Perl scripts on nearly any machine, and libraries are generally portable among the different implementations. Perl offers an incredibly powerful set of tools for managing arrays and finding and modifying text, and it is not difficult to learn. Perl is well suited to interpret the information provided by the server and produce complex documents with a minimum of programming, especially with the assistance of the CGI.pm module that is now a part of the Perl distribution.

Perl was created by Larry Wall, originally as a way to avoid the more mundane tasks of UNIX system administration. By creating a tool that could handle these tasks, he transformed his laziness into an incredibly useful language. The Perl community accepts two canonical interpretations of the acronym Perl: Practical Extraction and Reporting Language, and Pathologically Eclectic Rubbish Lister. Laziness, impatience, and hubris are said to be the three great virtues of Perl programmers—Perl makes it easy to accomplish seemingly difficult tasks quickly and fairly painlessly with its remarkable toolset and the many libraries that programmers have posted to the Web to make development easier.

For an excellent one-stop Perl resource, visit **http://www.perl.com**. The latest versions of Perl, and an enormous collection of libraries, documentation, and other resources are available at this site.

Much of Perl's syntax resembles C, though the way that it handles many tasks is quite different—it stores all variables as strings, for instance, and handles all math as floating point. Perl programs are not really compiled; in

Perl 5 (as of this writing) the program is compiled at the start of execution
and then run. While this does not provide excellent performance, it does
make Perl development much easier by avoiding the compilation step. For
reasons of space, this chapter will not provide an introduction to Perl itself,
just explanations of a few features that will be especially useful to CGI
developers working with cookies.

For a complete introduction to Perl, I strongly recommend **Learning Perl**,
known as the llama book for the animal on its cover. **Learning Perl on
Win32 Systems** provides the same information but is focused on the
needs of Windows developers and carries a gecko on its cover. Finally,
Programming Perl, written originally by Larry Wall, provides a complete
explanation of Perl, including many of its stranger and more powerful
features.

Perl's string and array handling features can reduce the burden of CGI
development significantly. Perl's tools are far more flexible than those of
the scripting languages explored in Chapter 4, though at first they may
seem considerably more forbidding. Perl uses the regular expression syntax
used by other UNIX tools like `grep` and `awk` to process strings, making it
easy to substitute and parse text. While Perl doesn't provide the escape and
unescape functions of JavaScript, recreating them isn't very difficult in
Perl—and the `cgi.pm` library that comes with Perl Version 5.004 and later
takes care of the translation. Unfortunately, `cgi.pm` doesn't make its
escape and unescape methods available by default to programs that use the
library, but many of the tools, including those for cookies, use them. Eager
developers can search the code of `cgi.pm` and find these jewels, and modify the `%EXPORT_TAGS` hash if they need access to these methods regularly
or included them in the *use* declaration. Developers can even modify
`cgi.pm`—they must just be sure to read the copyright notice.

One problem with cross-platform CGI development is that while all of
these programs use Perl, the links they need to make to database systems
will vary widely depending on what database software is used on what kind
of server, and what kind of connection is used between the Perl program
and the database. As a result, the examples in this chapter will stick to a
simpler set of tools, using Perl's ability to write to files as a means of storing data on the server. These examples will also rely more heavily on
information stored in the cookies themselves than do the examples in later
chapters.

Getting Started: Reading and Writing Cookies

The Perl examples in this chapter will all use the cgi.pm module that became a part of the Perl distribution as of Version 5.004. While there may be some situations that still call for hand-coding an application line-by-line, use of Lincoln Stein's cgi.pm library produces far cleaner code, that library is readily available with the standard Perl distribution (or by download from **http://www-genome.wi.mit.edu/ftp/pub/software/WWW/ cgi_docs.html**), and, most important, avoids the constant reinvention of the wheel. There are other CGI libraries (including one of my old favorites, cgi-lib.pl), but none of them provides as comprehensive a set of tools or is as widely supported.

Including the cgi.pm module requires an extra declaration near the top of the Perl program:

```
use CGI qw(:standard);
```

Programmers who want to include less of the library, but still need the cookie and form interpretation functionality, can use

```
use CGI qw(:cgi);
```

instead. Developers who need all public sessions of the library available, including the cookie functionality and all versions of HTML, can use

```
use CGI qw(:all);
```

Most of cgi.pm is fairly easy to use, and the documentation that accompanies it provides a fairly complete tutorial. The cookie() method is quite flexible, and deserves extra attention. Because cgi.pm uses Perl 5's objects, the notation may be unfamiliar to some developers who have worked with Perl 4. The same method is used for reading and writing cookies; depending on the values it receives, the cookie() method will either create a new Set-Cookie header or interpret the HTTP_COOKIE environment variable.

Developers who want to reach the HTTP_COOKIE variable for their own direct manipulation can use either cgi.pm's raw_cookie() method or $ENV{'HTTP_COOKIE'}. Printing Set-Cookie headers directly can be done with a print statement—just make sure to print all the headers before printing any HTML.

Retrieving a cookie value with the `cookie()` method is simple, and can be done at any time within a CGI script:

```
$myvalue=cookie('mycookie');
```

or

```
$myvalue=cookie(-name=>'mycookie');
```

Both versions are calling the `cookie()` method with only a name parameter; the second version explicitly names the parameter. The `cookie()` method will return a completely unescaped version of the cookie value associated with the name `mycookie`, if there is one. If there isn't, it returns an empty string.

Setting cookies is more complex. First, the cookie needs to be created. The `cookie()` method will return cookie values as scalar variables (effectively strings, in this case), which then need to be fed to the `header()` method. Although it isn't required to use named parameters, these can make cookie development much easier and debugging less painful. Creating a cookie requires, at minimum, a name and a value.

```
$myCookie=cookie(-name=>'mycookie',-value=>'myvalue');
```

or

```
$myCookie=cookie('mycookie','myvalue');
```

This will create a cookie with the name `'mycookie'` and the value `'myvalue'` that disappears at the end of the session. All of the cookie variables are available, however, and one, Expires, has been made much simpler with the addition of a relative time scheme that allows developers to specify how long the cookie should last instead of the date and time at which it should expire. The `cookie()` method handles the translations.

```
$myCookie=cookie(-name=>'mycookie',-value=>'myvalue', -
expires=>'+1y');
```

This call will create the same cookie as the calls above, except that it will last for a year before expiring, if the user lets it. The `cgi.pm` module can accept values that use s for second, m for minute, h for hour, d for day, M for month, or y for year. It will also accept the date as a string in the GMT format presented in Chapter 4. The Domain, Path, and Secure values are also available; note that Secure must be explicitly given the value of `true`, and not merely be present, for it to be set.

```
$myCookie=cookie(    -name=>'mycookie',
                     -value=>'myvalue',
```

```
            -path=>'/',
            -domain=>'mydomain.com',
            -expires=>'+1y'
            -secure=>1);
```

To make this readable, I have taken advantage of Perl's generosity in allowing statements to continue across multiple lines until they reach the semicolon. Whitespace is also unimportant, making it possible to keep a complex declaration from getting jumbled.

Now that the cookie value is ready, it has to be sent to the browser. The `header()` method provides a complete (and extensible) solution to the need to print HTTP headers on a regular basis. For the purposes of this chapter, we will not need to change the caching rules, generate content of types other than text/html, or create our own headers. The only parameter needed is the cookie parameter, which accepts cookie values (even multiple cookies) and puts them in the header:

```
print header(-cookie=>$mycookie);
```

To set multiple cookies, just give the cookie parameter an array:

```
print header(-cookie=>[$mycookie,$yourcookie];
```

The `cgi.pm` module offers a wide array of features that have nothing to do with cookies; many of them are used in the following examples. For more information, check the documentation that comes with the module or the chapter on CGI programming in **Learning Perl**.

The first example will check to see if a user has a `firstVisit` cookie. If there is one, the program will display it; if not, the program will set it.

```
#!/usr/bin/perl

use CGI qw(:standard);
# check for the firstVisit cookie
if (cookie('firstVisit')) {
  #if present, a returning visitor
  #collect cookie value for later presentation
  $firstVisit=cookie('firstVisit');
  $first="not ";
  #print header with no cookies.
  print header();
} else {
  #set firstVisit cookie
  $firstVisit=localtime;
  $cookie = cookie(-name=>'firstVisit',
                   -value=>$firstVisit,
                   -expires=>'+2y',
```

```
                                -path=>'/');
   #print header with firstVisit cookie
   print header(-cookie=>$cookie);
   $first="";
}
$currentDate=localtime;
#use cgi.pm's methods for creating HTML.
print start_html("First Visit Check"), h1("Visitor Status");
print p("This is $first your first visit.");
#use Perl's . concatenation operator to split
#multi-line strings within method call
print p("We have marked your first arrival at $firstVisit".
        " and we will celebrate it as a holiday each year".
        " at that time");
print hr();
print p("It is now $currentDate.");
print end_html();
```

Users who have never visited the site before (or who don't have cookies for other reasons) will receive a cookie containing the current time and date, shown in Figure 6-1.

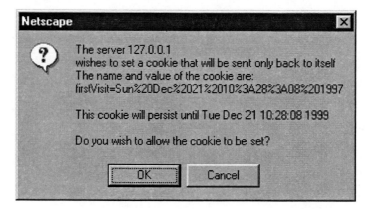

New users will be welcomed to the site and informed that this is their first visit, as shown in Figure 6-2.

If a firstVisit cookie already exists, the program extracts the time and date of the first time the user visited from that cookie and does not send any further cookies. Users who have been to the site before will be welcomed back to the site and told when they first visited, as shown in Figure 6-3.

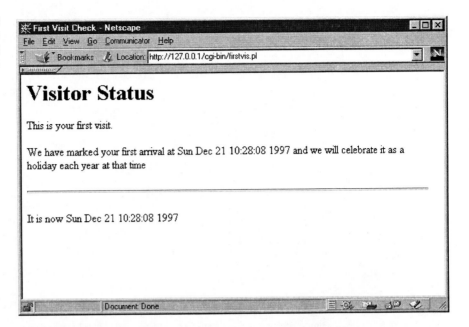

Figure 6-2
Welcoming
New Users

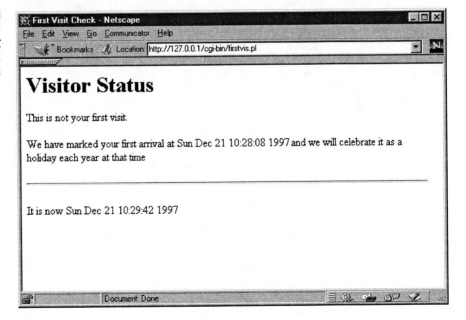

Figure 6-3
Welcoming
Back Users
with Cookies

Our next CGI example will collect the cookies created by the Notepad application in Chapter 4 and store them to a directory on the server for later processing. This script requires that users authenticate themselves to the server; a program willing to accept anonymous input need not worry about this step, though the submit.pl script will need minor modification. Users are warned throughout of the public nature of their comments. The first page just displays the comments and offers the opportunity to submit them. Users who are not quite sure that submitting these comments is a good idea have one last chance to turn back.

```perl
#!/usr/bin/perl
# need to include cgi.pm library with use CGI
use CGI qw(:standard);
# header() prints text/html, cookies, etc.
print header();
#start_html() prints top lines of page, inc. title
print start_html("Comments Submission"), h1("Comments Submission");
#note how tags are created using methods of same name
print p("Your comments are currently:");
#horizontal rule
print hr();
# note cookie method
print p(cookie('NotePad'));
print hr();
print p("Your comments, once submitted, will be available to all
project management personnel as well as any technical personnel. While
most users are restricted from seeing all comments from all personnel,
they should not assume that comments are private.");
# I still like to hand-code links, but not necessary.
print p("To submit your comments, <A HREF='submit.pl'>click
here.</A>");
# end_html closes BODY and HTML tags
print end_html();
```

The comments receive center stage, with the warning at the bottom above the submit link, as shown in Figure 6-4.

The submit.pl script reads in the NotePad cookie. If the cookie has any contents, it opens a file on the server and appends the value of the cookie to that cookie, with the authenticated name of the user and the time it was submitted.

```perl
#!/usr/bin/perl

use CGI qw(:standard);
# Collect cookie, write file
#get username - requires authentication
$username=remote_user();
#get cookie
$comments=cookie('NotePad');
# Need date to identify when submitted
$datestamp=localtime;
#check to see if comments not empty
if (($comments) && ($comments ne " ")) {
  #open the file for appending (>>)
  #COOKLIST is filehandle
  #note use of forward slashes, even in
  #Win32 environ. More easily converted
```

Figure 6-4
Preparing to
Submit Comments

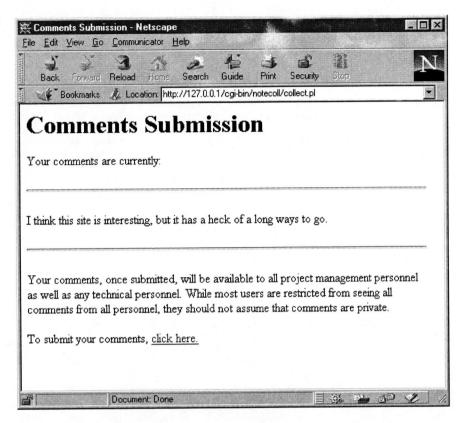

```
#to Unix environ, also avoids need to escape
#backslashes. die useful only for debugging
#from command line.
open (COOKLIST, ">>C:/comments/$username.txt") || die "open: $!";
#write to file with print
print COOKLIST p("$username, $datestamp");
print COOKLIST p($comments);
close (COOKLIST);
#no new cookies to send, normal header
#Developers who want to clear the NotePad
#cookie should do so here - send a blank (" ")
#value or expire the cookie. Notepad client page
#has delete option built-in.
print header();
print start_html("Comments Submission"), h1("Comments Submission");
print p("Thank you for submitting your comments. The full list of
your comments follows:");
print hr();

#read file, print to screen
open (COOKLIST, "C:/comments/$username.txt") || die "open: $!";
while (<COOKLIST>) {
  chomp;
```

```
    print "$_ <BR>";
  }
  close (COOKLIST);

  print hr();
  #long paragraph, not pretty-printed
  #easier option than . concatenation,
  #though it breaks up indents.
  print p("Your comments, once submitted, will be available to all
project management personnel as well as any technical personnel. While
most users are restricted from seeing all comments from all personnel,
they should not assume that comments are private.");
}
#Notepad cookie was empty - rejection notice
else {
  print header(), start_html("Please enter some comments");
  print h1("No comments submitted");
  print p("We can't accept your comments until you have entered
      some.");
  print p("Please <A HREF='../../notepad.htm'>enter some
      comments.</A>");
}
#end_html called for both circumstances
print end_html();
```

If users have not entered any comments, they will receive the rejection
notice shown in Figure 6-5. Users who do have comments will be thanked
for their contribution and shown a list of all their prior comments, as
shown in Figure 6-6.

Figure 6-5
Rejection Notice,
No Comments
Submitted

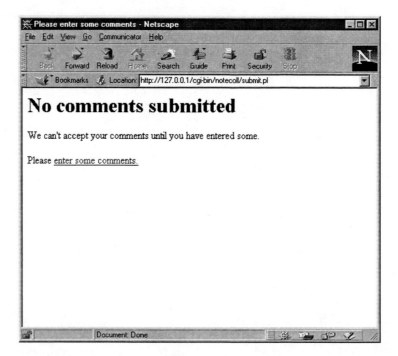

Figure 6-6
Comments
Accepted, the Full
Set Displayed

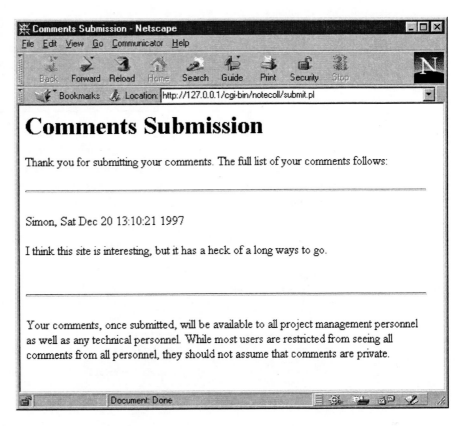

Figure 6-6
Comments
Accepted, the Full
Set Displayed

Border Crossings with CGI

Cookies and CGI scripts can be used to make sure that users have the privileges they need to visit certain areas of a site. While they are not as useful as access control lists and authentication for site-wide security management, they can be effective for areas of the site that use scripting. (Converting all the HTML files on a site to Perl scripts and using cookies to check on users is not recommended for ordinary projects.) This example uses CGI to limit user access to rooms in a maze, keeping track of their permissions in files on the server. Those permissions are linked to the user through a username cookie. This application could have been implemented with client-side cookies that contained all of the permissions, but border crossings are considerably more secure when permissions are stored on the server.

To improve the security of this application, some form of reversible encryption for usernames would be useful. At present, users could edit a username cookie and take over someone else's permissions without the program's detecting it. (They are prevented from simply entering another user's name, however.)

The entryway to the maze checks to see if the user already has a `MazeID` cookie. If there is one, the entryway redirects the user to the next page, `submit.pl`, which presents a welcome to the maze. If there is no `MazeID` cookie, the entryway presents a form that requests the user to enter a name, which will then also be sent to `submit.pl`.

```perl
#!/usr/bin/perl

use CGI qw(:standard);
#if they've been here before, send
#them on their way
if(cookie('MazeID')) {
  print redirect('http://127.0.0.1/cgi-bin/maze/submit.pl');
} else {
#new users need to enter an ID
  print header(), start_html('Maze Entry Area');
  print h1('Welcome to the Maze');
  print start_form('POST','submit.pl');
  print p("What is your name? ",textfield("name"));
  print end_form();
  print end_html;
}
```

Users who haven't visited the maze before will receive the greeting shown in Figure 6-7.

The next script is considerably more complex, acting as the administrator of user identities. If the user has just filled out the entryway form, the script checks to make sure there isn't already a user by that name. If there is, our user is asked to try again with a different name. If there isn't, a user by that name, the script assigns initial permissions, just enough to let the user into room #1. If the user who has arrived with a `MazeID` is welcomed back to the maze; any permissions from the last visit will still be in force. Users who show up with no form data and no cookie are redirected to the `entry.pl` script, where they will have to enter a name.

```perl
#!/usr/bin/perl
use CGI qw(:standard);
#check for form data
if (param('name')) {
  $username=param('name');
  #see if a user by that name exists
  #by checking if permissions file exists
  $filecheck=(-e "C:/mazeperm/$username.txt");
```

Figure 6-7
Entering an
ID for the Maze

```
   if ($filecheck){
     #if file there, it's taken. Try again.
     print header(),start_html('Name already taken');
     print p("$username is already in use. Please <A
HREF='entry.pl'>choose</A> a different name.");
     print end_html();
   } else {
     #file not there - available.
     #create permissions file for user.
     $username=param('name');
     open (COOKLIST, ">C:/mazeperm/$username.txt") || die "open: $!";
     print COOKLIST "$username,1,0,0,0,0,0,0,0,0";
     close (COOKLIST);
     #create cookie to link user to permissions file
     $cookie = cookie(-name=>'MazeID',
                 -value=>$username,
                 -expires=>'+1y',
                         -path=>'/');
     #print header with cookie
     print header(-cookie=>$cookie);
     print start_html('Welcome to the Maze');
     print h1('Welcome to the maze!');
     print p("Welcome, $username");
     print p("Please <A HREF='maze1.pl'>enter</A>.");
     print end_html();
   }
 } else {
   if (cookie('MazeID')) {
```

```
#if they have a cookie, they can rejoin
#their old permissions
$username=cookie('MazeID');
print header();
print start_html('Welcome to the Maze');
print h1('Welcome to the maze!');
print p("Welcome, $username");
print p("Please <A HREF='maze1.pl'>enter</A>.");
print end_html();
}
else {
#no form data and no cookie? Reject.
print redirect('http://127.0.0.1/cgi-bin/maze/entry.pl');
}
}
```

Users who already have cookies and users who have entered names that do not duplicate already-existing names will receive the welcome shown in Figure 6-8. Users who duplicate an existing name will get the offer to enter a different name as shown in Figure 6-9. Users who did not enter a name and have no cookie will get sent back to the form shown in Figure 6-7.

Figure 6-8
Welcoming a
User to the Maze

The actual maze files are all quite similar, except for the final one. They contain a set of data about what room they are, the routes to other rooms they contain, and the keys they provide users for reaching those rooms. The `createPage()` subroutine checks that data against the permissions file of the current visitor, and either welcomes the visitor to the page or sends the visitor away. If the user did not previously have the permissions this room provides, notification of the permissions is made. (The fact that a user is not constantly reminded the keys possessed provides most of the challenge in this simple game.)

Figure 6-9
Duplicate
Name Rejection

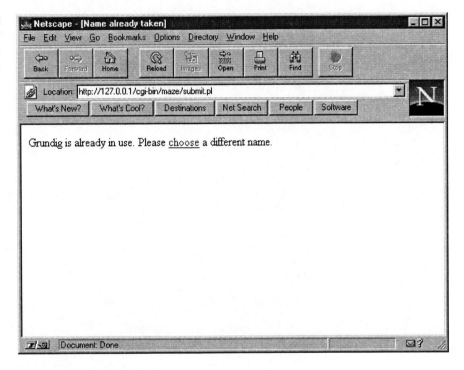

```perl
#!/usr/bin/perl
#import CGI module
use CGI qw(:standard);
#room settings - different for every room
$room=1;
$unlock=7;
@doors=(6,7,8);
#get user name
$username=cookie('MazeID');
#check to see if they have a username
if($username) {
#if okay, build page
createPage();
} else {
#no ID, no page - send to entry form
print redirect('http://127.0.0.1/cgi-bin/maze/entry.pl');
}

sub createPage {
```

```
#open file with permissions
open (COOKLIST, "C:/mazeperm/$username.txt") || die "open: $!";
while (<COOKLIST>) {
#get permissions
  $perm=$_;
}
close (COOKLIST);
#use Perl split() function
#much like JavaScript with different syntax
@perms=split(/,/, $perm);
print header(),start_html("Room #$room");
if (@perms[$room]) {
  #if they have permissions, welcome
  print h1("Welcome to Room $room");
  if (!(@perms[$unlock])) {
    #is this a new key?  If so, inform
    print p("You have unlocked the door to room # $unlock.");
    #set new permissions
    @perms[$unlock]=1;
    $newperms=join(",",@perms);
    #write permissions to file
    open (COOKLIST, ">C:/mazeperm/$username.txt") || die "open: $!";
    $newperms=join(",",@perms);
    print COOKLIST "$newperms";
    close (COOKLIST);
  }
#alert user of rooms they may visit
print p("You may go from here to:");
for ($i=0; $i<3; $i++){
  #note single/double quote issue in HREF.
  #string is really a double-quote string,
  #and contents will be parsed.
  #CGI.pm includes a() method as well;
  #I prefer to code my own links and tables.
  print p("<A HREF='maze@doors[$i].pl'>Room # @doors[$i]</A>");
}

} else {
#forbidden entry.
print h1("No entry");
print p("You don't have that key. You may <A HREF='maze1.pl'>start
over</A> if you like.");
}
print close_html();
}
```

Figure 6-10 shows a room the user has permissions to enter, in this case Room #1.

Figure 6-11 shows the less-polite version for users barging in where they don't belong.

Figure 6-10
Welcome to
a Room for
which the User
has Permissions

Figure 6-11
Forbidden Entry

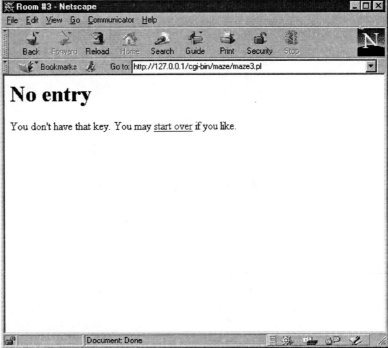

All of the remaining rooms use the same formula, except for the last room, which is maze9.pl in this case.

There is no reason this maze could not have many more than nine, and much more ornate rooms, even with the simple mechanisms used here. Key snatchers could lock rooms back up if the developer wanted to make the maze really difficult.

```perl
#!/usr/bin/perl
#import CGI module
use CGI qw(:standard);
#only need to declare room number
#no keys or doors
$room=9;
$username=cookie('MazeID');
if($username) {
createPage();
} else {
#redirect to entry if no username
print redirect('http://127.0.0.1/cgi-bin/maze/entry.pl');
}

sub createPage {
  #check permissions file, as before
  open (COOKLIST, "C:/mazeperm/$username.txt") || die "open: $!";
  while (<COOKLIST>) {
    $perm=$_;
  }
  close (COOKLIST);
  @perms=split(/,/, $perm);
  print header(),start_html("Room #$room");
  if (@perms[$room]) {
  #user has made it!
    print h1("Welcome to Room $room");
    print h2("Congratulations!");
    print p("You've completed the maze. Rest and celebrate!");
  } else {
  #forbidden, as usual.
    print h1("No entry");
    print p("You don't have that key. You may <A HREF='maze1.pl'>start
over</A> if you like.");
  }
print close_html();
}
```

Lucky users will reach the congratulations notice, shown in Figure 6-12. Unlucky users may never see it. On the bright side, if they return later, their permissions will stay with them, thanks to the persistent cookie.

Figure 6-12
The
Congratulations
Notice

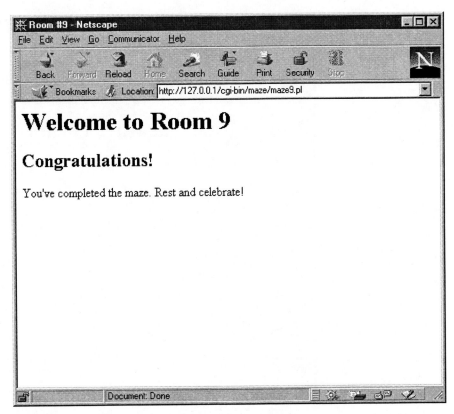

Building a Shopping Cart with CGI and Cookies

Although they may have drawbacks for border-crossing applications, client-side cookies are perfectly adequate for the task of building a shopping cart. The worst users can do is disrupt their own orders, and the program provides plenty of confirmation before actually placing an order. This application keeps track of a user's purchases with a very simple client-side cookie, building a list of goods for later processing by a commerce-enabled application. (In this case, the commerce-enabled application is a pair of payment collectors making C.O.D. deliveries.)

When the user first arrives at Josie's Fine Caramel Treats, there is the counter shown in Figure 6-13. Much like an old-style store, before the advent of the shopping cart, this presents a central view of all the items available for purchase, and tells the user what options are available.

Figure 6-13
First Arriving
at Josie's

Figure 6-13
First Arriving at Josie's

This central view handles all the processing for the site, accepting the orders users enter in the item descriptions and keeping a central tabulation of their potential purchases.

```perl
#!/usr/bin/perl

use CGI qw(:standard);

#preprocessing - gather cookies and form fields
@names=(Squirrels,Rabbits,Dogs,Cows,Trees);
@prices=(5,6,4,6,12);
$basket=cookie('basket');
if ($basket){
  #split quantities out of cookie
  @quantity=split(/,/, $basket);
  $goods=join(",",@quantity);
} else {
  # no cookie - set to zero
  $goods='0,0,0,0,0';
}
```

```perl
if (param('item')) {
#add the item from the form to the cart
#hitch is that zero doesn't work from form
#so form submits one higher, that one
#subtracted here
@quantity[param('item')-1]=param('quant');
$goods=join(",",@quantity);
}
# if a change, write a cookie
if ($goods ne $basket) {
  $cookie = cookie(-name=>'basket',
          -value=>$goods,
          -expires=>'+15m',
                -path=>'/');
  print header(-cookie=>$cookie);
} else {
  #no change, no new cookie
  print header();
}
# send out the page
print start_html("Josie's Fine Caramel Treats");
print h1("Josie's Fine Caramel Treats");
print p("Welcome to Josie's Fine Caramel Treats, where we treat you
like a fine treat.");
print p("Caramel lovers the world over have visited our store in
search of the finest caramels.");
print hr();
#Table contains goods, prices, quantities,totals
print "<TABLE BORDER=1>";
print "<TR><TH>Item</TH><TH>Price/lb.</TH><TH>Quantity
(lbs.)</TH><TH>Total</TH></TR>";
for ($i=0; $i<5; $i++) {
  $item=$i+1;
  print "<TR><TD><A HREF='item$item.pl'>Caramel
@names[$i]</A></TD><TD>";
  print "\$@prices[$i].00</TD><TD>";
  print "@quantity[$i]</TD><TD>";
  print '$',@quantity[$i]*@prices[$i],'.00</TD></TR>';
  $total+=@quantity[$i]*@prices[$i];
}
print "</TR><TD></TD><TD></TD><TD></TD><TD>\$$total.00</TD></TR>";
print "</TABLE>";
#when they're ready, move to checkout
print "<A HREF='register.pl'>Advance to the checkout</A>";
print end_html();
```

The items are on simple forms with descriptions that allow the user to order if an item is desired. All quantities are in pounds of caramel. The item forms read the cookie to see if the user has placed an order previously. If there is already an order, they place that in the form field as the default to make it easier for the user to make changes.

```perl
#!/usr/bin/perl

use CGI qw(:standard);
#check for cookie.
#No cookie gets sent to main form to be
#set up. This page could also set cookie
```

```
#if developer thought appropriate.
if (!(cookie('basket'))) {
print redirect('http://127.0.0.1/cgi-bin/shopping/main.pl');
}
else {
  $basket=cookie('basket');
  @quantity=split(/./, $basket);
  #this item uses 0 - switch for room
  #this entire page could be generated automatically
  #from database with minor changes.
  $current=@quantity[0];
  print header(), start_html('Caramel Squirrels');
  print h1('Caramel Squirrels');
  print p('Our Caramel Squirrels have been a favorite for years. Bird-
watchers who have lost birdseed to the ever-charming rodents can exact
their revenge on these replicas in fine caramel. Guaranteed caramel
pleasure!');
  #use cgi.pm's form capacities
  print start_form('POST','main.pl');
  #note naming conventions for form field
  #parameters; much like cookie()
  print p('How many pounds would you like? ',textfield(-
name=>"quant",-value=>$current));
  #item number carried as hidden field.
  print hidden('item',1);
  print submit('Enter your order');
  print end_form();
  print end_html;
}
```

Users who visit this page with see something like Figure 6-14. They can enter the number of pounds they want, and hit the submit button to add to their order and return to the main screen.

The main screen keeps totals using the information from the client cookie. Figure 6-15 shows a cookie being set after a user has visited several of the screens and ordered a good deal of caramel. Note the escaping that the `cookie()` method has performed on the value.

After several such visits, the user's cart might look like Figure 6-16, which is positively overflowing with caramel.

At this point, it is time to head to the cash register. The cash register in this example is really a mechanism for turning the shopping cart information over to another application for processing. All of the information is put in hidden fields for the processor, which will also accept name, address, and payment collection information. I would suggest that that final application clear the cookie when the order is complete; clearing the cookie on this page might cause some users to lose orders if they changed their minds and went back to the previous page.

Figure 6-14
97 Pounds of
Caramel Squirrels
for the Holidays

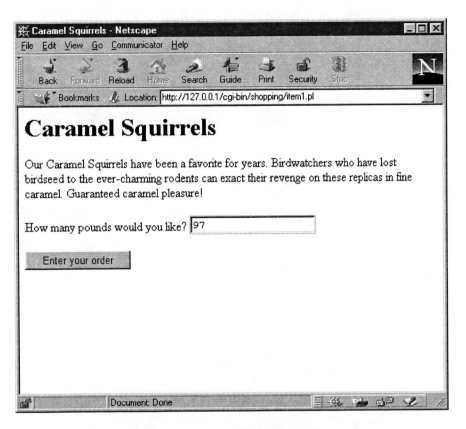

Figure 6-15
Shopping Cart
Cookie in Action

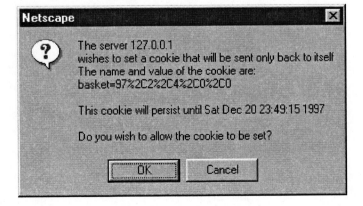

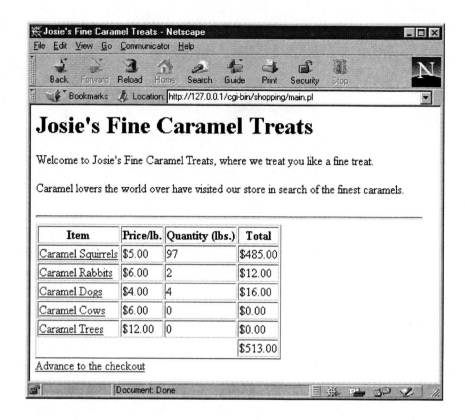

```
#!/usr/bin/perl

use CGI qw(:standard);
if (!(cookie('basket'))) {
  print redirect('http://127.0.0.1/cgi-bin/shopping/main.pl');
} else {
  #preprocessing - gather cookies and form fields
  @names=(Squirrels,Rabbits,Dogs,Cows,Trees);
  @prices=(5,6,4,6,12);
  $basket=cookie('basket');
  @quantity=split(/,/, $basket);
  print header();

# send out the page
  print start_html("Josie's Fine Caramel Treats");
  print h2("Josie's Fine Caramel Treats");
  print p("Welcome to the checkout, where you can prepare to pay for
your caramels.");
  print hr();
  print start_form('POST','final.pl');
  #similar to previous page, but removes
  #HREFs and adds hidden fields
  print "<TABLE BORDER=1>";
  print "<TR><TH>Item</TH><TH>Price/lb.</TH><TH>Quantity
(lbs.)</TH><TH>Total</TH></TR>";
  for ($i=0; $i<5; $i++) {
```

```
      $item=$i+1;
      print "<TR><TD>Caramel @names[$i]</TD><TD>";
      print "\$@prices[$i].00</TD><TD>";
      print "@quantity[$i]</TD><TD>";
      print '$',@quantity[$i]*@prices[$i],'.00</TD>';
      print hidden(-name=>"item$item",-value=>@quantity[$i]);
      $total+=@quantity[$i]*@prices[$i];
      print '</TR>';
   }
   print "</TR><TD></TD><TD></TD><TD></TD><TD>\$$total.00</TD></TR>";
   print "</TABLE>";
   print '<P>All orders are shipped personally by our payment collec-
tion specialists, Guido and Fluffy. If we have to hunt you down, we
will.<BR>';
   print 'Name:',textfield('name');
   print ' Phone Number:', textfield('phone'), '<BR>';
   print 'Address:<BR>',textarea(-name=>'address',-rows=>4,-
columns=>20),' ';
   print submit('Submit your order');
   print end_form();
   print end_html();
}
```

The cash register looks like Figure 6-17. Users who submit their orders will be getting a visit from Guido and Fluffy, along with a lot of candy.

Figure 6-17
Entering the
Cash Register

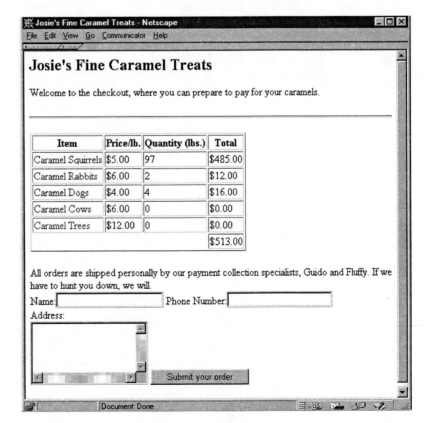

These examples have just scratched the surface of Perl's development capabilities. Although Perl probably isn't the right language for writing accounting or relational database systems, it offers powerful tools to developers who need to do nearly anything with text. Perl can connect to databases, providing much better control over large quantities of data than the simple file-and-cookie schemes presented here. In many ways, Perl is the ideal glue language, allowing developers to transform textual information into requests that are intelligible by back-end processing systems. Unlike JavaScript and VBScript, Perl wasn't developed specifically for the Web, but as a result it has a richer vocabulary. CGI doesn't have state management tools that rival the powers of the environments presented in the next chapters, but it has enough of a foundation so that developers can, with some extra work, create environments of equal power.

Cookies
and Netscape
Server-Side
JavaScript

LiveWire, recently redescribed by Netscape as Server-Side JavaScript (SSJS), was one of the first proprietary tools for server-side programming, applying JavaScript to Netscape Enterprise Server and FastTrack server development. SSJS is a richer environment than CGI, offering additional toolsets for processing requests, especially requests that require information from a database. This environment handles much of the overhead of interpreting requests and creating responses, leaving the developer free to focus on manipulating data. SSJS provides a mix of relatively weak tools for cookie handling and strong tools for session management.

Netscape's choice of "Server-Side JavaScript" as the replacement title for LiveWire may mislead some developers into thinking that Netscape's SSJS might be compatible with Microsoft's version of server-side JavaScript, Active Server Pages, which will be covered in Chapter 8. SSJS is definitely **not** compatible with Active Server Pages. It runs only on Netscape's FastTrack and Enterprise servers.

Building Applications on Netscape Servers

Netscape's approach to SSJS is different from its approach to client-side JavaScript. Developers use the same language in both situations, but the object models surrounding that language and the process of building applications are very different. SSJS applications are compiled into bytecodes by the jsac compiler before being used, while client-side JavaScript is interpreted every time the page is loaded. The tools provided for manipulation with JavaScript are very different, reflecting the needs of HTTP request handling and database connectivity rather than user interaction. Developers can mix and match client and server code to meet their needs, but must always remember which side of the transaction they are on.

SSJS provides the full facilities of the JavaScript language—control structures and syntax, for example. It also allows access to LiveConnect, a key Netscape library that allows JavaScript and Java to communicate and share information. Most of the rest of the tools developers are used to working with on the client side—the document object and all of its contents—are replaced with server-specific tools. There are also a few significant changes in comparison operators and prototype usage between JavaScript 1.1 and JavaScript 1.2 that are covered in the Netscape documentation.

Unlike CGI programs, SSJS programs can be a mixture of HTML and script, and the jsac compiler will create a program that combines both—multiple pages and code files are combined into a single application. SSJS applications are more like small web sites, containing a number of pages and their accompanying code. An initial page is run by the server when the application is first started, allowing the program to initialize itself if necessary. The default page will be the document presented to the user when the application is opened. Pages within a JavaScript application can refer to each other as if they were in the same directory, and users can refer to the pages contained in a single JavaScript application directly with URLs.

SSJS applications must be installed on the Enterprise Server using the applications manager. Doing this generally requires administrative privileges. Contact your system administrator if you are not sure how to install your programs. Also note that none of the programs in this chapter uses the start page option—I create a blank `start.htm` file and set that as the start page during application installation so that I can easily add information there later if needed.

JavaScript files in an SSJS application must end with the `.js` extension and contain only JavaScript code, not HTML. All functions in `.js` files that are compiled into an application are available to all the HTML files that are a part of that application—there is no need for a `<SERVER SRC="zzzz.js">` attribute. Scripts within HTML files that are to run on the server are indicated with the `<SERVER>` tag or by a backward quote (`` ` ``) enclosing a JavaScript expression within an HTML tag. All code within `<SCRIPT>` tags will be ignored by the compiler and passed through for execution on the client browser. For example:

```
<HTML>
<HEAD>
<TITLE>Server-Side Java Script</TITLE>
</HEAD>
<BODY BGCOLOR="#FFFFFF">
<P>This is ordinary HTML.</P>
<SERVER>write("<P>This was written with JavaScript!</P>");</SERVER>
<P>This is ordinary HTML again.</P>
</BODY></HTML>
```

Once compiled with the `jsac` compiler and installed with the application manager, this simple script will produce output that is a combination of the raw HTML and the output from the JavaScript write statement, as shown in Figures 7-1 and 7-2.

Remember, server-side code doesn't worry as much about what kind of code will run on the user's browser. By the time this output reaches the browser, it has been converted into innocuous HTML, without a trace of the server-side JavaScript that created it. Server-side programs that generate HTML or client-side Java that is not compatible with all browsers may run into difficulty, but all the examples in this chapter should work with browsers from both Microsoft and Netscape.

Figure 7-1
Server-Side
JavaScript Output
in Netscape
Communicator

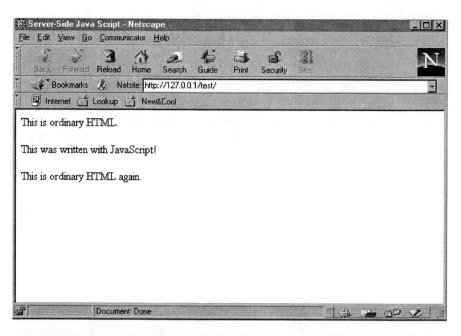

Figure 7-1
Server-Side
JavaScript Output
in Netscape
Communicator

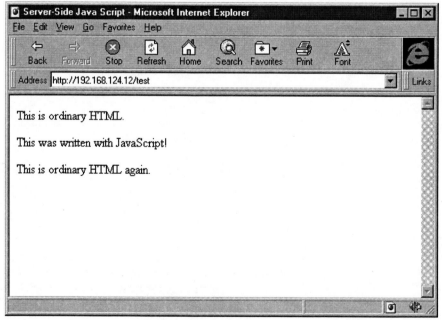

Figure 7-2
Server-Side
JavaScript
Output in
Internet Explorer

Netscape provides a set of objects that insulate developers from having to interpret the CGI variables by themselves. The request object contains information about the HTTP request made by the user. A list of the request object's properties (and some of their CGI equivalents) is shown in Table 7-1.

Property	Contents
agent	Provides the name and version of the client software that originated the request; similar to HTTP_USER_AGENT
auth_type	Provides information about the type of authorization, if the user has logged in (authenticated); similar to AUTH_TYPE
auth_user	If the user of the client has had to authenticate, provides the username given; similar to REMOTE_USER
ip	Provides the IP address of the client; similar to REMOTE_ADDR
method	Provides the HTTP method used to make this request, typically GET, POST, or head; similar to REQUEST_METHOD
protocol	The HTTP protocol level supported by the client (HTTP/1.1, for example.); similar to SERVER_PROTOCOL
query	Provides the information in the URL that appeared after the ? separator; similar to QUERY_STRING
imageX	Provides the horizontal position of the cursor, if the user clicked on an image map; only available for requests generated by image maps
imageY	Provides the vertical position of the cursor, if the user clicked on an image map; only available for requests generated by image maps
uri	The request's local URI, providing the information that followed the hostname and the optional port; similar to SCRIPT_NAME

One of the most important things about this table, however, is what is missing. None of these options includes cookie values. Getting cookie values directly from the request requires extra work, and writing them will also require effort. The request object also has a method, httpHeader(), that returns all the information from the HTTP request header the client submitted. Examining the cookie string in the header is easy with the following diagnostic program:

```
<HTML>
<HEAD>
<TITLE>Server-Side Java Script - Headers</TITLE>
```

```
</HEAD>
<BODY BGCOLOR="#FFFFFF">
<SERVER>
var header=request.httpHeader();
write("cookie:"+header["cookie"]+"<BR>\n");
</SERVER>
</BODY></HTML>
```

Figure 7-3 shows the results after a few cookies have been set. Like the `document.cookie` object in client-side JavaScript, the cookie name-value pairs are all presented on a single line, URL-encoded and separated by semicolons. Because they use the same format, the JavaScript `readCookie()` function from Chapter 4 can be used with very little modification:

```
function ReadCookie(name){
var header, allCookie, CookieVal, length,start,end;
header=request.httpHeader();
cookieVal="";
name=name+"=";  //append equals to avoid false matches.
allCookie= header["cookie"];
if (allCookie) {
  length=allCookie.length;
  if (length>0) {//no cookies - user is probably incinerating cookies.
    start=allCookie.indexOf(name,0)
    if (start!=-1) {//if string appeared - otherwise cookie wasn't
set.
      start+=name.length;
      end=allCookie.indexOf(";",start);
      if (end==-1) {end=length;}
      cookieVal=unescape(allCookie.substring(start,end));
    }
  }
else {
  cookieVal="";
  }
}
return(cookieVal);
}
```

Netscape's facility for handling responses is similarly limited. Responses are manipulated with the `write()` function used above, and the `addResponseHeader()` and `removeResponseHeader()` functions. The `write()` function can be used any time during the course of an SSJS program, but the header functions need to be used before the first 64K of the response has been written to the buffer—the response will already have gone to the client. All cookie setting must be performed near the start of a document, though it doesn't need to be in the first line written.

The `WriteCookie()` function needs only slight modifications to work in this environment. Instead of writing its results to the `document.cookie` object, it creates `Set-Cookie` headers with the server-side `addResponse-Header()` function. It cannot check to make sure the cookie was accepted, because it won't know until another request comes back from the browser. As a result, that functionality has been deleted.

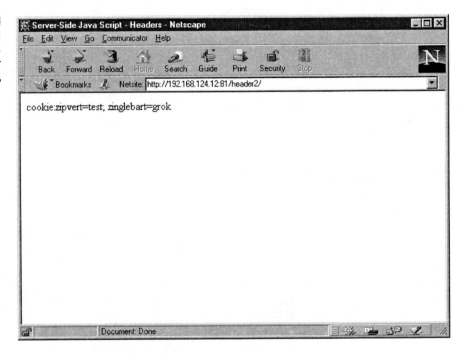

```
function WriteCookie(name,value,expires,domain,path,secure){
var CookieVal,CookError;
CookieVal=CookError="";
if (name) {
CookieVal=CookieVal+name+"=";
    if (value) {
    CookieVal=CookieVal+escape(value);
     if (expires) {
     CookieVal=CookieVal+"; expires="+expires.toGMTString();
     }
     if (domain){
     CookieVal=CookieVal+"; domain="+domain;
     }
     if (path) {
     CookieVal=CookieVal+"; path="+path;
     }
     if (secure) {
     CookieVal=CookieVal+"; secure";
     }
    }
    else {CookError=CookError+"Value failure";}//need valid value
}
else {CookError=CookError+"Name failure";}//need valid name
if (!CookError) {
```

```
    //sets cookie with header
    addResponseHeader("Set-Cookie",CookieVal);

}
return CookError;
}
```

These two slightly modified functions can be used with their unmodified companions, `combine()` and `breakdown()`, for a variety of cookie handling tasks. Store them in a new `.js` file—`svcooklb.js` or something similar, and be sure to add them to the `jsac` command line every time you compile a program that requires them.

Session Management with Netscape Server Side JavaScript

Netscape's server-side tools for directly managing cookies are extremely weak, but the program makes up for this with a strong set of session management tools. The Netscape server console allows developers to choose from among five different methods for preserving state beween multiple sessions, even after the application has been compiled and installed. Different applications on the same server can even use different methods. Developers can use client-side cookies while they debug their programs to watch variables, and then switch to server-side cookies to avoid bombing users with multiple cookies. They can even use SSJS's built-in URL encoding or IP tracking tools to avoid using cookies altogether.

The session management tools work only while the user is still in the same browser session—they do not support persistence.

Netscape's session management services take advantage of three objects which reside on the server, providing functionality beyond that afforded by the simple request object. The client object contains information relevant to the particular browser making the request. The project object contains information that is available to all requests that access this particular application. The server object contains information that is available to all applications running on a particular server. (Netscape considers multiple virtual servers listing on different ports to be separate servers, so applications running on servers listening to port 80 and port 8080 can't communicate.)

All of these objects have limited lifetimes. All objects, including the server object, are destroyed any time the server is stopped. The project object is also destroyed when it is stopped at the application console. The information in the client object is destroyed when the client makes no requests in a preset time, or when either the application or the server is stopped. Any information that needs to be stored persistently must be written to a file, a database, or a persistent cookie on the client.

The Server and Project Objects

The Project and Server objects maintain state for applications and groups of applications, respectively. They can be very useful for storing information needed for a future request (the next available userID, for instance), and can store object values, unlike the client object. Because both objects face the prospect of multiple simultaneous reads and write from a variety of requests being processed, they require the use of a fairly sophisticated lock and unlock mechanism that protects information from being modified inapproriately. The project application will prove useful for the shopping cart-application at the end of this chapter.

The Client Object

The Client object handles most of the session management functionality appropriate to typical Web applications. Developers can add properties to the Client object, and are restricted only by the limitations of the method they choose for maintaining that object. The Client object's properties may be stored on either the client or the server, and Netscape provides a number of options for controlling the server's maintenance of those properties.

Choosing the method the server uses for Client Object Maintenance can have a significant impact on the kinds of use developers can reliably make of the Client object. Each of the five methods has its advantages and limitations, as shown in Table 7-2.

The server administrator sets the technique used for Client Object Maintenance from the server administration console shown in Figure 7-4. Developers should plan their application around one of these settings and be prepared to work around its shortcomings.

Table 7-2
Client Object
Maintenance
Techniques

Technique	How it Works	Advantages and Limitations
client-cookie	All Client object properties are stored as corresponding cookies on the client machine. Each property gets its own cookie, named NETSCAPE_LIVEWIRE. *propertyName.*	This requires little overhead on the server. Users can leave a session open and return hours later (as long as they do not quit their browsers) and the session will still be available. Properties can be manipulated directly by client-side scripting. Users must accept cookies. Users who accept some cookies and reject others may disrupt program logic. Sessions may be disrupted by users quitting (or crashing) browsers. The contents of the client object face have the same size limitations cookies have—no more than 20 from same domain, no more than 4K per cookie.
client-url	All client properties are stored as request strings encoded to URLs.	Users do not receive cookies, so possible rejection is avoided. This is a fairly well-automated process, but useful only when small amounts of data are stored—this can generate enormous URLs. The process should not be used with forms that employ the GET method. There is some increase in processing overhead. The process usually breaks when a user leaves site and returns, but may be bookmarked.
server-ip	All client properties are stored on the server, which uses the IP address of the requesting client to keep track of which properties go to which client.	This is extremely efficient and completely unobtrusive. Unfortunately, it breaks down completely when users are behind proxy servers, an increasingly likely probability. The process is useful only on intranets where all users will reach the server directly with their own IP addresses intact.

continued

Technique	How it Works	Advantages and Limitations
server-cookie	All client properties are stored on the server. A single cookie (which expires at the end of the session) containing an ID value is sent to the client. The server uses this value to connect users with the values it has stored.	This requires users to accept cookies. Sessions will not be disrupted by users quitting (or crashing) browsers unless a session expires. All client properties are stored on the server, adding to server overhead. A session expires after a preset period of user inactivity.
server-url	All client properties are stored on the server. An ID value is encoded into all URLs referring back to this application. The server uses this value to connect uses with the values it has stored.	There are requirements for users to accept cookies. Sessions may be disrupted by users quitting (or crash-ing) browsers. This is a fairly well-automated process for generating URLs. It should not be employed with forms that use the GET method. All client properties are stored on the server, adding to server overhead. A session expires after a preset period of user inactivity.

Figure 7-4
Using the
JavaScript
Application
Managers to Set
Client Object
Maintenance

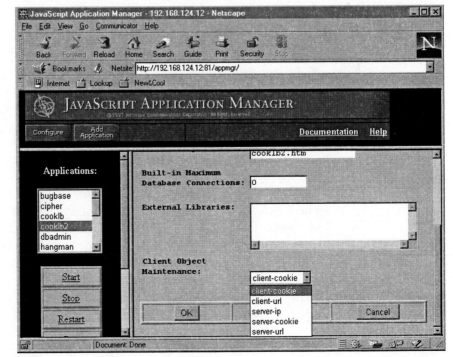

Netscape affords some very powerful mechanisms for providing URL encoding. When the server is using URL encoding, the JavaScript processor will actually parse a document to find URLs, and insert query strings as needed. This mechanism has a few limitations, however. First, only URLs that are embedded in HTML receive this treatment. This means that all URLs created with the `write()` function need some extra help—the `addClient()` function. The `addClient()` function checks to see what method the server is using for client object maintenance. If the server is using one of the URL encoding methods, the `addClient()` function will append the needed query string to the end of the URL. If not, the `addClient()` function leaves the URL alone. The `addClient()` function takes as its argument the opening tag of an HTML link:

```
addClient("<A HREF='http://www.netscape.com'>");
```

The second limitation of the automatic parsing is that the processor will append query strings to all URLs. URLs that should not be receiving query strings (links to other sites and applications, and `mailto:` links, for instance) need to be skipped. The easiest way to force the processor to skip them is to mark them as calculated JavaScript sections with the backquote (`` ` ``). For instance,

```
<A HREF="www.netscape.com">Netscape</A>
```

would become

```
<A HREF=`"www.netscape.com"`>Netscape</A>
```

When using client-URL maintenance, the `addClient()` function encodes the most recent values of the client properties into the URL. If a URL is encoded at the top of the page and a client property is modified afterward, subsequent URLs will have different query strings than the first one encoded. While this can be used as a feature, it is generally a trap. Applications that plan to use client-URL maintenance should handle all client object manipulation before writing the page.

The Client object contains no predefined properties, but developers can add properties as needed. All properties of the Client object are stored as strings; there is no direct way to store an array or an object to a client property. (The `combine()` and `breakdown()` functions provided in Chapter 4 could allow developers to combine multiple values for storage in a single client property; JavaScript's `split()` and `join()` functions will work for arrays.) Property names, like those of JavaScript variables, are case-sensi-

tive. The properties are referred to directly with the JavaScript dot notation, and no `var` declaration is required. To set a client property called
`firstName`, just write:

```
client.firstName="your name here";
```

To write the `firstName` property into the HTML, just use

```
write(client.firstname);
```

Netscape provides two tools for controlling the lifespan of these Client
objects. The first, `client.destroy`, obliterates the Client object on the
server immediately. All applications using a server-side method of maintaining Client objects will lose that information. Applications using client-side
maintenance tools will have a problem, however. The values stored on the
client will come back to the server with new requests. To destroy cookies,
call the `client.expiration` method with an argument of zero:

```
client.expiration(0);
```

The `expiration()` function also sets the timeout for the client objects
stored on the server when it uses on of the server maintenance methods.
(The default is 10.) Sites using client-URL maintenance should call
`client.destroy()` at the top of the page, and generate a new page which
will not have any URL encoding. Users can still use the back button to
return to the session, and developers should be prepared for the possibility.

The Client object also has two methods for manipulating the ID
values used to keep track of client objects: `ssjs_getClientID` and
`ssjs_generateClientID`. The `ssjs_getClientID` function returns a
meaningful value only to applications using one of the server-side maintenance techniques, and reflects the ID value used by the server to keep track of
which user goes with which Client object. The `ssjs_generateClientID`
function creates a new client value every time it is called. It is most useful with
the client-side methods for Client object maintenance, creating an ID that can
be stored in the Client object itself or in other objects to uniquely identify a
user for the duration of a transaction. The ID values returned by both of these
functions can be used with the Project and Server objects to store more complex data objects or share database connections.

Building a Mutating Site with the Client Object

This simple example will demonstrate the Client object and its application
using all of the Client-object maintenance mechanisms. While it does

nothing especially useful, the same concepts can be applied to personalization, art sites (it could create a strange hall of mirrors), and even border controls. The site consists of four pages, all of which have links to the other pages. The information displayed on a page varies depending on the page visited previously. The background color, text color, and content of the page will all change—all the page itself includes is links to other pages and a simple set of instructions. This site uses only the Client object, not directly manipulated persistent cookies.

All four rooms have a similar structure, and are named `roomx.htm`, where x is the room number.

For `room1.htm` we write:

```
<HTML>
<SERVER>
room=1;
backColor="red";
textColor="yellow";
buildRoom(room, backColor, textColor);
</SERVER>
</BODY></HTML>
```

For `room2.htm` we write:

```
<HTML>
<SERVER>
room=2;
backColor="black";
textColor="white";
buildRoom(room, backColor, textColor);
</SERVER>
</BODY></HTML>
```

For `room3.htm` we write:

```
<HTML>
<SERVER>
room=3;
backColor="white";
textColor="black";
buildRoom(room, backColor, textColor);
</SERVER>
</BODY></HTML>
```

For `room4.htm` we write:

```
<HTML>
<SERVER>
room=4;
backColor="green";
textColor="white";
buildRoom(room, backColor, textColor);
</SERVER>
</BODY></HTML>
```

The real action takes place in the `rooms.js` file, which contains the `buildRoom()` function. The `buildRoom()` function displays the page based on the settings given it by the *previous* room, then adjusts the settings so that the next room will behave according to the settings given it by this room. It sets background color, text color, and displays a quote from a text file stored elsewhere on the server.

```javascript
function buildRoom(room, bgColor, txtColor) {
//check to see if they've been here before
if (client.started=="true") {

//get values set by previous page
  oldRoom=client.oldRoom;
  oldBgColor=client.bgColor;
  oldTxtColor=client.txtColor;

//set values for next page
//have to do this before addClient() call
  client.oldRoom=room;
  client.bgColor=bgColor;
  client.txtColor=txtColor;

//display room number
  write("<HEAD><TITLE>Mutant Room #" + room +"</TITLE></HEAD>");

//set background and text according to settings
//from previous page
  write("<BODY BGCOLOR='" + oldBgColor);
  write("' TEXT='" + oldTxtColor +"'>");

//tell them where they are now
  write("<H2>Welcome to Room #" + room +"</H2>");

//tell them where they came from and what it did
  write("<P>You came here from room #" + oldRoom +".");
  write(" It set the background color to " + oldBgColor);
  write(" and the text color to " + oldTxtColor + ".</P>");

//provide links to other rooms
//note use of addClient()
  write("<P>You may visit rooms:</P>");
  for (i=1; i<5; i++) {
    write(addClient("<A HREF='room" + i +".htm")+"'>");
    write(i+"</A> ");
  }

//show quote
//This reads from file outside of main http doc
//tree - a good way to include info not otherwise
//available through HTTP
  write("<P>The previous page asked that this page show you the fol-
lowing quote:</P>");
  var fileName="D:\\netscape\\suitespot\\quotes\\quote" + oldRoom
+".txt";
  var readFile= new File(fileName);
  noErr=readFile.open("r");
  if (noErr) {
```

```
        while (!readFile.eof()) {
            line=readFile.readln();
            write(line+"<BR>");
        }
    readFile.close();
    }
}
else {
//display start page to new visitors
//start by setting values for next page.
    client.started="true";
    client.oldRoom=room;
    client.bgColor=bgColor;
    client.txtColor=txtColor;
    write("<HEAD><TITLE>Mutant Room Start</TITLE></HEAD>");
    write("<BODY BGCOLOR='white' TEXT='black'>");
    write("<H2>Welcome to mutant room #"+room +".</H2>");
    write("<P>Because you haven't visited any of these strange rooms
yet, ");
    write("you're seeing this strange plain page with no colors and no
quote.<P>");
    write("<P>Of course, these quotes are from <I>Macbeth</I>, so you
may ");
    write("prefer to avoid them anyway.</P>");
    write("<P>You may visit rooms:</P>");

//provide menu - note use of addClient()
    for (i=1; i<5; i++) {
        write(addClient("<A HREF='room" + i +".htm")+"'>");
        write(i+"</A> ");
    }
}
}
```

 Developers who do not want to or cannot (because of security or administrative concerns) include quote files can leave out that section. The text files I used are ordinary text files, named `quote1.txt` through `quote4.txt`.

Install this application, and choose any mechanism for client object maintenance—it will work with any of them, unless you are behind a proxy (in which case `server-ip` may return the wrong pages); or rejecting cookies (in which case neither of the cookie mechanisms will work.) To keep track of the methods that send cookies, tell your browser to alert you when cookies are set.

Opening this application for the first time brings up the screen shown in Figure 7-5, an uncustomized page that does not display a quote. Behind the scenes, however, this page is setting the values that will give the next page its personality.

Figure 7-5
The Opening Page

As users move from page to page, they see pages that follow settings from previous pages. Reloading a page will change the display as the page accepts the values it set the first time it was loaded. Each page's personality is determined by the page that preceded it, as shown in Figures 7-6 and 7-7.

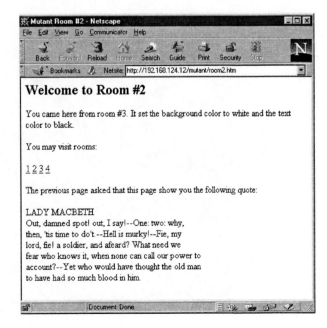

Figure 7-6
Room 2 after
Visiting Room 3

Figure 7-7
Room 4 after
Visiting Room 2

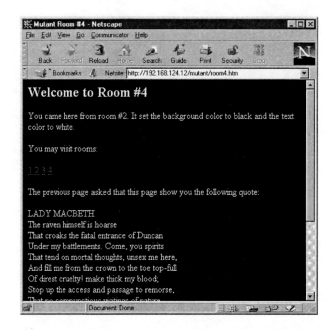

While the content of the page will not change with the technique used for client object maintenance, the URLs and the cookies sent will. Figure 7-8 shows Room 3 when it has been reached using the `client-url` method. Note the enormous URLs that provide information on each client property.

Figure 7-8
Room 3 with
`client-url`
Maintenance

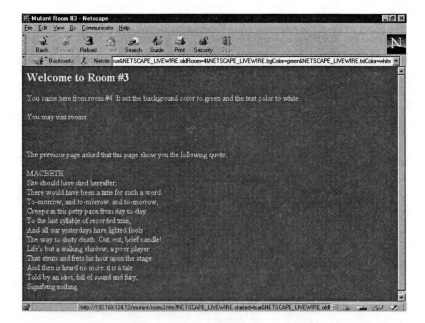

`Client-cookie` will provide the same information as the `client-url` method except that it puts the information into separate cookies instead of building an enormous query string. `Server-cookie` keeps all the information on the server, but builds an enormous ID value for the linking cookie, shown in Figure 7-9.

Figure 7-9
A `server-cookie`
ID as Reported
by Netscape
Communicator

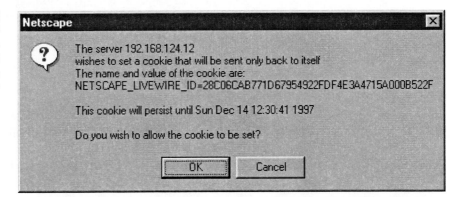

The `server-url` puts that enormous ID value into a URL, as shown in Figure 7-10. Large as this URL may be, it is still much smaller than the URL generated by `client-url`.

Figure 7-10
A Page using
`server-url` ID

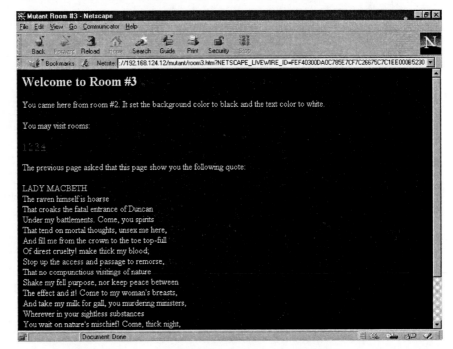

Building Applications with Cookies

Netscape's SSJS allows developers to combine the kinds of JavaScript cookie functions developed for the client with its client-state management tools, database tools, and access to the file system. Applications that need only to maintain state for the duration of a browser session can be created easily with little extra effort, while applications that preserve information for a longer period can take advantage of SSJS's access to databases and the file system.

Collecting the Notepad Cookie

The first task we will assign SSJS is the collection of the cookies created with the Notepad application in Chapter 4. To make certain that users identify their comments, we will use the authentication username as a file name and require that users have been authenticated to the server. Users can save multiple comments; all new comments will be appended to the current file. Users will also be able to view previous comments submitted.

This application will contain several parts. Many of its pages will need the server-side library `svcooklb.js`. Then, the application needs an entryway page that authenticates the user and provides an alert to the user that comments are about to be submitted. This page will display the comments and offer a last chance to turn back, as well as the option of seeing previous comments. The last page in the series shows all comments so far collected.

Remember that all of these files need to be compiled into a single .web file with a single call to the jsac compiler. For my files, that was jsac -v -o notepad.web svcooklb.js entry.htm record.htm list.htm. Then that application needs to be installed with the server's application manager.

The entryway page (`entry.htm`) does not have to take on the business of authentication by itself—that task can be handled by the server's access control list. What the page *does* have to do is find the username of the person accessing it, collect the notepad cookie, and display the warning message that comments will be distributed. Finally, the page presents links that allow the user to submit comments or visit a page displaying previous comments.

```
<HTML>
<HEAD><TITLE>Comment Submission</TITLE></HEAD>
<BODY BGCOLOR=#FFFFFF>
<SERVER>
var who, comments;
```

```
//get user - authentication must be performed
//by server
who=request.auth_user;
write("<H2>Welcome, " + who + "!</H2>");
write("<P>Your current comments are:</P><HR>");
//get cookie
comments=ReadCookie("NotePad");
write("<P>"+comments+"</P>");
</SERVER>
<HR><P>Please note - Comments are visible over the web only to the
user who submitted them. They are, however, used by the company in
pursuit of better sites and should not be assumed to be private once
submitted.</P>
<P>If you would like to save your comments to the server (where they
will be publicly available and identified with your name), click <A
HREF="record.htm">here</A>.</P>
<P>You may also see a <A HREF="list.htm">list</A> of your previous
comments.</P>
</BODY></HTML>
```

When users arrive at this page after making some comments with Chapter 4's Notepad application, they will see something like Figure 7-11.

Figure 7-11
Cookie Collection
Welcome Screen

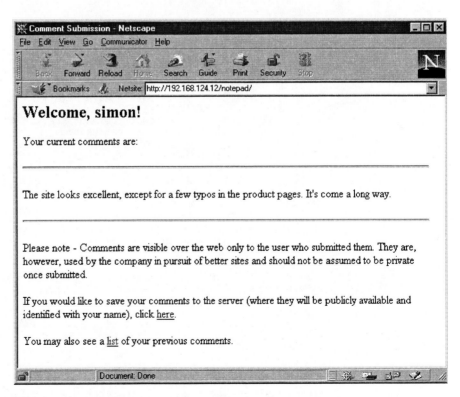

The next page (`record.htm`) does the work of collecting the cookies, taking advantage of SSJS's abilities to read and write text files to the server's hard drive. Note that this page writes the files to a location outside the Web page hierarchy, so users cannot stumble into the comments directory and read everyone's comments. The only users allowed to read all the comments have a separate set of privileges for accessing that directory.

```
<HTML>
<HEAD><TITLE>Comment Submission</TITLE></HEAD>
<BODY BGCOLOR=#FFFFFF>
<SERVER>
var who=request.auth_user;
//Gets cookie using library functions
var rawComments=ReadCookie("NotePad");
var comments=unescape(rawComments);
//note the extra backslashes used to escape a backslash
//Unix developers may use single forward slashes.
var fileName="D:\\netscape\\suitespot\\comments\\" + who +".txt";
var today= new Date();
var dateText= (today.getMonth() + 1) + "/" + today.getDate() + "/"
    +today.getYear();
if (comments!="") {
    var saveFile= new File(fileName);
    noErr=saveFile.open("a");
    if (noErr) {
        saveFile.writeln(who + "<BR>");
        saveFile.writeln(dateText+ "<BR>");
        saveFile.write("<P>" + comments + "</P>");
        saveFile.writeln("");
        noErr=saveFile.close();
        if (noErr) {
            write("<H2>Your comments have been saved, " + who +
                ".</H2>");
            write("<P>Your current comments are:</P><HR>");
            write("<P>"+comments+"</P><HR>");
        }
        else {write("Save Error ");}
    }
    else {write("Save Error ");}
}
else {
    write("<H1>No comments to save</H1>");
    write("<P>If you would like to enter some comments, visit the <A
HREF='../notes.htm'>commenting area</A>.</P>")
}
</SERVER>
<P>Remember: comments are visible over the web only to the user who
submitted them. They are, however, used by the company in pursuit of
better sites and should not be assumed to be private once submit-
ted.</P>
<P>You may also see a <A HREF="list.htm">list</A> of your previous
comments or return to the <A HREF="entry.htm">welcome</A> page.</P>
</BODY></HTML>
```

Usually, users will be greeted with the message that their comments were saved and with the opportunity to check the log of all the comments they have submitted, as shown in Figure 7-12. A lot more error checking goes into this program, because it has more complex things to deal with. Users who haven't typed in any comments, for instance, are offered the chance to do so, as shown in Figure 7-13.

Figure 7-12
A Successful Save

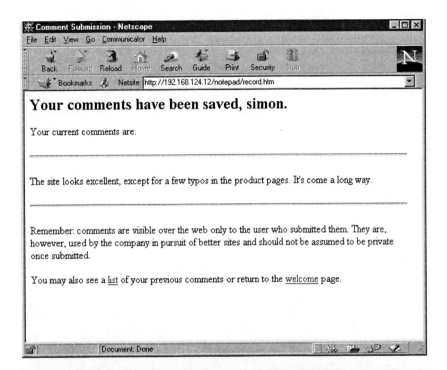

Figure 7-13
Try again—No
Comments
Submitted

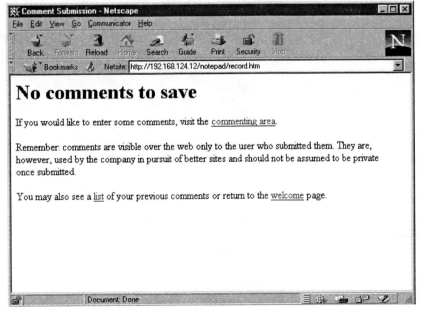

The last file (`list.htm`) does not worry about cookies at all. It just reads the file that contains all the previous content submissions and displays it to the user.

```
<HTML>
<HEAD><TITLE>Comment Submission</TITLE></HEAD>
<BODY BGCOLOR=#FFFFFF>
<SERVER>
var who=request.auth_user;
//note the extra backslashes used to escape a backslash
//Unix developers may use single forward slashes.
var fileName="D:\\netscape\\suitespot\\comments\\" + who +".txt";
var readFile= new File(fileName);
noErr=readFile.open("r");
if (noErr) {
    write("<H2>"+ who + "'s Comments</H2><HR>");
    while (!readFile.eof()) {
        line=readFile.readln();
        write(line);
    }
readFile.close();
}
else {write("File does not exist!");}

</SERVER>
<HR><P>Please note - Comments are visible over the web only to the
user who submitted them. They are, however, used by the company in
pursuit of better sites and should not be assumed to be private once
submitted.</P>
<P>You may return to the <A HREF="entry.htm">welcome</A> page.</P>
</BODY></HTML>
```

The listing shows the users the information available to the comment administrators, as shown in Figure 7-14.

Figure 7-14
Saved Comments

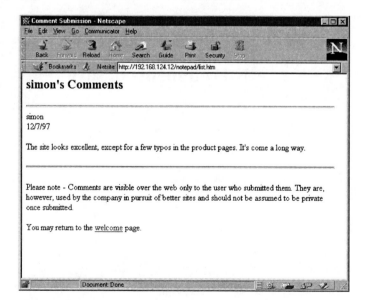

Building the Maze

SSJS can also manage border control, storing information in client-side cookies or in server-side files or databases linked to users by a cookie. Taking advantage of SSJS's modularity, we will create two versions of the maze, identical except for a core processing module, demonstrating both means of storing the data. (Both versions use the svcooklb.js file created above to manage their cookies.) Users will think both modules look the same, unless they explore the contents of the cookie. Users of the client-side version will be able to see their username and their maze information, while users of the client side will only see an ID field that links them to their information on the server.

The registration page finds out if users have visited before with the `readMazeUser()` function, stored in the central code file. If there has been a previous visit, users are immediately redirected to the welcome page. If not, they are asked to enter their names:

```
<SERVER>
username=readMazeUser();
if (username!="") {
redirect("welcome.htm");
}
</SERVER>
<HTML><HEAD><TITLE>Register for the Maze!</TITLE></HEAD>
<BODY>
<H2>Identify yourself to the maze</H2>
<FORM ACTION="welcome.htm" METHOD="GET">
<INPUT TYPE="TEXT" NAME="UserName" SIZE=60>
<INPUT TYPE="SUBMIT">
</FORM>
</BODY></HTML>
```

The welcome page checks to see if a query string is appended to the URL for this page. If there is one, it assumes that this is a new user registration and sends the information to the `register()` function stored in the central code file.

```
<SERVER>
var querystring = request.query
if (querystring) {
   username=register(querystring);
   //write cookie, init maze (locked)
}
else {
   username=readMazeUser();
   //read cookie, get prior visit info
}
//check to make sure they didn't sneak in
//or use an empty username
if (username=="") {
  redirect("register.htm");
```

```
}
</SERVER>
<HTML><HEAD><TITLE>Welcome to the Maze!</TITLE></HEAD>
<BODY>
<H2>Welcome to the Maze, <SERVER>write(username);</SERVER></H2>
<A HREF="maze1.htm">Enter the Maze</A>
</BODY></HTML>
```

The maze rooms all follow the pattern of room 1, providing their room number, the number of the room they unlock (the key), and the three rooms that can be reached from this room.

```
<SERVER>
thisRoom=1;
key=7;
door1=6;
door2=7;
door3=8;
room(thisRoom, key, door1, door2, door3);
</SERVER>
```

All this data is sent to the `room()` function in the central code file which uses the information to build a complete page, checking to see if the user has the required permission to be in the room. If the permission exists, the user gets the key to another room and can move forward. If there is no permission, the user gets a brief message of rejection.

There are two different sets of code that provide these functions. The first, displayed below, stores all information in a cookie on the user's browser. The information could be more throughly encoded if security were an issue, but for this demonstration it will remain in plain text. The `register()` function sets a complete cookie including the username and initial maze privileges—room 1 and nothing else. The `readMazeUser()` function retrieves only the first part of the cookie—the username. The `room()` function provides the core functionality, reading in the cookie and interpreting it to determine the user's permissions. Based on those permissions, it rejects the user, gives new permissions, or allows the user to wander through areas previously visited.

```
function register(rawInput) {
//get username from string
username=rawInput.split("=");

//put entire set of maze info in cookie
cookieVal=username[1]+",1,0,0,0,0,0,0,0,0";
expiration=new Date(1999,12,25);

//call WriteCookie(); svcooklb.js is required
WriteCookie("MazeName",cookieVal,expiration);
return (username[1]);
}
```

```
function readMazeUser() {
//get username from cookie
cookieVal=ReadCookie("MazeName");
username=cookieVal.split(",");
return (username[0]);
}

function room(thisRoom, key, door1, door2, door3) {
//get maze cookie - split into array for easy access
cookieVal=ReadCookie("MazeName");
MazeValues=cookieVal.split(",");

//create the page
write ("<HTML><HEAD><TITLE>Room #" + thisRoom +".</TITLE></HEAD>");
write ("<BODY BGCOLOR=#FFFFFF>");
if (MazeValues[thisRoom]==1) {
    if (thisRoom!=9) {
        write ("<P>Welcome to room number " + thisRoom +"</P>");
        if (MazeValues[key]!=1) {
            write ("<P>You received key number " + key +"</P>");
        }
        write ("<P>You can go to room <A HREF='maze"+door1+".htm'>number
" + door1 +"</A>.</P>");
        write ("<P>You can go to room <A HREF='maze"+door2+".htm'>number
" + door2 +"</A>.</P>");
        write ("<P>You can go to room <A HREF='maze"+door3+".htm'>number
" + door3+"</A>.</P>");

//unlock the door
        MazeValues[key]=1;

//set the cookie
        cookieValNew=MazeValues.join(",");
        expiration=new Date(1999,12,25);
        WriteCookie("MazeName",cookieValNew,expiration);
    }
    else {
//hey - this is the last page!
        write("<H2>Congratulations!</H2>");
        write("<P>You made it through the maze, " +
MazeValues[0]+"!</P>");
    }
}
else {
//rejected
    write("<P>I'm sorry, but you don't have that key.</P>");
    write("<P>You can always <A HREF='maze1.htm'>start over</A>.");
}
write ("</BODY></HTML>");
}
```

The server version of these functions is similar, but calls to a file that stores its maze-tracking information. For convenience, the file is in the same format as that used by the client-side cookie. The cookie stored on the user's computer only contains the username, which links the user to the maze tracking file.

```
function register(rawInput) {
username=rawInput.split("=");

//create file; check for previous use
var fileName="D:\\netscape\\suitespot\\permits\\" + username[1]
+".txt";
var checkFile=new File(fileName);
Err=checkFile.open("r"); //true if file exists
checkFile.close();
if (Err) {  //file exists for previous user.
  redirect("duplicate.htm"); //sorry!
}
else { //no previous user
  var writeFile=new File(fileName);
  noErr=writeFile.open("w");

//set user privileges. Same format as client cookie
  writeFile.writeln(username[1]+",1,0,0,0,0,0,0,0,0");
  writeFile.close();
  var expiration=new Date(1999,12,25);
  WriteCookie("MazeName",username[1],expiration);
  return (username[1]);
}
}


function readMazeUser() {
cookieVal=ReadCookie("MazeName");
username=cookieVal;
//much simpler than client because
//only username information stored in cookie
return (username);
}


function room(thisRoom, key, door1, door2, door3) {
cookieVal=ReadCookie("MazeName");
//retrieve values from file named after cookie
var fileName="D:\\netscape\\suitespot\\permits\\" + cookieVal +".txt";
var readFile=new File(fileName);
Err=readFile.open("r"); //true if file exists
fileVal=readFile.readln();
readFile.close();
MazeValues=fileVal.split(",");

//create page - same logic as client version
write ("<HTML><HEAD><TITLE>Room #" + thisRoom +".</TITLE></HEAD>");
write ("<BODY BGCOLOR=#FFFFFF>");
if (MazeValues[thisRoom]==1) {
   if (thisRoom!=9) {
      write ("<P>Welcome to room number " + thisRoom +"</P>");
      if (MazeValues[key]!=1) {
         write ("<P>You received key number " + key +"</P>");
      }
      write ("<P>You can go to room <A HREF='maze"+door1+".htm'>number
            " + door1 +"</A>.</P>");
```

```
                    write ("<P>You can go to room <A HREF='maze"+door2+".htm'>number
                        " + door2 +"</A>.</P>");
                    write ("<P>You can go to room <A HREF='maze"+door3+".htm'>number
                        " + door3 +"</A>.</P>");
                    MazeValues[key]=1;

//save new permissions to server-side file
                    cookieValNew=MazeValues.join(",");
                    var writeFile=new File(fileName);
                    noErr=writeFile.open("w");
                    writeFile.write(cookieValNew);
                    writeFile.close();
            }
            else {
//they made it!
                    write("<H2>Congratulations!</H2>");
                    write("<P>You made it through the maze, " +
                        MazeValues[0]+"!</P>");
            }
    }
    else {
//rejection
            write("<P>I'm sorry, but you don't have that key.</P>");
            write("<P>You can always <A HREF='maze1.htm'>start over</A>.");
    }
    write ("</BODY></HTML>");
    }
```

The file storage mechanism for the server creates another minor problem: the possibility of duplicate usernames. The registration function handles this simply, redirecting duplicate users to an error message stored in duplicate.htm:

```
<HTML>
<HEAD><TITLE>Duplicate Username</TITLE></HEAD>
<BODY BGCOLOR=#FFFFFF>
<H2>Name in Use</H2>
<P>That username is already taken by another user.</P>
<P>Please try a different name</P>
</BODY></HTML>
```

For the most part, these two systems produce identical sites. When users arrive at the site for the first time, they will see the screen in Figure 7-15. If they have registered previously, they will immediately be redirected to the welcoming page shown in Figure 7-16.

Depending on the version of the application employed, users will experience two different kinds of cookies. Figures 7-17 and Figure 7-18 show the client-storage version's cookies at two different stages in maze exploration, while Figure 7-19 shows the unchanging cookie users will receive when they first enter the site.

Figure 7-15
The Registration
Page that Collects
Information for
the Cookie

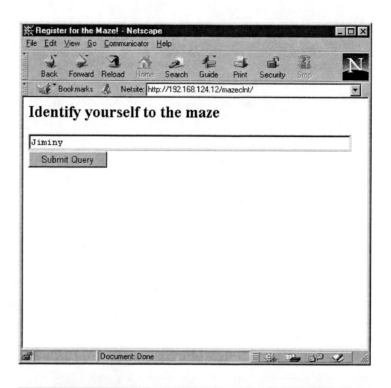

Figure 7-15
The Registration
Page that Collects
Information for
the Cookie

Figure 7-16
The Welcome
Page that Sets
the Cookie if
Necessary

Figure 7-17
Client Cookie
Information
at Start

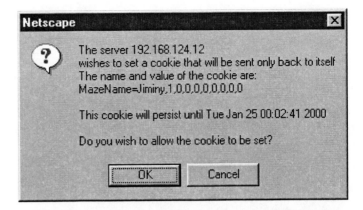

Figure 7-18
Client Cookie
Information
Later in the Maze

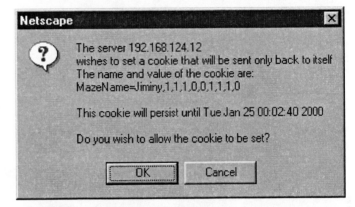

Figure 7-19
The Server
Version's
Simpler Cookie

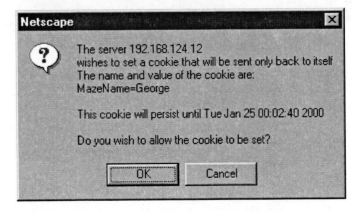

Users traversing the maze will be allowed into rooms based on their permissions. Figure 7-20 shows a typical room, Figure 7-21 shows a rejection notice, and Figure 7-22 shows the notification users will receive when they finally reach the last room.

Figure 7-20
Caught in
the Maze

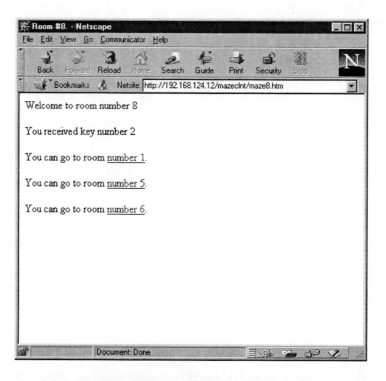

Figure 7-21
No Entry, a
Rejection Notice

Figure 7-22
Victory at Last

Although these mechanisms are simple, they can easily be extended to cover larger sites. Storing permissions on the client in the cookie is risky and certainly insecure, but may be adequate for many basic needs. Storing the permissions on the server is both more extensible (the file could contain many more elements, or even be stored in a database) and more secure (the user cannot change the permissions). Sites that need more security will need to combine this cookie-based system with a full authentication mechanism. This site keeps users out of each other's permissions, as shown in Figure 7-23.

Figure 7-23
Name Already
in Use

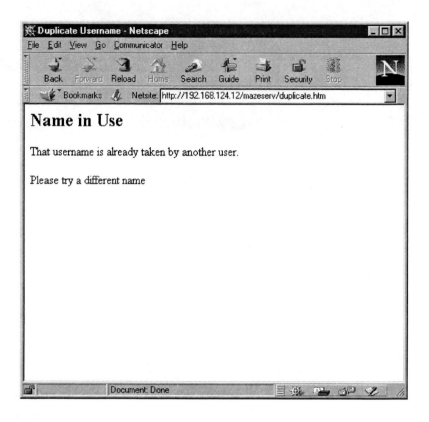

Simple Shopping Cart

Netscape's built-in client object makes constructing shopping carts fairly simple. Its lack of support for arrays introduces a few complications, but nothing that cannot be easily remedied. The information stored in the client object is supplemented in this case by information in the project object, which makes it easier to keep track of the information available to the entire application. This shopping cart example will provide services for a small store, though the client object could be used to store information for much larger operations.

The focus of this application is on state management, not the host of services needed to support electronic commerce; the final page will store orders to a file for processing, not a complex transaction system. Developing reliable transaction systems and payment processors is a topic worthy of several books, and has very little to do with cookies once the information is turned over.

Jim's Chocolate Coatings sells a variety of items, all of which are edible and have chocolate coatings. All of these chocolates are sold in bulk to local customers. Each item will have its own descriptive page, as well as a link to the central catalog page. Orders may be placed on each descriptive page, and a cash register is maintained at the central page to let users know how much they have spent.

On this site, unlike the previous sites, the application will take advantage of the project object to store information about the items for sale. Client objects will store information about how much the user is ordering, which will connect to the project information through item numbers. In this case, the item numbers run from 1 to 5—Jim's Chocolate Coatings is only getting started on a Web site, and wants to make certain this works before posting the entire inventory and letting the competition in on some of their stranger specialties.

To initialize the store, this application uses a `start.htm` page which sets up the inventory and makes it available to all requests. The `start.htm` file takes advantage of the project object's ability to hold arrays to create a list of products and and prices. For now that information is embedded in the code; a larger (or more rapidly changing) inventory will require a more automated process that reads the information in from a file or database.

```
<SERVER>
product=new Array();
price=new Array();
product[1]="Chocolate-covered bubble gum";
price[1]="1.5";
product[2]="Chocolate-covered peanuts";
price[2]="1.25";
product[3]="Chocolate-covered pretzels";
price[3]="1.0";
product[4]="Chocolate-covered mangoes";
price[4]="2.5";
product[5]="Chocolate-covered grasshoppers";
price[5]="3.5";
project.products=product.join(";");
project.prices=price.join(";");
</SERVER>
```

The pages listing the actual products use a simple form that describes the product and allows the user to order candy by the pound. This form does not need to contain much detail, though it *does* dip into the pricing information established above. (A more sophisticated catalog could draw all of this, including the description, from files using the item number.)

```
<HTML>
<SERVER>
order=client.order.split(";");
quantity=order[1];
</SERVER>
```

```
<HEAD><TITLE></TITLE></HEAD>
<BODY BGCOLOR=#FFFFFF>
<H2>Chocolate-covered Bubble Gum</H2>
<P>Gum-chewers looking for a great kick before they get into the joys
of chewing should try our flavorful chocolate-covered gum. Comes in an
assortment of milk, dark, and white chocolate coverings, with a sur-
prising variety of bubble gum flavors underneath. Guaranteed chocolate
chewing satisfaction.</P>
<B>Price: $
<SERVER>
price=new Array();
price=project.prices.split(";");
write(price[1]);
</SERVER>
per pound</B>
<HR>
<FORM ACTION="welcome.htm" METHOD="GET">
<INPUT TYPE="HIDDEN" VALUE=1 NAME="item">
Pounds on order:<INPUT TYPE="TEXT" NAME="quantity" VALUE=`quantity`>
<INPUT TYPE="SUBMIT" VALUE="Order">
</FORM>
</BODY></HTML>
```

The welcome page is both the front door for this application and the cash
register, keeping a running total of the user's current purchase based on the
catalog pages visited. The welcome page interprets query strings and converts them to orders.

Do not use this shopping cart mechanism as is with any of the URL-
based client object maintenance methods. The URL-encoding of the client
information will interfere with the purchasing information.

```
<HTML>
<HEAD><TITLE>Jim's Chocolate-Covered Creations</TITLE></HEAD>
<BODY BGCOLOR="#FFFFFF">
<H2>Welcome</H2>
<P>At Jim's Chocolate-Covered Creations, we pride ourselves on having
the best in chocolate-covered surprises. While some parts of our prod-
uct line are conventional, other parts are considerably more daring.
Be assured, however, that all of our creations are both edible and
delicious.</P>
<TABLE BORDER=1>
<TR>
<TH>Item</TH>
<TH>Price/lb.</TH>
<TH>Your order</TH>
<TH>Total</TH>
</TR>
<SERVER>
if (!client.order) {
  client.order="0;0;0;0;0;0"
}
```

```
product=price=new Array();
total=subtotal=0;
product=project.products.split(";");
price=project.prices.split(";");
order=client.order.split(";");
if (request.query) {
  //split out the request string
  parts=request.query.split("&");
  itemRequest=parts[0].split("=");
  quantity=parts[1].split("=");
  order[itemRequest[1]]=quantity[1];
}
client.order=order.join(";");
for (i=1; i<6; i++) {
  write ("<TD>");
  write ("<A HREF='item" + i +".htm");
  write ("'>" + product[i] + "</A></TD><TD>");
  write ("$" + price[i]+"</TD><TD>");
  write (order[i] +"</TD><TD>$");
  subtotal=price[i]*order[i];
  total+=subtotal;
  write (subtotal);
  write ("</TD></TR>");
}
  write("<TR><TD></TD><TD></TD><TD></TD><TD>$");
  write(total+"</TD></TR>");
  write("</TABLE>");
  write("<A HREF='submit.htm'>Place your order</A>");
</SERVER>
</BODY></HTML>
```

The last page in this application (`submit.htm`) is just a mechanism for converting the information from the client object into hidden fields for processing by an order entry system. For now, Jim's is using a very simple collection method, so appropriate warnings are provided.

```
<HTML>
<H2>Your order</H2>
<FORM ACTION="processor.cgi" METHOD="POST">
<TABLE BORDER=1>
<SERVER>
if (!client.order) {
  redirect("welcome.htm");
}
product=price=new Array();
total=subtotal=0;
product=project.products.split(";");
price=project.prices.split(";");
order=client.order.split(";");
if (request.query) {
  //split out the request string
  parts=request.query.split("&");
  itemRequest=parts[0].split("=");
  quantity=parts[1].split("=");
  order[itemRequest[1]]=quantity[1];
}
client.order=order.join(";");
for (i=1; i<6; i++) {
```

```
  write ("<TD>");
  write ("<A HREF='item" + i +".htm");
  write ("'>" + product[i] + "</A></TD><TD>");
  write ("$" + price[i]+"</TD><TD>");
  write (order[i]);
  write ("<INPUT TYPE=HIDDEN NAME='item"+i+"' VALUE='"+order[i]+"'>");
  write ("</TD><TD>$");
  subtotal=price[i]*order[i];
  total+=subtotal;
  write (subtotal);
  write ("</TD></TR>");
}
  write("<TR><TD></TD><TD></TD><TD></TD><TD>$"+total+"</TD></TR>");
  write ("</TABLE>");
  write("<A HREF='submit.htm'>Place your order</A>");
</SERVER>
<HR>
<P>Please enter your name, address, and phone number. All orders will
be verified and shipped C.O.D. by our specially trained payment col-
lection specialists.</P>
Name:<INPUT TYPE="TEXT" NAME="Customer" SIZE=40>
Phone Number:<INPUT TYPE="TEXT" NAME="Phone" SIZE=20><BR>
Address:<TEXTAREA COLS=40 ROWS=4 NAME="Address"></TEXTAREA>
<BR>
<INPUT TYPE="SUBMIT" VALUE="Order this!">
</FORM>
</BODY></HTML>
```

The result of all this work is a simple on-line store. Customers are greeted
with an empty order form that invites them to browse the inventory, as shown
in Figure 7-24. Clicking on an item brings up a more complete description
and a space for ordering it by the pound, as shown in Figure 7-25.

Figure 7-24
First Arrival
at Jim's

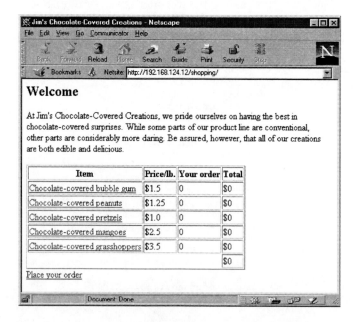

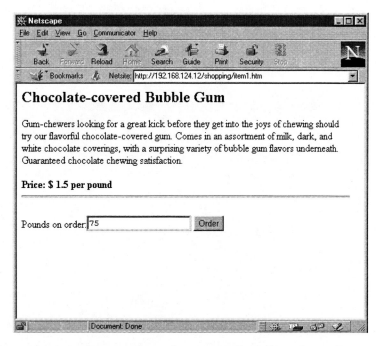

As the customer places orders, they are reflected at the welcome page, which keeps a running total of purchases, as shown in Figure 7-26.

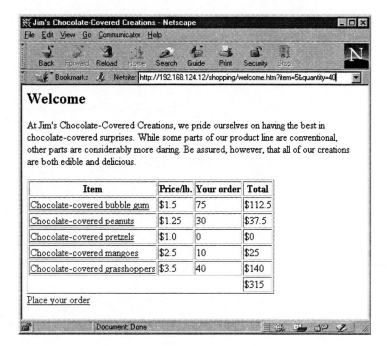

A customer ready to complete the order, can visit the checkout page shown in Figure 7-27, which presents the order once more and collects the necessary shipping information. Once the information is collected, this page will submit the details gathered by the client object to an order-processing system.

Figure 7-27
Order Entry and
a Warning

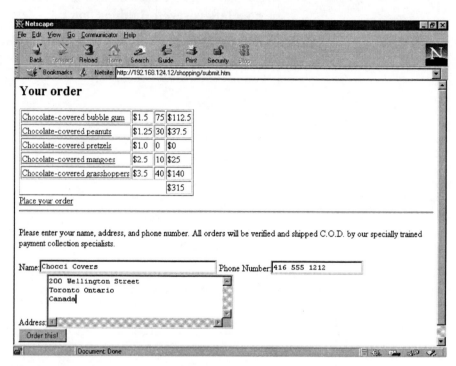

For situations like shopping carts, where the transaction lasts minutes or hours instead of days, weeks, months, or years, Server-Side JavaScript's client object offers a simpler solution than direct cookie manipulation, managing the storage of client information and potentially saving the programmer hours of effort.

Cookies and Active Server Pages

Microsoft's server-side solution also offers tools for managing state with cookies. Like Internet Explorer, Active Server Pages (ASP) allow developers to choose JavaScript, VBScript, or a mixture of the two as their scripting language. ASP work in the same basic framework as CGI and Netscape LiveWire, but follow a set of standards created by Microsoft for use with its Internet Information Server and its own set of database interfaces. Cookie management with ASP uses some of the same tools as cookie management in the browser. We will use several of the same scripting techniques we employed on the client side in Chapter 4 to power our ASP state management system.

ASP—An Introduction

ASP offers many of the options provided by CGI and LiveWire and has its own strong built-in mechanism for state management. Microsoft initially developed ASP for their Internet Information Server (IIS) 3.0. ASP also works with Peer Web Services for Windows NT Workstation, as well as the Personal Web Server for Windows 95 and 98. O'Reilly and Associates includes an Active Server Pages engine with their WebSite 2.0 server, and Chili offers Chili!ASP for a number of servers, including Netscape servers. All examples in this chapter were created and tested with Internet Information Server 3.0 running under Windows NT Server 4.0.

If you have Internet Information Server 2.0 (which comes with Windows NT Server 4.0) or Peer Web Services (which comes with Windows NT Workstation 4.0), you will need to add the Active Server Pages component of IIS 3.0. Visit **http://www.microsoft.com/iis/** and go to the download IIS 3.0 area. You will be presented (after filling out many forms) with a list of parts which comprise IIS 3.0, including FrontPage extensions and NetShow. The only part actually needed for the examples in this book is Active Server Pages. The Personal Web Server for Windows 95 that comes with FrontPage 97 and 98 already has ASP installed.

ASP performs the same function as CGI and LiveWire; all of these products are meant to make it possible for servers to respond more interactively than simple file requests will permit. Microsoft isolates developers to a certain extent from the HTTP request process, but the information is still available through server-side objects accessible by scripts. The ASP engine itself is an interface that uses Microsoft's ISAPI to combine HTTP with an application model and database access through Microsoft's ODBC and Active Database Object (ADO) interfaces, using familiar client-side scripting languages as the glue.

Fortunately, the scripting engines in the Active Server Pages component of Internet Information Server 3.0 are slightly more recent than those in Internet Explorer 3.0, saving developers from having to worry about users with old versions of the browser. Properly written Active Server Pages will look like normal HTML pages to the browser—checking the source will show only the HTML produced by the ASP code, not the ASP code itself. Although it is possible (and often desirable) to deploy Web pages that include client-side scripting as well as server-side scripting, the server side of ASP is independent of the client. ASP created with VBScript will work perfectly well in Netscape Navigator, as long as they do not include VBScript intended for the browser.

The other key tool that ASP provides is a link to databases through Open Database Connectivity (ODBC), Microsoft's operating system-level technology for connecting programs to databases. Using ODBC, you can connect your pages to an Microsoft Access database, a Microsoft SQL Server database, or nearly any other database available from other vendors. This book will only explore database connectivity as far as is needed for the cookie examples; many more detailed discussions of ASP database connectivity and ODBC are available. The examples in this chapter will use an Access database to store information. For a production environment where more than 10 users may be connected at the same time, Access will prove inadequate, and developers should use a database intended for larger-scale operations.

Active Server Pages are a combination of script and HTML, somewhat like LiveWire. To indicate that a file is an ASP, use the extension `.asp` instead of `.htm` or `.html`. Ordinary HTML can be renamed with the `.asp` extension and nothing much will happen to it—the server will read the file, but will not find any scripts to execute, so it will just return the HTML file. The results of ASP processing are ordinary HTML files, sent to the browser as type text/html just like a normal file. The file the browser receives will bear no trace of its origin as an ASP file—unless, of course, there's an error and the file does not parse properly.

The Active Server Page Object Model

ASP provides a server-side object model that simplifies development considerably. ASP includes five objects available for scripting: the Server, Application, Session, Request, and Response objects. The Server object is mostly a utility object that provides some key functionality for extending ASP. The Application object stores information for the application as a whole—creating variables accessible to any ASP script. Session objects provide state management for sessions with individual users. The Request and Response objects provide the script with access to the HTTP request that came in and the response that is going out, respectively.

Leaving out the Server object, the object model for ASP can be represented as shown in Figure 8-1. The Application object contains information available to all the scripts running from the same `global.asa` file, no matter which user is making the request. The Session object uses cookies to remain persistent—all requests from a single user will keep the same Session object. The Session object can also make use of the `global.asa` file, which will be explored in detail later in the chapter. Request and Response objects come and go with every request from a user.

Figure 8-1
ASP Object Model

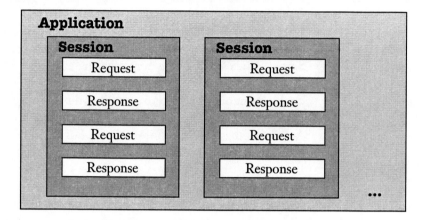

The Session object provides a lot of state management functionality in a convenient package. Using cookies that last the duration of the user's browser session, it lets a program keep an entire set of information on a session, using only one small cookie. Most of this chapter will describe how to use and extend the Session object, while using the Request and Response objects to make the pages work.

Scripting Active Server Pages

Adding scripts to ASP can be done in three ways. The first method uses the familiar SCRIPT element, with a new attribute: RUNAT. Since only the server and ASP recognize the RUNAT attribute, the only reasonable value for RUNAT is SERVER. SCRIPT elements in ASP accept the LANGUAGE attribute, but not the SRC attribute. (There is another mechanism for including library code that will be covered shortly.) All SCRIPT elements are assumed to use VBScript unless the LANGUAGE attribute explicitly states otherwise. A single ASP file may contain scripts written in multiple scripting languages. SCRIPT elements in ASP are limited to holding complete subroutines and functions—no loose code is allowed to float as it can on a browser client. An acceptable SCRIPT element might look like:

```
<SCRIPT LANGUAGE="JavaScript" RUNAT="SERVER">
function today() {
    Response.Write("Today is a day just like any other day.");
}
</SCRIPT>
```

The today function can now be called (by scripts in any permitted language) from scripts enclosed in "script delimiters"—the <%, <%=, <%@, and %> markers. Although they look a bit like HTML tags, scripts in an ASP file do not have to nest the way HTML tags are normally required to. Script delimiters can even appear inside of an attribute value. Because ASP are just a another way to create text files which will later be parsed by a web browser, there are no rules prohibiting the appearance of script delimiters anywhere in an ASP file—except of course, within other script delimiters and within server-side SCRIPT elements. The %> delimiter will always close a script; nesting scripts will be closed unexpectedly, so always be careful to close a script before opening a new one.

The <%@ opening delimiter is used only to define what language will be used by default for scripts enclosed in delimiters encountered during parsing. If no language is declared explicitly, VBScript will be assumed. To use JavaScript (or JScript as Microsoft has preferred to call its version), insert <%@ LANGUAGE="JScript" %> or <%@ LANGUAGE="VBScript" %> at the top of the file. While ASP is quite capable of coping with different languages in SCRIPT elements, it is a better idea to stick to one script language or the other for scripts that appear using delimiters.

The <% delimiter is used to open a script. Scripts inside of delimiters will be run as they are encountered. Scripts can output text using the Response.Write method. These scripts may call other functions and subroutines, but they cannot define functions or subroutines. Scripts may even start loops and leave them to be finished by another script that appears in a different delimited section. A typical script might look like this:

```
<H1>Hello from the HTML!</H1>
<% Response.Write "Hello from the Script!" %>
<H2>Hello from the HTML again!</H2>
```

The last opening delimiter, <%= , is used to open a section that is written directly to the HTML, like an enormous string. HTML should be kept in quotes; scripts can be concatenated to the HTML with either the & (VBScript) or + (JavaScript) operator. A typical script written using this mechanism might look like:

```
<%="Today is " & date %>
```

I tend to use <%= to store only information generated by the script itself, allowing the surrounding HTML to provide other content. This is a matter of preference; use whichever method seems more efficient.

The last way to include scripts is effectively a replacement for the SRC attribute of the SCRIPT tag, but allows developers to do much more as well. All ASP files will be parsed for server-side includes before the script parsing begins. This means that libraries of scripts, as well as HTML, can be included in an ASP file by reference to an outside source. To include a file using a relative path, use the FILE keyword; to include a file using an absolute path specified from the root of the current server, use the VIRTUAL keyword.

```
<!-- #include file="usefulASPscript.inc" -->
<!-- #include virtual="/scripts/ASPlib.inc" -->
```

The top include statement will retrieve the contents of the file usefulASPscript.inc, which is assumed to be in the same directory as the ASP file that includes it. The bottom include statement will check the server's top-level scripts directory for the ASPlib.inc file and include its contents where the include statement appeared.

Making full use of ASP, even for simple cookie work, will require extensive use of all of these features, as well as the scripting techniques already covered in Chapter 4. The examples in this chapter will primarily use VBScript. VBScript should cause far fewer problems here than it did in the browser, because the object model for ASP was written around VBScript's capabilities instead of being a port of an originally JavaScript environment. Cookie values, for instance, are automatically encoded and decoded as appropriate without any need for the escape() and unescape() functions. ASP can use the full range of VBScript 2.0 functions; developers need not worry about whether or not the more advanced features will be available. All code in this chapter that is not otherwise labeled should be assumed to be VBScript.

Perl hackers who have found themselves stuck on an ASP project may be happy to hear that a Perl scripting engine is under development and available for ASP development. Visit **http://www.ActiveState.com/** for more information and downloads. The Perl scripting will not be quite like the CGI programming most Perl developers are used to, but PerlScript makes it possible to apply much of that familiar power to Web development with ASP.

Cookie Management in ASP: Working Directly

ASP uses cookies in several ways. Developers can read and write cookies directly through the Request and Response objects, or use the built-in state management of the Session object. Before moving on to the automation provided by the Session object, we will explore the direct cookie access that ASP provides. In addition to allowing developers to interact with cookies created by client-side scripts, these tools are necessary for applications that need to maintain state over more than the duration of a browsing session.

Reading Cookies

Our first experiment with ASP will retrieve some cookies that were created in the Web browser. Our notepad page provides an easy test subject for an inital experiment using ASP to collect cookies. The ASP Request object includes a cookies collection that makes it easy to extract a particular name-value pair. In this case, the cookie we need to retrieve is called NotePad. All our initial ASP page will do is retrieve the contents of that cookie and dump them on the screen.

```
<HTML><HEAD><TITLE>NotePad Cookie Contents</TITLE></HEAD>
<BODY><H1>
<% Response.Write (Request.Cookies("NotePad")) %>
</H1></BODY></HTML>
```

This simple bit of ASP scripting works equally well in VBScript or JavaScript. By default, it will be interpreted as VBScript. To test it out in JavaScript, just add <%@ LANGUAGE="JavaScript" %> to the beginning of it.

While the results are hardly stunning, they do offer a tremendous return for very little code, as shown in Figure 8-2.

Our next step will be to find out the author of this note. ASP scripts can request users to authenticate, if they have not already done so. (Users of Internet Explorer for Windows 95 and NT who are connecting to an intranet may already be authenticated through their Windows logon.) This technique is a convenience; users who choose to cancel can remain anonymous. If authentication really needs to take place, use the regular security tools provided by the web server for better-enforced authentication.

Figure 8-2
An Extremely
Simple Cookie
Reader

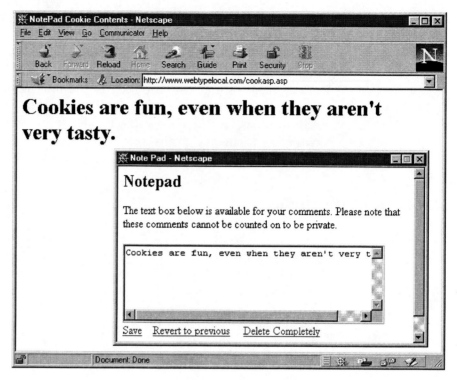

Figure 8-2
An Extremely
Simple Cookie
Reader

```
<%
If Request.ServerVariables("LOGON_USER") = "" Then
    Response.Status = "401 access denied"
End If
%>
<HTML><HEAD>
<TITLE>NotePad Cookie Contents</TITLE></HEAD>
<BODY BGCOLOR=#FFFFFF><H1>
<% Response.Write (Request.Cookies("NotePad")) %></H1>
<BR>
<%= Request.ServerVariables("LOGON_USER") %>
</BODY></HTML>
```

Forcing the authentication request is easy—it just takes a check of the
LOGON_USER server variable (or REMOTE_USER) to see if the users have
authenticated. If they haven't, the 401 result will make their browsers
immediately present them with an authentication dialog box before allowing them to proceed. If they have authentication, the rest of the script will
execute, displaying the contents of the cookie as well as the username of the
person who probably wrote in. Note that there are two different methods
for writing script results into the HTML. The first uses the Response
object's Write method to put text into the HTML file, while the second

just uses the <%= script delimiter to enter its results directly into the file. The results of this adventure are promising, as shown in Figure 8-3.

Figure 8-3
Cookie Value
and Owner

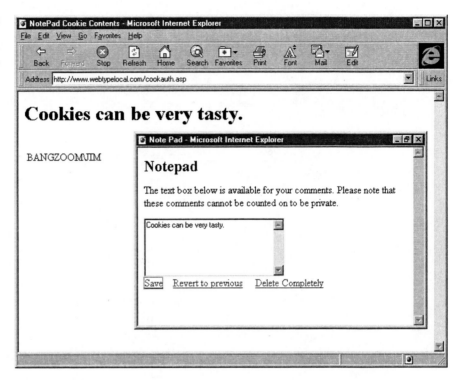

The next challenge is storing this information in a meaningful way. ASP allows direct access to ODBC data sources through the ADO. For this example, we need only open the datasource, write two fields to it, and close the data source. The data source will be an Access database, set up as a System DSN in the ODBC (or 32-bit ODBC on a Windows 95) Control Panel.

Developers interested in the details of setting up DSNs can check the help files provided with the ODBC control panels. They are quite useful, except that they never explain what DSN stands for. Data Source Name seems likely.

The DSN for this program (and the others in this chapter) is called `ASPtest` and will store our note cookies. It contains one table—Notes, which contains rows of username and comments. All that our ASP page has to do is collect the cookies; while username would be helpful, the point of this application is collecting the comments. For this example, we will allow our scenario to be all-Microsoft: users will be connecting to this page with Internet Explorer 3.0 or 4.0 through an intranet already using a Windows NT domain structure. To reduce comment duplication, users will have to navigate through a front door that requests authentication and makes certain they want to turn in their cookies before collecting them.

```
<%
If Request.ServerVariables("LOGON_USER") = "" Then
    Response.Status = "401 access denied"
End If
%>
<HTML><HEAD>
<TITLE>NotePad Cookie Collector</TITLE></HEAD>
<BODY BGCOLOR=#FFFFFF>
<H1>Cookie Collection</H1>
<P>The current value of your comment cookie is:</P>
<P><EM><% Response.Write (Request.Cookies("NotePad")) %></EM></P>
<P>The server has identified you as <%=
Request.ServerVariables("LOGON_USER") %></P>
<P>Are you sure that you want to submit your comments?</P>
<A HREF="submit.asp">Yes</A><BR>
<A HREF="elsewhere.htm">No</A>
</BODY></HTML>
```

By showing users their cookie contents, and alerting them that we know who they are, the page attempts to ward off diplomatic disasters. The next page actually collects the cookie contents.

```
<!-- #include virtual="/ASPSAMP/SAMPLES/ADOVBS.INC" -->
<%
'Authentication block
    If Request.ServerVariables("LOGON_USER") = "" Then
    Response.Status = "401 access denied"
    End If

'Data Handling block (uses constants from #include)
'Get UserID
UserID=Request.ServerVariables("LOGON_USER")

'Open cookie and encode quotes
origCookie=Request.Cookies("NotePad")
partEncodedCookie=replace(origCookie,Chr(39),"&#39")
encodedCookie=replace(partEncodedCookie, Chr(34), "&#34")

'If all values are acceptable, create and execute SQL
If UserID <> "" and encodedCookie<> "" then

    'Open a connection
    set DataObj=Server.CreateObject("ADODB.Connection")

    'Choose a Mode - in this case, write.
    DataObj.Mode=adModeWrite

    'Open the System DSN
    DataObj.Open "ASPtest"
```

```
'Build and execute the SQL call
   SQLtext="INSERT INTO Notes (UserName,Comments) VALUES ('" & UserID
         & "','" & encodedCookie & "')"
   DataObj.Execute SQLtext, numChanged, adCmdText

   'Close the database connection
   DataObj.Close
End If
%>
<HTML><HEAD>
<TITLE>NotePad Cookie Collector</TITLE></HEAD>
<BODY BGCOLOR=#FFFFFF>
<H1>Cookie Collection</H1>
<!-- Response varies with data -->
<% If UserID <> "" and encodedCookie<> "" then %>
<P>Thank you for your submission.</P>
<% End If %>
<% If UserID="" then %>
<P>Please authenticate to submit your comments.</P>
<% End If %>
<% If encodedCookie="" then %>
<P>Please enter comments before submitting them.</P>
<% End If %>
<A HREF="elsewhere.htm">Return home</A>
</BODY></HTML>
```

The first line includes a file, adovbs.inc, that defines key constants needed by the ADO data connector. The adojavas.inc file is the equivalent in JavaScript, defining the same set of constants. Keeping scripts that use ADO readable generally requires using this file.

The data handling block collects the UserID and the cookie contents. While most forms of UserID should be syntactically safe for inclusion in a SQL statement, the cookie is not as reliable. Without some forethought, the script will spew errors at users who include either single quotes (') or double quotes (") in their comments. To avoid this nightmare, we use VBScript 2.0's Replace function to replace these characters with an equivalent that will display properly in an HTML browser. (If a database developer must use the comments without running them through a Web browser, a search and replace on the comments field will be required first.) While this is not a perfect solution, it ensures that the characters will display properly if the comments are read through another Web page. An if statement also protects the script from passing empty values for UserID and comments— empty values will cause errors. Putting the if statement before the database connection decreases the number of useless database connections, reducing the load on the server.

```
'If all values are acceptable, create and execute SQL
If UserID <> "" and encodedCookie<> "" then
```

The next few lines open the database connection. First, the ASP page uses the server object to create an ADO connection object.

```
'Open a connection
set DataObj=Server.CreateObject("ADODB.Connection")
```

Once the object has been created, but before the script opens a connection, it needs to be set to an appropriate mode. Because the only activity performed on the database by this script is adding data, the mode it needs is write-only. The Mode property of the `DataObj` object created in the previous lineis set to the `adModeWrite` constant, defined in the `ADOVBS.INC` file.

```
'Choose a Mode - in this case, write.
DataObj.Mode=adModeWrite
```

The next line opens our `ASPtest` database.

```
'Open the System DSN
DataObj.Open "ASPtest"
```

It is not always necessary, but it is good practice, to construct database calls as separate variables before appying them. The SQL statement used to add the username and comments to the database is an `INSERT INTO`. This `INSERT` tells the database to create a new row in the table Notes, and provides the UserID and encodedCookie variables for their values. All `VALUES` must be surrounded by single quotes, making encoding of quotes, as was done earlier, mandatory in applications that use SQL.

```
SQLtext="INSERT INTO Notes (UserName,Comments) VALUES ('" & UserID
        & "','" & encodedCookie & "')"
```

If you are unfamiliar with SQL, don't panic. Tools like the query builders in Visual InterDev can create SQL with visual tools, producing code that can be added to ASP with a mouseclick.

The line that follows executes the SQL specified in `SQLtext` on the database opened through the `DataObj` object. The Execute method takes three arguments. The first is the command to be executed, in this case `SQLtext`. The second is a variable whose value will change to reflect the number of rows changed by this operation. (In this case, it should return the value 1, for the one row being added.) The last value is a constant, which defines how the first argument should be interpreted. Most of the examples in this chapter will use the `adCmdText` constant (defined in `ADOVBS.INC`) to specify that the first argument is a SQL command in text that needs to be parsed. Other values are used for tables and stored procedures.

```
DataObj.Execute SQLtext, numChanged, adCmdText
```

The next line is critical. Leaving out this command will generate memory leaks that can quickly paralyze a busy server. Always close a database connection when the page is done with its operations.

```
'Close the database connection
   DataObj.Close
```

The `End If` statement that follows closes out the database activity on the page. The ensuing lines thank users for comments or tell why the server cannot accept their comments. This script has opted to require authentication information, but other scripts might permit users to submit their comments anonymously. The database will return an error if fed an empty value, but a script that accepts anonymous comments might substitute `UNKNOWN` or a similar string for a user name if none is available.

The next section thanks the users for their input or alerts them that their information was not correct. If their data was not correct, it has not been entered in the database, but we still need to inform the user of the situation:

```
<!-- Response varies with data -->
<% If UserID <> "" and encodedCookie<> "" then %>
<P>Thank you for your submission.</P>
<% End If %>
<% If UserID="" then %>
<P>Please authenticate to submit your comments.</P>
<% End If %>
<% If encodedCookie="" then %>
<P>Please enter comments before submitting them.</P>
<% End If %>
```

If users have provided authentication information and a cookie to collect, they will see the page displayed in Figure 8-4. If they have not authenticated, they will see the page displayed in Figure 8-5.

On the database side, the information has been gathered in a table that can be used like other Access data, as shown in Figure 8-6.

Figure 8-4
Results of
a Proper Cookie
Submission

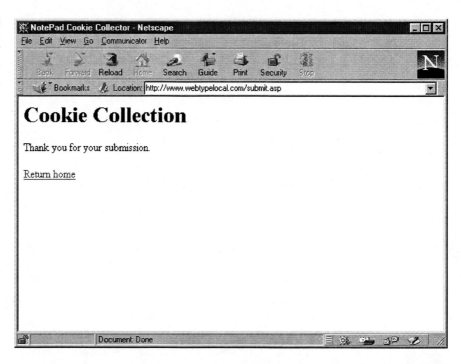

Figure 8-5
Results of an
Anonymous
Cookie
Submission

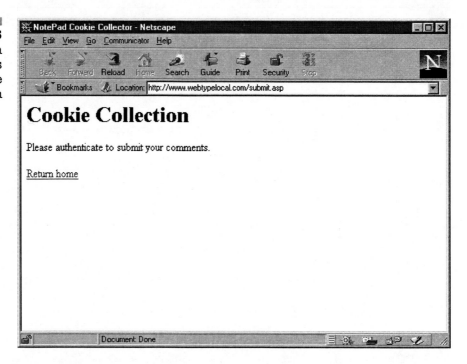

Figure 8-6
Collected
Information
Displayed in an
Access Form

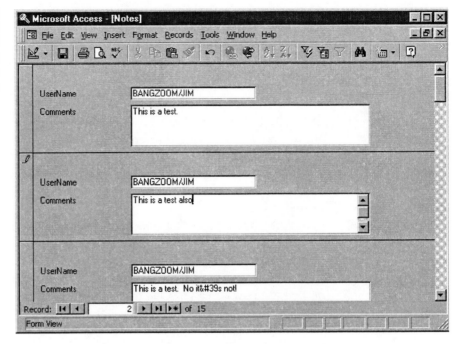

Creating a report using that data, either in Access or through another ASP file, can now be done using other tools.

Writing Cookies

In the previous example, our ASP page just collected cookie information gathered by a client-side script. In our next example, we will write a cookie to the user's machine that indicates the first date on which the page was visited. This level of demographic information unlikely to infuriate too many visitors, and we will take extra care to store it in a format that curious users can inspect.

Writing cookies is done through the `Response.Cookies` collection, which is an associative array indexed by the name of the cookie. To set the value of the cookie `"firstVisit"` to `"11/12/97"`, an ASP page would use code that looks like

```
Response.Cookies("firstVisit")="11/12/97"
```

The Expires, Domain, Path, and Secure properties are also available, and easily addressed as properties of this cookie object. All of these properties are write-only; they cannot be read once they have been written, though they can be overwritten with a new value before the cookie is sent to the user.

```
Response.Cookies("firstVisit").Path="/"
```

The Expires property is considerably more forgiving than it was on the client—it accepts values stated as *"Month Day, Year"* or in `"MM/DD/YY"` format. `"April 4, 1999"` would be an acceptable value. Because we no longer need to create the full date and time string specified in GMT, VBScript is an acceptable tool for manipulating this information without further assistance from JavaScript. The ASP engine will handle all overhead associated with converting the date to the official version required by the cookie standard.

Making the `firstVisit` cookie work requires a little more infrastructure than did the comments collector above. Because this application may need to keep track of visitors to every page, the code behind it will be stored in two separate `.inc` files accessible to pages that use it, making any needed changes far easier. One piece holds the code for writing the cookie; the other holds the code for reading the cookie and taking note of the visit. I strongly recommend using the cookie-writing code only on your site's main point of entry, though making the code modular is intended to make it easier to use on multiple sites or at multiple points of entry on a large site. While the code could be placed on every page, users who have asked to be alerted to cookies will be subjected to a blizzard of cookies if they refuse to accept them. Remember—always keep to a minimum the number of times a cookie is set, whenever possible. The `firstVisit` cookie will only contain a date in this example, providing a minimal but useful amount of information about patterns of site visitation.

Like its predecessors, this chapter is not going to go into much detail on the creation and maintenance of ASP connections to back-end databases. Explaining the SQL query langugage and ASP's mechanisms for handling database sources is worthy of several additional books, many of which are available at your local bookstore.

The cookie-writing module only has a few tasks to accomplish. First, it reads the `firstVisit` cookie to see if it has a value. If it does not, the cookie-writing module will create a new `firstVisit` cookie to be sent back to the user. The `firstVisit` cookie will contain a date value.

```
<SCRIPT RUNAT=SERVER LANGUAGE=VBSCRIPT>
sub cookieWrite
firstVisit=Request.Cookies("firstVisit")
```

```
if firstVisit="" then
   Response.Cookies("firstVisit")=Date()
   Response.Cookies("firstVisit").expires="December 31, 1999"
end if
end sub
</SCRIPT>
<% cookieWrite %>
```

This piece of code must be included in pages that need to write the firstVisit cookie before any HTML markup code is written, to get out the Set-Cookie header it produces before the HTML begins. The code to read the cookie, on the other hand, can float anywhere in the document, since all it does is read the value of the cookie and store it in a database—no further interaction with the document is necessary.

```
<!-- #include virtual="/ASPSAMP/SAMPLES/ADOVBS.INC" -->
<SCRIPT RUNAT=SERVER LANGUAGE=VBSCRIPT>
sub cookieRead
firstVisit=Request.Cookies("firstVisit")
if firstVisit<>"" then
   pageAt=Request.ServerVariables("URL")
   'Open a connection
   set DataObj=Server.CreateObject("ADODB.Connection")
   'Choose a Mode - in this case, write.
   DataObj.Mode=adModeWrite
   'Open the System DSN
   DataObj.Open "ASPtest"
   'Build and execute the SQL call
   SQLtext="INSERT INTO dateLog (FirstVisit,Page) VALUES ('" &
         firstVisit & "','" & pageAt & "')"
   DataObj.Execute SQLtext, numChanged, adCmdText
   'Close the database connection
   DataObj.Close
end if
end sub
</SCRIPT>
<% cookieRead %>
```

For the most part, this code is identical to the one we used to collect the comment cookies, using the ADO database connectivity built into ASP to store the information from the cookies in an Access database. Instead of collecting the username and comments of visitors, this stores the firstVisited date along with the URL of this page in the database. Someone else will have to develop analysis tools on the database that can translate this table of first visits and URLs into an explanation of how long it takes users to reach various levels of the site.

Including these files in ASP documents is easy, requiring one INCLUDE line per module. (Remember that all pages using this code must be ASP pages—server-side code included in a document identified as a regular HTML file will not execute.) A point of entry page might look like this:

```
<!--#INCLUDE FILE="cookwrite.inc" -->
<!--#INCLUDE FILE="cookread.inc" -->
<HTML>
<HEAD><TITLE>Welcome!</TITLE></HEAD>
<BODY BGCOLOR=#FFFFFF>
<H1>Welcome to our site</H1>
<P>This site is being used for a navigation analysis experiment.
Please be aware that our system will be sending cookies to your
browser to record the date you first visited. No information other
than the date will be tracked; we just want to find out how long it
takes users to explore various areas of our site.</P>
<P>Please note: turning off or rejecting cookies will not interfere
with your use of this site.</P>
<P>Visit our <A HREF="level2.asp">second level</A> to continue the
tour...</P>
<P>The current value of your firstVisit cookie is:
<%= Request.Cookies("firstVisit") %>
</BODY></HTML>
```

Visiting this page warns users of the cookie experiment in progress and also shows them the value of their cookies, as seen in Figure 8-7.

Figure 8-7
Entryway to the
Cookie Navigation
Tracking Site

To create a file that only reads the cookies, include only the cookread.inc file:

```
<!--#INCLUDE FILE="cookread.inc" -->
<HTML>
<HEAD><TITLE>Level2</TITLE></HEAD>
<BODY BGCOLOR=#FFFFFF>
<H1>Further Information</H1>
<P>Thank you for participating in our navigation analysis experi-
ment.</P>
<P>The current value of your firstVisit cookie is:
<%= Request.Cookies("firstVisit") %>
</BODY></HTML>
```

This second level only reads the cookie, to keep cookie-hating users from becoming too annoyed with the site. As shown in Figure 8-8, the cookie code has very little effect on the contents of the document, except for the last line.

Figure 8-8
A Second-level
Screen that Only
Reads Cookies

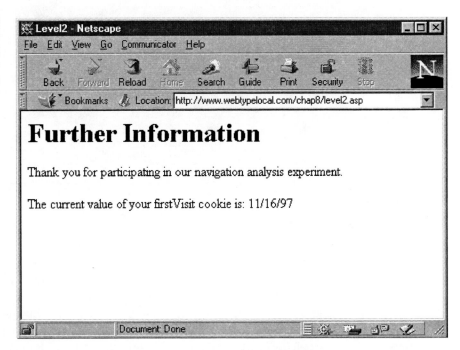

Meanwhile, the database has tracked our user through two pages, as shown in Figure 8-9. Apparently, users are willing to explore at least one level beyond the front door before giving up.

The Access database is keeping track of the date and time of visit in a separate field called "Date". In this case, the Date field has a default value of =Now(), which allows the database to handle this part of the tracking without further intervention from the page. Developers using other databases should check their documentation to see if this is possible; if it isn't, pass the Now() value to the database from the script.

Figure 8-9
The Results of
this Tracking in
Access

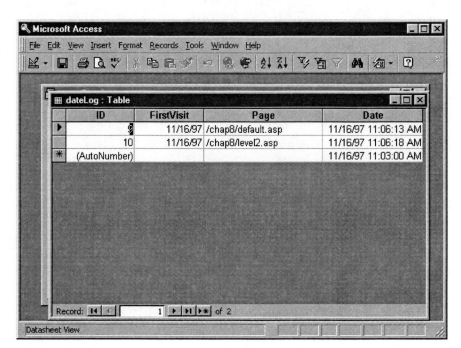

Cookies and Keys

A considerable amount of the code in Chapter 4 went into creating cookies that could contain more than one value, sparing users the hassle of constantly having to approve multiple cookies from the same page. ASP's cookie tools automate this process, providing built-in mechanisms that allow developers to include more than one value in a single cookie. While ASP's mechanisms do not have quite the flexibility of the JavaScript cookie object we built, they do make it very easy to manage reasonably simple sets of information. Cookies in ASP may have "keys"—a set of names and values that together will make up the value of the cookie as finally set.

Setting the values of keys of a cookie uses similar syntax to setting the value of the cookie itself:

```
Response.Cookies("cookieName")("keyName")=keyValue
```

Because all the keys of a cookie will be stored in a single cookie, the total size of all of the keys when combined may not exceed 4K. Still, this mechanism provides an excellent way to store several small chunks of information in a single cookie. Reading the keys back is very similar:

```
variable=Request.Cookies("cookieName")("keyName")
```

Before reading the cookie keys, developers should check to make sure that this cookie does in fact have keys. The `HasKeys` attribute of the cookie object will return true if the cookie contains keys, and false if the cookie does not exist or has no keys.

To demonstrate the use of multiple keys, we will create a form that requests the name and birth date of a user, and then personalize a page using that information.

```
<HTML>
<HEAD><TITLE>Personal Information Collection</TITLE></HEAD>
<BODY BGCOLOR=#FFFFFF>
<FORM ACTION="personalSubmit.asp" METHOD="GET">
First Name: <INPUT TYPE="Text" NAME="First" SIZE=25><BR>
Last Name: <INPUT TYPE="Text" NAME="Last" SIZE=40><BR>
Birthdate: <INPUT TYPE="Text" NAME="Birthdate" SIZE=8
VALUE="MM/DD/YY"><BR>
<INPUT TYPE="SUBMIT" VALUE="Submit information">
</FORM>
</BODY></HTML>
```

This form will then submit the information to the following page, which turns the form data into a cookie with keys. The `Response.Query` collection works much like `Response.Cookies`—to extract the value of a form field, put the name of the field (defined in the `NAME` attributes above) in quotes and use it as an argument for `Response.QueryString()`.

```
<SCRIPT RUNAT=SERVER LANGUAGE=VBSCRIPT>
sub collector
Response.Cookies("personalInfo")("First") =
Request.QueryString("First")
Response.Cookies("personalInfo")("Last") = Request.QueryString("Last")
Response.Cookies("personalInfo")("Birthdate") =
Request.QueryString("Birthdate")
end sub
</SCRIPT>
<% collector %>
<HTML>
<HEAD><TITLE>Thank you</TITLE></HEAD>
<BODY BGCOLOR=#FFFFFF>
Thank you for submitting your information. To see the results, visit
<A HREF="checkit.asp">the demonstration reader</A>.
</BODY></HTML>
```

The demonstration reader takes the information from the cookie keys and creates a personalized page with that information:

```
<%
if Request.Cookies("personalInfo").HasKeys then
    FirstName=Request.Cookies("personalInfo")("First")
    LastName=Request.Cookies("personalInfo")("Last")
    Birthdate= Request.Cookies("personalInfo")("Birthdate")
    if IsDate(Birthdate) then
        if (Day(Birthdate)=Day(Date())) AND
            (Month(Birthdate)=Month(Date())) then
            Birthday=true
        end if
    end if
end if
%>
<HTML><HEAD><TITLE>Personalized</TITLE></HEAD>
<BODY BGCOLOR=#FFFFFF>
<H2>Welcome to our page!</H2>
<P>Hello 
<% if FirstName <>"" then %>
<%= FirstName %> 
<% end if %>
<% if LastName <>"" then %>
<%= LastName %>
<% end if %>
!</P>
<% if Birthday=true then %>
<H1>Happy Birthday!</H1>
<% end if %>
</BODY></HTML>
```

Users who visit the demonstration page on their birthday (or the day they told the page was their birthday), will get an extra surprise, shown in Figure 8-10.

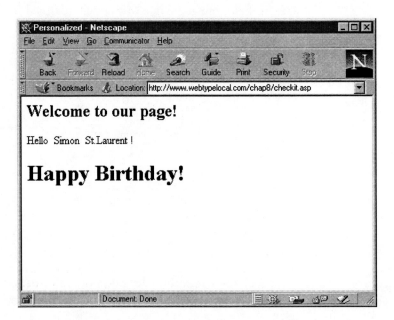

This example was implemented with no form validation and only a simple check to make sure the date value is actually a date before attempting to extract a date from it. Most developers will want to use client-side or server-side scripting to check the values entered by users before storing them as cookies. Users who enter an invalid date, for instance, will not get to enjoy the birthday greetings provided here.

State Management in ASP: Session Management

ASP has a very bad habit of dropping cookies everywhere. Trying the examples above with a browser set to alert the user of cookies will produce a flood of ASPSESSIONID alerts. ASP will drop an ASPSESSIONID cookie with every ASP request until a session is begun by the ASP page. (It is possible to disable this behavior in the registry; it also destroys all use of the Session object.) Starting a session, which allows your server to keep tabs on particular users, will end the flood of cookies. The ASPSESSIONID cookie sent with a page that makes use of the Session object will be stable, persisting until the user exits their browser. Effectively, ASP forces developers to enable tracking of their users to avoid a situation in which they antagonize the users most upset by that tracking in the first place.

Despite ASP's strange behavior, the Session object provides a powerful tool for keeping track of users for the duration of their browser session. Every time a user requests an ASP file, the page has an opportunity to use the Session object. Once the Session object has been called into being, the information kept there is available to all future connections with the user whose request created it. The ASPSESSIONID cookie will maintain its value until the user quits the browser or the Session object times out.

The Session object is an associative array that allows developers to store pieces of information about the current session on one request and retrieve them later in a new request. Setting values in the Session object is much like setting the value of a cookie:

```
Session("FirstName")="Jim"
```

Sessions can store data of nearly any kind, even object references that include information particular to a user. (Assigning an object to a Session Object value requires using the Set keyword: Set Session("MyObject")="ZZZZ.ServerSideControl", for instance.) Using the Session object, developers can, for example, maintain information about a particular interaction without having to write it out as a cookie or refer to a database. This can dramatically reduce the amount of overhead needed to implement tasks that require several pieces of information.

Another powerful feature of the Session object is that ASP pages can defer to a central file that begins and ends all Session objects without requiring every ASP page to carry initialization information. The `global.asa` file centralizes processing and reduces overhead by maintaining a central source for Session (and Application) object information. Developers who need to stop the flood of `ASPSESSIONID` cookies but are not allowed to edit the registry can create dummy entries in the `global.asa` file that will start sessions, even if the developer is not using them. This way, users get hit one time only with `ASPSESSIONID` cookies. More important, developers who need to open database entries for users or set up other initialization parameters can use the Session object event handlers defined in the `global.asa` file to build a framework.

There are two Session object events available to developers in the `global.asa` file: `Session_OnStart` and `Session_OnEnd`. Most developers will need to use `Session_OnStart`; only applications that need explicit cleanup after they have completed will use `Session_OnEnd`. `Session_OnStart` is a good place to do things like increment visitor counters, check other cookies to see if the user has been here before, create database objects for use by this session, and possibly redirect the user to the "official" front door of a site or the beginning of a process. As an example, the following `global.asa` file takes the user to the personal information page created above on first arrival at the site. Later pages can access that personalization information through the Session object when they need it. The `global.asa` file contains:

```
<SCRIPT LANGUAGE="VBSCRIPT" RUNAT="SERVER">
sub Session_OnStart
'Initialize the fields to be used for personalization
'good practice
Session("First")=""
Session ("Last")=""
Session("Birthdate")=""
'Redirect to personalization page if on a different page
'code from Microsoft Adventure Works ASP demo
personalize="/personalize.asp"
currentPage= Request.ServerVariables("SCRIPT_NAME")
if strcmp(currentPage, personalize,1) then
   Response.Redirect(personalize)
end if
end sub

sub Session_OnEnd
'empty placeholder for now.
end sub
</SCRIPT>
```

> One significant drawback is that this redirection can lock out users who are rejecting cookies or using browsers that cannot handle cookies. In certain situations where the success of a transaction depends on state management, this may be acceptable. Try to use this technique only when absolutely necessary.

The personalization page is a slightly altered version of the previous example, allowing the user to edit information submitted during the same session:

```
<HTML>
<HEAD><TITLE>Personal Information Collection</TITLE></HEAD>
<BODY BGCOLOR=#FFFFFF>
<FORM ACTION="personalSubmit.asp" METHOD="GET">
First Name: <INPUT TYPE="Text" NAME="First" SIZE=25 VALUE=<%=
            Session("First")%> ><BR>
Last Name: <INPUT TYPE="Text" NAME="Last" SIZE=40 VALUE=<%=
            Session("Last")%>><BR>
Birthdate: <INPUT TYPE="Text" NAME="Birthdate" SIZE=8 VALUE=<%=
            Session("Birthdate")%>><BR>
<INPUT TYPE="SUBMIT" VALUE="Submit information">
</FORM>
</BODY></HTML>
```

The page that processes this form now responds more fully, and welcomes the user to the site.

```
<SCRIPT RUNAT=SERVER LANGUAGE=VBSCRIPT>
sub collector
Session("First") = Request.QueryString("First")
Session("Last") = Request.QueryString("Last")
Session("Birthdate") = Request.QueryString("Birthdate")
end sub
</SCRIPT>
<% collector %>
<HTML>
<HEAD><TITLE>Thank you</TITLE></HEAD>
<BODY BGCOLOR=#FFFFFF>
<P>Thank you for submitting your information. To see the results on
other pages, visit <A HREF="checkit.asp">the demonstration
reader</A>.</P>
<P>You are currently registered as
<B><%=Session("First")%> <%=Session("Last")%></B>, with a
birthdate of <B><%=Session("Birthdate")%></B>. You can <A HREF=
"personalize.asp">change</A> any of this information if needed.</P>
</BODY></HTML>
```

Because the application can count on the `Session_OnStart` function to have sent people to the personalization page, other pages using that information can now do less error-checking.

```
<%
Birthdate= Session("Birthdate")
   if IsDate(Birthdate) then
      if (Day(Birthdate)=Day(Date())) AND
         (Month(Birthdate)=Month(Date())) then
         Birthday=true
      end if
   end if
end if
%>
<HTML><HEAD><TITLE>Personalized</TITLE></HEAD>
<BODY BGCOLOR=#FFFFFF>
<H2>Welcome to our page!</H2>
<P>Hello 
<%= Session("First") %> 
<%= Session("Last") %>
!</P>
<% if Birthday=true then %>
<H1>Happy Birthday!</H1>
<% end if %>
</BODY></HTML>
```

Although we have added extra functionality here, all of it (except for the redirection based on the Session object) could have been accomplished using our previous keyed cookie. However, the Session object is much more convenient and encourages developers to make better use of the information available.

The Session object has two properties and a method that developers should be aware of. The `SessionID` property returns the value of the `ASPSESSIONID` cookie; most developers will not have much cause to use this. The `Timeout` property is more useful; it returns the length of time (in minutes) that the ASP engine will wait for the user to respond before destroying the Session object and calling the `Session_OnEnd` subroutine. By default, this value is set to 20 minutes, which should provide enough time for most transactions. If users complain that they are losing information because the computer cuts them off too quickly, increase the value. If a server has too many Session objects stored in memory and begins to break down, decrease this value. Users will have to respond more quickly, but the weight of opened but useless sessions will have less impact. To set the `Timeout` value to ten minutes, use

```
Session.Timeout=10
```

The last method of the Session object is especially useful when a user wants to clear out the entire shopping cart or record of a visit at one blow. The Abandon method ends the session (calling the `Session_OnEnd` subroutine in the `global.asa` file) and frees all the resources it used. The visitor can come back to the site, but will receive a new `ASPSESSIONID` cookie and none of the information from the previous session will be retained. To abandon a Session, just use:

```
Session.Abandon
```

Cookie Munging

Until recently, ASP's session management tools only worked with browsers that accepted cookies. Older browsers and users who had decided to reject cookies could make ASP programs malfunction horribly, keeping users from reaching information. While some developers simply added warnings about their sites requiring cookies for proper functioning, others stayed away from the Session object completely. (It is even possible to turn off session tracking completely, though it takes an adventurous foray in the registry.) Some developers implemented their own state management tools with hidden form fields and manual URL encoding, but these relatively ungainly techniques required considerable effort on the part of the programmer and were likely to fall apart when users entered a process in the middle.

Microsoft has released a small program that helps resolve this difficulty by converting the ASPSESSIONID cookies to URL extensions. The Cookie Munger is probably better described at this point in its development as a technology demonstration instead of a beta release, but it can provide developers, especially developers with a C++ background, with a useful tool that allows their site to use ASP session tracking while remaining cookie-free. The Cookie Munger is currently available from Microsoft at **http://www.microsoft.com/iis/UsingIIS/Developing/Samples/ default.asp**, and comes complete with source code. Developers with a C++ background can rebuild the Munger to their own specifications.

The Cookie Munger parses incoming and outgoing requests. When an HTTP request is received, the Munger parses the URL it requests and extracts any ASPSESSIONID information from the URL, converting it into cookie information that can be used by the ASP processor. (Munging is the process of converting URLs and cookies back and forth.) When pages are sent back out, the Munger parses the headers and extracts the ASPSESSIONID cookie. It then parses the rest of the document and appends the ASPSESSIONID information to all relative URLs (it ignores the absolute ones) in the document. This drastic measure preserves state information without using cookies by creating document personalized for every user. The Cookie Munger is somewhat "smart"; the first time it responds to a particular user, it can transmit the cookies and also munge the URLs. When it receives a response, it checks to see if the cookie was accepted. If not, it will continue to munge; if the cookie was accepted, it will stop munging documents for that user.

Developers who drop the Cookie Munger into their IIS server will quickly find that Cookie Munger has some significant drawbacks. Parsing every outgoing and incoming request significantly increases the overhead on transactions. On a lightly-trafficked server this may be acceptable, but any server approaching its performance limits will have a difficult time absorbing this extra load. The "smart" munging can reduce this load, but still imposes significant overhead. The "smart" features of the Munger are limited, though. The Munger cannot tell the difference between ASP responses and documents coming from other sources, like CGI applications, and will strip the cookies from those documents as well. Worse yet, the Munger interferes with the delivery of normal HTML files—Microsoft suggests that Cookie Munger users rename all of their `.htm` and `.html` files to `.asp`. This gets the files past the Cookie Munger, but imposes a tremendous cost in performance—every HTML file will get parsed by the ASP processor as well as the Cookie Munger!

The Cookie Munger has considerable room for improvement, but at least it is a start. Microsoft has promoted the Cookie Munger on the Site Builder network and sounds interested in further Cookie Munger development. With luck, future versions of ASP will include this kind of cookie-free session management, without the tremendous costs the Cookie Munger now imposes.

State Management in ASP: Border Crossings

Implementing our border-crossing scenario in ASP can be done two ways. Our script can check for the identity cookie of our users with every request, or it can use the identity cookie to identify the user the first time, and then rely on the ASP session mechanisms to sustain that identity. To make the most use of ASP's built-in functionality, the demonstration will use the latter approach which takes full advantage of ASP's capabilities, while still using the parts developers will need if they want to check the identity cookie at every step. This example, like its predecessors, is quite simple, focusing on managing the border crossings at appropriate points rather than creating a large database for security management.

The first thing the border-crossing program needs is a passport store. For this application, the passport information will be kept in an Access table named **Passports**. The Passports table will contain an automatically generated UserID field that can be kept in a persistent cookie for storage between sessions. Access provides an easy, if insecure, mechanism for generating and retrieving UserID values. By allowing Access to create sequential primary keys, the developer can then retrieve the latest (highest-valued) key and use it as a UserID. This is a good solution for lightly-trafficked sites where no more than one user is likely to arrive at a time, but sites that need more dependability will probably want to use other mechanisms. The keys returned by Access will start out low; rather than leaving them as 1,2,3,4, the program will multiply them by an unusual non-prime number: 39. This makes it harder for average users to figure out the system and adopt someone else's privileges, though someone actively trying to get in on another's ID will be able to spot the pattern fairly quickly by making repeated requests. In addition, if the developer wishes, the passports database could also contain authentication information and deny users access on the basis of mismatches between UserID values and their associated authentication. For the purpose of the fun-house this example creates, such measures are overzealous at best. Permissions for specific pages are held in fields named `maze1-maze9`.

A larger site would, of course, need a more sophisticated database structure than the flat-file one presented here.

The site consists of nine pages, `maze1.asp-maze9.asp`. The `maze1.asp` file is the front door of the maze. Each page has three links. The right of a user to explore those links is determined by values set during visits to other pages; each page provides a key to another page, though it may not be a directly linked page. All the permissions information is kept in the Passports table in the same database, and a list of the permissions is kept in the Session object as an array. The information in the Session object will be used to grant and deny permission to visit another page based on the pages previously visited. When the user is finished (or the session is abandoned), the permissions achieved are written back into the database. The Session object handles permissions information while the user is connected, and a persistent cookie and database store that permission when the user is disconnected.

When a user connects to the system, the `Session _OnStart` method of the `global.asa` has to check to see if the user has a UserID cookie. If there is one, that ID will be compared with the Passports table and the permissions retrieved from that table. Permissions are retrieved through an ADO recordset. Once this has been accomplished, the user can begin running the maze.

```
<SCRIPT LANGUAGE="VBSCRIPT" RUNAT="SERVER">
sub Session_OnStart
'no includes permitted in global.asa file
'have to define needed constants here
Const adModeRead = 1
Const adModeWrite = 2
Const adModeReadWrite = 3
Const adOpenKeyset = 1
Const adCmdText = &H0001
Const adCmdTable = &H0002

if Request.Cookies("UserID")="" then
   UserName="Blank" 'script could add functionality
   set DataObj=Server.CreateObject("ADODB.Connection")

   'Choose a Mode - in this case, read and write.
   DataObj.Mode=adModeReadWrite

   'Open the System DSN
   DataObj.Open "ASPtest"

   'Build and execute the SQL call
   SQLtext="INSERT INTO Passports (UserName) VALUES
           ('" & UserName &"')"
   DataObj.Execute SQLtext, numChanged, adCmdText

   'Get UserID as NewID using MAX
   SQLtext="SELECT MAX(UserID) FROM Passports"
   Set RcdSetObj=DataObj.Execute (SQLtext, numChanged, adCmdText)
   NewID=RcdSetObj(0)

   'Close the database connection
   DataObj.Close
   Response.Cookies("UserID")=NewID*39
   Response.Cookies("UserID").expires="December 31,1999"
else
   NewID=Request.Cookies("UserID")/39
end if

'Set up session object and permissions
   dim permissions(9)
   set DataObj=Server.CreateObject("ADODB.Connection")
   DataObj.Mode=adModeReadWrite
   DataObj.Open "ASPtest"
   SQLtext="SELECT DISTINCTROW Passports.* FROM Passports WHERE
           (((Passports.UserID)= " & NewID & "))"
   Set RcdSetObj=DataObj.Execute (SQLtext, numChanged, adCmdText)
'collect the permissions information from the database
   for i=1 to 9
     mazeName="maze" & i
     permissions(i)=RcdSetObj(mazeName)
   next
   'Close the database connection
```

```
      DataObj.Close
'store database information in Session object
      Session("PermArray")= permissions
      Session("UserID")=NewID
end sub

sub Session_OnEnd
'constants
Const adModeReadWrite = 3
Const adOpenKeyset = 1
Const adCmdTable = &H0002

'Write all the Permissions back into the recordset.
permissions=Session("PermArray")
set DataObj=Server.CreateObject("ADODB.Connection")
set RcdSetObj=Server.CreateObject("ADODB.Recordset")
DataObj.Mode=adModeReadWrite
DataObj.Open "ASPtest"
RcdSetObj.Open "Passports", DataObj, adOpenKeySet, adCmdTable
RcdSetObj.Filter="[UserID] = '" & Session("UserID") &"'"

for i=1 to 9
  mazeName="maze" & i
  RcdSetObj(mazeName)=permissions(i)
next
RcdSetObj.Update 'write the recordset to the database

'Close the database connection
DataObj.Close
end sub
</SCRIPT>
```

The `Session_OnEnd` subroutine closes down the maze program—it writes all the permissions currently held by this session back into the database. That way, when users return, they don't have to start at the beginning. Effectively, it is the `Session_OnStart` subroutine in reverse.

Relying on `Session_OnEnd` is not necessarily a good idea. ASP seems to forget to call it when a page uses `Session.Abandon`, so make sure you have an alternate solution for users who need to save their work. In this demonstration, the `quit.asp` page duplicates much of the functionality of the `Session_OnEnd` subroutine. It is to be hoped that ASP 2.0 will fix this problem.

The actual maze pages all use a shared set of code. The individual pages are shells, containing only a few variables that the `mazeCode.inc` file will need to assemble the page. The `maze1.asp` file, for instance, is:

```
<% Page=1
   Unlock=7
   Connect1=6
   Connect2=7
```

```
    Connect3=8
%>
<!--#include file="mazeCode.inc"-->
```

The `mazeCode.inc` file handles all the processing, giving users keys and keeping them abreast of their progress (or lack of it) through the maze. It retrieves the permissions array from the Session object, and tests to see if users have the needed permissions for any page. If they don't, users can go no further. A message offering to take them to the beginning is presented for the benefit of users who tried to start someplace other than `maze1.asp`. If users can visit this page, and they haven't visited it before, their permissions are updated to reflect the new key they have picked up by visiting, and they are notified. Then the program creates the menu of pages they can try to reach from the current page.

```
<%
permissions=Session("PermArray")
if permissions(page)<>-1 then
    Response.Write("I'm sorry, but you don't have that key.<BR>")
    Response.Write("You can go back to the <A HREF=
                    'maze1.asp'>beginning</A> if you like.")
else
    Response.Write("<P>Welcome to room #" & Page &".</P>")
    if permissions(unlock)<>-1 then
        Response.Write("<P>You now have key #" & unlock &".</P>")
    end if
    permissions(unlock)=-1
    Response.Write("<P>From here you may visit:</P>")
    Response.Write("<A HREF='maze" & Connect1 &".asp'>Room Number " &
                    Connect1 & "</A><BR>")
    Response.Write("<A HREF='maze" & Connect2 &".asp'>Room Number " &
                    Connect2 & "</A><BR>")
    Response.Write("<A HREF='maze" & Connect3 &".asp'>Room Number " &
                    Connect3 & "</A><BR>")
    Session("PermArray")=permissions
    Response.Write("<P>Frustrated? <A HREF='quit.asp'>Quit</A> and
                    come back later.</P>")
end if
%>
```

Figures 8-11 and 8-12 show typical pages created by this code.

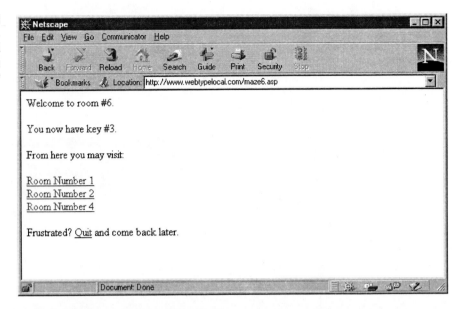

Figure 8-11
A Newly Opened
Page Giving the
User a Key

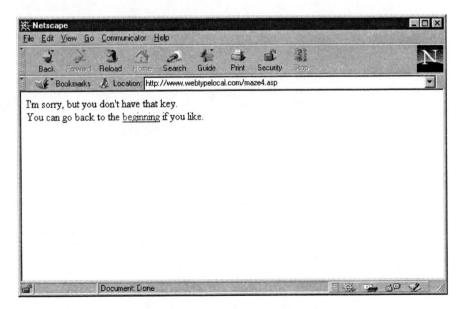

Figure 8-12
A Page
Rejecting a User
Without a Key

Lucky users may finally reach `maze9.asp`, the goal, shown in Figure 8-13.

```
<HTML>
<HEAD><TITLE>Congratulations!</TITLE></HEAD>
<BODY BGCOLOR=#FFFFFF>
<P>You found all the keys!</P>

<P>To save your work, <A HREF="quit.asp">quit</A>.</P>
</BODY></HTML>
```

Figure 8-13
The Final Maze

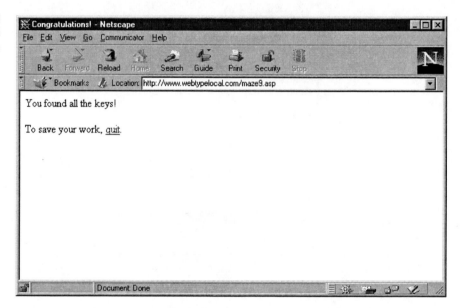

Users who are fed up with the whole maze—not a surprising possibility, as this is really a technology demonstration and not particularly entertaining—can quit. The `quit.asp` function will save all they have accomplished so far, much like the `Session_OnEnd` subroutine. If ASP picks up on the `Session.Abandon` call at the end of this page, `Session_OnEnd` will duplicate some effort.

```
<!-- #include virtual="/ASPSAMP/SAMPLES/ADOVBS.INC" -->
<%
'Write all the Permissions back into the recordset.
permissions=Session("PermArray")
set DataObj=Server.CreateObject("ADODB.Connection")
set RcdSetObj=Server.CreateObject("ADODB.Recordset")
DataObj.Mode=adModeReadWrite
DataObj.Open "ASPtest"
RcdSetObj.Open "Passports", DataObj, adOpenKeySet, adCmdTable
RcdSetObj.Filter="[UserID] = '" & Session("UserID") &"'"

for i=1 to 9
  mazeName="maze" & i
  RcdSetObj(mazeName)=permissions(i)
```

```
next
RcdSetObj.Update 'write the recordset to the database

'Close the database connection
DataObj.Close
Session.Abandon
%>
<HTML>
<HEAD><TITLE>Come back again!</TITLE></HEAD>
<BODY BGCOLOR=#FFFFFF>
<P>All your permissions will be kept for your next visit.</P>
<P>Thank you for participating.</P>
</BODY></HTML>
```

The maze is a good example of a structured set of pages easily manipulated with a small set of controls, and takes advantage of ASP's ability to hide the processing behind the curtain of server-side processing. More complex sets of data will require more sophisticated database management and session objects, but the same principles should apply.

State Management in ASP: The Shopping Cart

The ASP Session object is an excellent tool for managing our shopping-cart application. It has the considerable virtue of being transient, while allowing our application to collect the needed information and submit it to another server for final processing. As long as users do not overburden the server with huge shopping carts, the Session object should be capable of storing significantly more information more efficiently than could a cookie containing all of the same information; the Session object can also process it more efficiently than could a series of write operations to a database. The Session object is an especially useful tool for implementing small sites that only need to keep track of a few basic items.

Our shopping-cart example will provide services to a small store, though the Session object could handle considerably larger tasks. Our focus here is on the state management mechanism of the Session object, not on the wide array of tools that ASP provide for creating large catalogs from databases. Using the Session object to maintain a list of the items in a shopping cart is a fairly simple task; assembling a functioning catalog containing thousands of items is much more complex. The store in this example will contain five product pages, plus a central page that displays the contents of the cart and a processing page that displays the user's final order. The Session object will contain an array that holds the quantities of items being ordered, and all of the pages on the site will reflect that information.

The `global.asa` file will initialize the store. More complex stores will use database connections like those used above, but Joe's Chewing Gum Warehouse only carries a few items:

```
<SCRIPT LANGUAGE="VBSCRIPT" RUNAT="SERVER">
sub Session_OnStart
dim Order(5), Flavor(5), Price(5)
'initialize order quantities, prices
for x=1 to 5
   Order(x)=0
   Price(x)=.25
next
'Banana Daiquiri is expensive
Price(3)=.50
'Set Flavor names for tables
Flavor(1)="Bubble-gum Bubble Gum"
Flavor(2)="Chocolicious Chewing Gum"
Flavor(3)="Banana Daiquiri Delight"
Flavor(4)="Strawberry Twist"
Flavor(5)="Raspberry Raspberry"
'Store arrays in Session object
Session("Order")=Order
Session("Flavor")=Flavor
Session("Price")=Price
end sub

sub Session_OnEnd
'placeholder - no databases to close out
end sub
</SCRIPT>
```

The catalog pages are named `item1.asp–item5.asp`. They contain information about the products and a simple form for adding products to the shopping cart stored in the Session object. The form allows users to indicate whether they want to place an order, and if so, how many items they would like:

```
<% Order=Session("Order")
   Quantity=Order(1)
   Price=Session("Price")
   MyPrice=Price(1) %>
<HTML>
<HEAD><TITLE>Bubble-gum flavor Bubble Gum</TITLE></HEAD>
<BODY BGCOLOR=#FFFFFF>
<H2>Bubble-gum Magic</H2>
<P>Bubble-gum flavor is back!  After years of chewing strange
concoctions, many of our customers asked us to bring back the original
flavor they had enjoyed for years. Our unique blend of bubble-gum
flavors will put a smile on your face as you chew.</P>
<FORM ACTION="default.asp" METHOD="POST">
<TABLE>
<TR>
<TD>Order?</TD>
<TD>Description</TD>
<TD>Price</TD>
<TD>Quantity</TD>
```

```
</TR>
<TR>
<TD><INPUT NAME="Order" TYPE="checkbox" <% if Quantity>0 then
    Response.Write("CHECKED") %>></TD>
<TD>Bubble-gum Bubble Gum</TD> <TD><%=FormatCurrency(MyPrice)%>
    ea</TD>
<TD><INPUT NAME="Quantity" TYPE="TEXT" SIZE=4 VALUE="<%=
    Quantity %>"></TD>
</TR>
</TABLE>
<INPUT TYPE="HIDDEN" VALUE=1 NAME="item">
<INPUT TYPE="SUBMIT" VALUE="Order"></FORM>
</BODY></HTML>
```

The `default.asp` file is the central switchboard of the application. It presents the catalog, and maintains the shopping cart. When it opens, it loads the Session object's information and checks to see if any additional order information has come in through a POST from an item page. If there is additional order information, it adds that to the session information for storage. Whether or not the page was reached from a form, the `default.asp` page displays the current order, and offers users the option of submitting it for fulfillment.

```
<% Order=Session("Order")
   Flavor=Session("Flavor")
   Price=Session("Price")
   'if we got here from an order form, process
   if Request.ServerVariables("REQUEST_METHOD")="POST" Then
     item=Request.Form("item")
     ordered=Request.Form("Order")
     if ordered="on" then
       Order(item)=Request.Form("Quantity")
     else
       Order(item)=0
     end if
   'store arrays in Session object to preserve state
   Session("Order")=Order
   Session("Flavor")=Flavor
   Session("Price")=Price
   end if
%>
<HTML>
<HEAD><TITLE>Joe's Chewing Gum Warehouse</TITLE></HEAD>
<BODY BGCOLOR=#FFFFFF>
<H1>Gum for the Chewers</H1>
<P>Joe's Chewing Gum Warehouse is committed to providing serious gum
chewers with the tastes they love, the textures they want, and the
flavors that last. Joe's special-orders all of its flavors and stocks
only limited quantities to ensure freshness.</P>
Our current selection, and your order. Quantities and price are per
piece.<BR>
<TABLE BORDER=1>
<TR>
<TD>Description</TD>
<TD>Price</TD>
<TD>Quantity</TD>
```

```
<TD>Total </TD>
</TR>
<% For x=1 to 5 %>
<TR>
<TD><A HREF="item<%=x%>.asp"><%=Flavor(x)%></A> </TD>
<TD><%=FormatCurrency(Price(x)) %> ea </TD>
<TD ALIGN="CENTER"><%= Order(x) %></TD>
<TD><%=FormatCurrency(Price(x)*Order(x))%></TD>
</TR>
<% Total=Total+(Price(x)*Order(x))
    next %>
<TR>
<TD></TD><TD></TD><TD></TD>
<TD><%=FormatCurrency(Total) %></TD>
</TR>
</TABLE>
<A HREF="pay.asp">Pay for your gum</A>
</BODY></HTML>
```

The last page of the shopping cart prepares the order for final submission, collecting a name and address (for shipment and payment enforcement) and giving users one last chance to back out of their order. Legal information regarding payment is provided, though Joe's low-tech means for securing payment don't require any special security processing by the order system.

```
<% Order=Session("Order")
    Flavor=Session("Flavor")
    Price=Session("Price")
    'This page only displays and formats the order
    'using the session object
    'The next page (not part of example)
    'places the order
%>
<HTML>
<HEAD><TITLE>Joe's Chewing Gum Warehouse - Ordering</TITLE></HEAD>
<BODY BGCOLOR=#FFFFFF>
<H2>Order Placement</H2>
<P>Joe's will process your order quickly. We trust you to pay up on an
invoice; our enforcers are always happy to take a chewer's gum away or
worse if they haven't paid up within 30 days.</P>
Your order. Quantities and price are per piece.<BR>
<TABLE BORDER=1>
<TR>
<TD>Description</TD>
<TD>Price</TD>
<TD>Quantity</TD>
<TD>Total </TD>
</TR>
<% For x=1 to 5 %>
<TR>
<TD><%=Flavor(x)%></TD>
<TD><%=FormatCurrency(Price(x)) %> ea </TD>
<TD ALIGN="CENTER"><%= Order(x) %></TD>
<TD><%=FormatCurrency(Price(x)*Order(x))%></TD>
</TR>
<% Total=Total+(Price(x)*Order(x))
    next %>
```

```
<TR>
<TD></TD><TD></TD><TD></TD>
<TD><%=FormatCurrency(Total) %></TD>
</TR>
</TABLE>
<FORM ACTION="submit.asp" METHOD="POST">
<% For x=1 to 5 %>
<INPUT TYPE="HIDDEN" NAME="item<%=x%>" VALUE="<%=Order(x)%>">
<% next %>
Name:<BR>
<INPUT TYPE="TEXT" NAME="Customer" SIZE=40><BR>
Address:<BR>
<TEXTAREA COLS=40 ROWS=4 NAME="Address"></TEXTAREA>
<BR>
<INPUT TYPE="SUBMIT" VALUE="Place Order">
</FORM>
</BODY></HTML>
```

When users first visit Joe's Chewing Gum Warehouse, they will see the default screen, with no order placed, as shown in Figure 8-14.

Figure 8-14
Joe's Chewing Gum, Initial Empty Cart

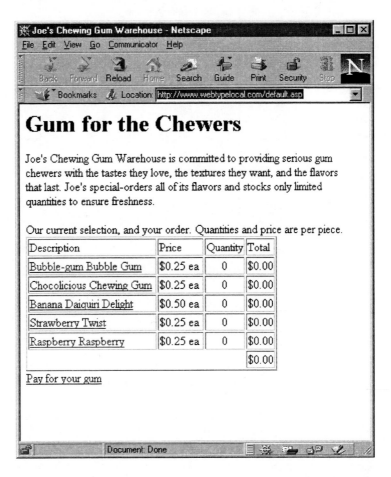

Clicking on one of the chewing gum varieties in the table will bring users to a page that describes the flavor and allows them to place an order, as shown in Figure 8-15. The checkbox provides an easy way for users to turn down their order without having to retype the quantity as zero.

Figure 8-15
Bubble-gum
Bubble Gum,
Adding to
the Cart

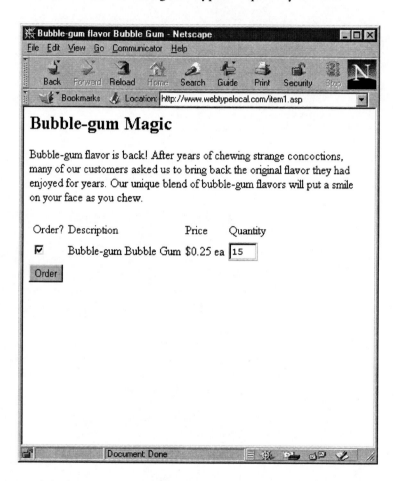

When the users return to the default page, their orders are added to the current list. After visits to several flavors, users may have racked up a small bill, as shown in Figure 8-16.

To place the order, users can click on the **Pay for your gum** link, which takes them to pay.asp, shown in Figure 8-17. This page presents the order and collects a name and address. It doesn't yet abandon the session—that will be the task of the final page in the order process. All needed session information is put into HIDDEN fields for processing by the next form down the line.

Figure 8-16
The Shopping
Cart, Filling Up

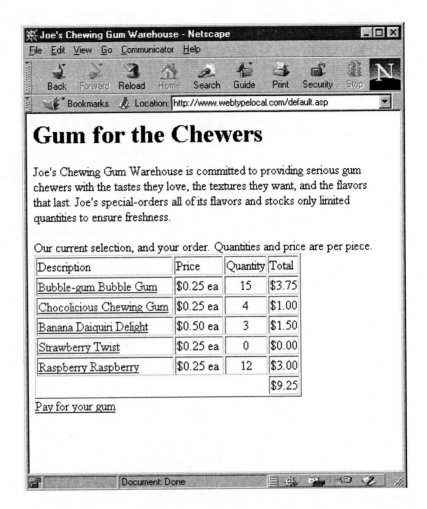

While not a full-fledged electronic commerce solution in itself, Active Server Pages are capable of handling the shopping-cart side of these transactions with a minimum of effort. Small sites like Joe's can be extremely efficient, using only a single, relatively small, cookie and calling to a database only at the end of the process when the order is placed.

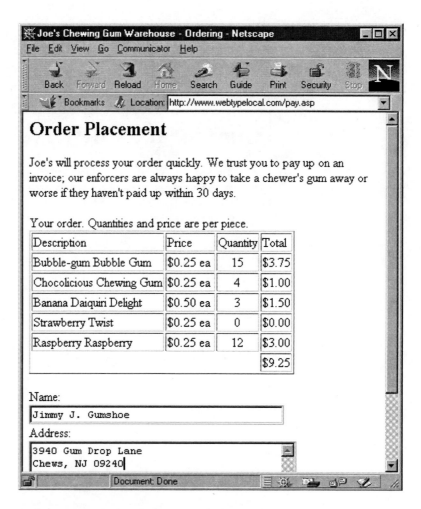

Figure 8-17
Taking the Cart
to the Register

ASP and State Management Architectures

ASP provide powerful tools for maintaining state that provide a useful medium between the twin concerns of maintaining all state information in the cookie itself and keeping all state information locked up in a database. While Active Server Pages do not create the most efficient pages on the market, the Session object offers mechanisms that avoid the inefficiencies of constant database calls and cookie transfers. The `global.asa` file, while unwieldy and difficult to debug, provides a very useful central switchboard for initializing transactions and preparing application structures. Developers working with Microsoft servers and databases will undoubtedly find ASP a handy tool for a wide variety of work, capable of handling difficult tasks with a minimum of developer effort.

NOTE Developers interested in putting even less effort toward ASP creation should look at Microsoft's Visual InterDev. At least for developers who have previously used Microsoft's Visual C++ or Visual J++ programming environments, Visual InterDev can be a significant time saver. Visual InterDev is capable of writing much of the code for developers, especially SQL code for database connectivity.

The Future of ASP: IIS 4.0 and Beyond

Internet Information Server 4.0 remains, at this writing, a moving target, but it will definitely include the next version of Active Server Pages—ASP 2.0. Microsoft has singled out state management as an area to improve. The Session object has picked up some new collections and properties to improve its ability to store and reference information. The `Session_OnStart` and `Session_OnEnd` event handlers and the `Abandon` method remain unchanged (though perhaps they will work more reliably).

The `SessionID` and `Timeout` properties will work as they have in ASP 1.0 (the version that shipped as part of IIS 3.0.) New properties include `CodePage`, used for symbol mapping, and `LCID`, a locale identifier for internationalized content. Two new collections, `Contents` and `StaticObjects`, provide new ways to access ASP objects. `StaticObjects` contains all the objects defined with the `OBJECT` element in the `global.asa` file. `Contents` contains all of the objects available through the Session object—it is comparable to the `document.all` collection in Internet Explorer 4 in that it lets developers retrieve nearly anything they can reference from one location.

ASP appears to be evolving gradually, without too much radical change. The cookies collections of the Request and Response objects appear to be remaining the same. While some of the changes may require developers to change their pages, none of the changes announced so far should break the mechanisms described in this chapter.

## CHAPTER 9

Cookies and Java

Cookies are comparative newcomers to Java, perhaps representing even a violation of the applet sandbox that has been a key part of Java's marketing. Java has also seen a great deal of growth on the server side, becoming more popular as a tool for creating servlets—applications that perform tasks similar to those performed by CGI, LiveWire, and ASP. While cookies are not an integral part of Java, they do afford functionality not completely provided for by the original Java client-side specifications and are a growing part of servlet development. While Java environments that use cookies remain in the minority, that segment is growing rapidly. This chapter provides an introduction to the mechanisms used to connect Java applications to cookie information. We will start on the browser side of Java cookie interactions and move to the server side. The two sides use completely different tools, requiring a different set of techniques.

A Tiny Crack in the Sandbox

When Java first appeared as a part of Netscape Navigator 2.0, Sun and Netscape went to great pains to make certain that Java applets could not write to the user's hard drive under any circumstances. Applets were run in the "sandbox"—a carefully secured set of virtual machine libraries that would keep applets out of mischief. Applets could make all the noise they wanted in a browser window, but under no circumstances was a rogue applet allowed to cause damage. Applets were inspected several times before being allowed to run on a user's machine, and then were allowed to make calls only to a "safe" subset of the Java API. JavaScript, which also shipped with Navigator 2.0, could write cookies, but Java applets could not.

Years later, applets are still restricted. Netscape Communicator 4.0 has lengthened the leash, allowing signed applets to undertake riskier tasks, but cookie support for applets has not yet crossed the browser developers' minds. However, a group of other enabling technologies (LiveConnect) has appeared, making it possible for developers to pass cookies to and from applets. Originally developed by Netscape to allow JavaScript, plug-ins, and applets to communicate, LiveConnect provides a set of interfaces that enable JavaScript functions to call Java methods and vice versa. Netscape Navigator 2.0 first allowed JavaScript to call Java methods, and Navigator 3.0 extended that functionality to allow Java to call JavaScript. Communicator and Navigator 4.0 both support this enhanced LiveConnect. Microsoft Internet Explorer 3.0 provided for JavaScript to Java communication; in Microsoft Internet Explorer 4.0, Microsoft also adopted Netscape's implementation of Java to JavaScript communication. The limitations on which browsers would support LiveConnect have kept developers from using it, but Microsoft's recent (and surprising) embrace of this technology should accelerate the use of these techniques.

Connecting cookie values to a Java applet requires the use of JavaScript. This is not a 100% pure Java application by any means. Calling Java from JavaScript is done one way; calling JavaScript from Java is done an entirely different way. Combining these different techniques may require some creativity as well as some technical knowhow. The LiveConnect cookie demonstration built here will give Java developers a sense of how to move their cookies from the browser scripting environment to their Java applet environment and back, but will not go into great detail about how a Java applet might apply cookies. Applets already afford a far more powerful development environment than client-side scripting does, one capable of far more powerful things than manipulating outlines and printing personalized messages. This demonstration is about passing cookies from the browser to an applet and back—not about Java development, or even applet interface.

There are several factors to consider in developing LiveConnect applications. First, it is entirely possible that the browser will call scripts before an applet is fully initialized, producing errors and failures. Developers should always make sure that the applet is ready before submitting cookie values. Another possible pitfall is Java's lack of mechanisms for handling cookie information. Java has no built-in mechanisms for escaping and unescaping text, so developers who need to make use of more complex cookies will have to remember to handle this conversion before passing cookie values to an applet. Passing dates (expiration dates, for instance) can also cause problems, depending on the browser on which the page has been loaded. Java is a much more strongly typed language than JavaScript—passing the wrong kind of data to an applet will produce angry error messages and probably stop the applet from working at all. The answer to most of these problems is simplification—passing data in the simplest possible forms. Strings and numbers may require extra effort to process, but the results will be more dependable.

The applet used to demonstrate passing a cookie value from JavaScript to Java is just a window displaying the value of a variable. Note that nothing in this applet requires it to hold the value of a cookie; all it does is display the value of a variable, called `cookieString` for convenience. For this part of LiveConnect, all the classes used by the applet are standard parts of the Java libraries.

```
import java.applet.Applet;
import java.awt.Graphics;
//LiveConnect Cookie Demonstration
public class cooktest extends Applet
{
    String cookieString;

    public void init(){
    cookieString= new String(Java Cookie Demo);
    }

    public void paint(Graphics g){
    g.drawString(showString, 20, 20);
    }

    public void setString(String yourString) {
    cookieString=yourString;
    repaint();
    }
}
```

The init() method sets the default string to **Java Cookie Demo**, giving us a value to change. The paint() method displays that string in the applet's designated space in a browser window. The method that will connect JavaScript to this display is the setString() method, which will be called from a JavaScript function and passed the value of a cookie. The applet will need to be compiled and stored as cooktest.class.

The HTML and JavaScript that enable this cookie reading take advantage of tools created in Chapter 4. The HTML file contains a form with a text entry field and two buttons. One of the buttons calls the bakeCookie() function, which sets the cookie to be fed to the applet, and the other calls feedCookie(), which uses the applet's setString() method to display the value of the cookie. Both of these functions use the simple JavaScript cookie library (jscooklb.js) to handle the cookie processing.

```
<HTML>
<HEAD><TITLE>LiveConnect Test</TITLE></HEAD>
<BODY>
<SCRIPT SRC="jscooklb.js" LANGUAGE="JavaScript">
</SCRIPT>
<SCRIPT LANGUAGE="JavaScript">
function bakeCookie(){
WriteCookie("JavaTest", document.inputPlace.words.value);
}
function feedCookie(){
cookieValue = ReadCookie("JavaTest");
document.cooktest.setString(cookieValue);
}
</SCRIPT>
<APPLET CODE="cooktest.class" NAME="cooktest" WIDTH=150 HEIGHT=25>
</APPLET><BR>
<FORM NAME="inputPlace">
<INPUT TYPE="text" SIZE=30 NAME="words"><BR>
<INPUT TYPE="button" VALUE="Set Cookie" onClick="bakeCookie()">
<INPUT TYPE="button" VALUE="Feed Applet" onClick="feedCookie()">
</FORM>
</BODY>
</HTML>
```

When initially loaded, the applet shows its default text and the HTML form, as in Figure 9-1.

Once the page is loaded, the user can type a string into the text field. To make that string appear in the applet, the user must click the **Set Cookie** and **Feed Applet** buttons in sequence, producing the screen shown in Figure 9-2.

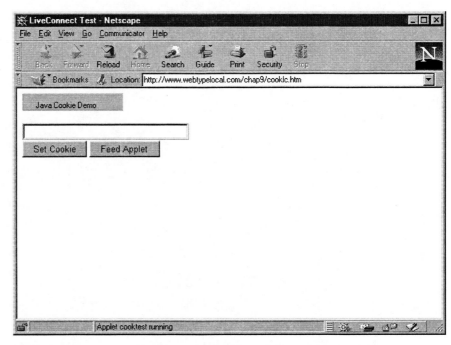

Figure 9-1
Cookie
LiveConnect
Demo at Start

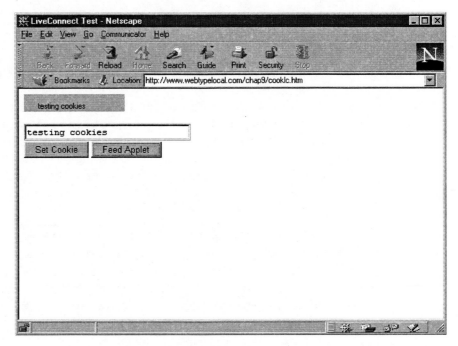

Figure 9-2
Applet after
Receiving Cookie
Value—Netscape

Skipping the **Set Cookie** button and clicking on **Feed Applet** will pass the applet the empty string (no cookie was found), unless someone set a persistent cookie named JavaText in a previous example. This example works just as well in Internet Explorer as it does in Netscape, as shown in Figure 9-3.

Figure 9-3
Applet after
Receiving Cookie
Value—Internet
Explorer

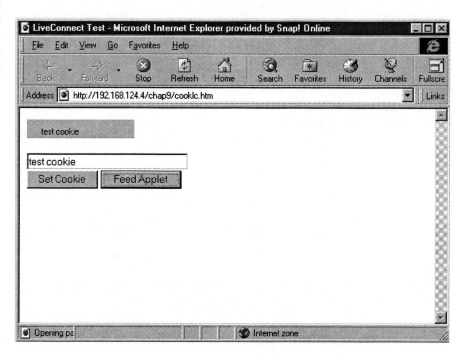

Allowing a Java applet to set a cookie is a more complicated matter. Netscape provides a set of classes—`netscape.javascript`—that allow Java applets to communicate with JavaScript in the browser. The JSObject class is a creaky tool for establishing communication, but it makes it fairly simple to call JavaScript functions—and change the values of JavaScript objects—from Java with its `call()` and `eval()` methods.

Unfortunately, Netscape hasn't provided its classes in a developer friendly form; my solution has been to find the `Java_30` file included with Netscape Navigator 3.0, open it as a zip file, and build my own `netscape.zip` class file that contains only the Netscape classes. Once you have extracted those classes, you can use them with the various Java development tools. I have successfully used them with Borland JBuilder, Visual J++, and the Sun JDK.

Most of the `cooktest2` applet should be familiar. The two major areas that have changed are the import statements (note the addition of `import netscape.javascript.*`) and the `setString()` method.

```
import java.applet.Applet;
import java.awt.Graphics;
import netscape.javascript.*;
// Cookies going back out
public class cooktest2 extends Applet
{
     String cookieString;

     public void init(){
     cookieString = new String("Java Cookie Demo");
        }

public void paint(Graphics g){
     g.drawString(cookieString, 20, 20);
        }

public void setString(String yourString) {
     cookieString = "Java:" + yourString;
     repaint();
     JSObject win= JSObject.getWindow(this);
     win.eval("cookieChange ('"+yourString+"','"+cookieString+"');");
        }
}
```

The `setString()` method now performs some additional functions. First, it adds `"Java:"` to the string sent it by the JavaScript function. (This way we can tell that the return value has actually changed.) Next, it creates an object named `win`, of type `JSObject`. The JSObject has no constructor method, so creating it requires a call to its `getWindow()` method. The keyword `this` refers to the applet, so `JSObject.getWindow(this)` will return an object that will allow the applet to address the window in which the applet first appeared. The last line of the method makes the actual call to the JavaScript `cookieChange()` function, shown below. Java still cannot address cookies directly; the `eval()` method will perform the JavaScript call made in the string it takes as an argument.

The JSObject class also includes a `call()` method that takes the name of the function to be called and an array of arguments. I find the `eval()` method to be more flexible (and much easier to debug), but either method will work.

The HTML for this example is very much like that of the previous example, with one change to the `APPLET` element and the significant addition of the `cookieChange()` function. The `APPLET` now has the `MAYSCRIPT` attribute. This tells the browser that this applet has been given "permission" by the developer to make calls to JavaScript. The `cookieChange()` function will act as the gateway for information coming back from the Java applet, accepting two arguments. The first is the "original" value of the `cookieString` inside the applet; the second is the new value. The `cookieChange()` function announces the old and new values, to demonstrate that something is actually changing, and then sets the cookie to reflect the new value.

```
<HTML>
<HEAD><TITLE>Java-to-JavaScript Communication</TITLE></HEAD>
<BODY>
<SCRIPT SRC="jscook1b.js" LANGUAGE="JavaScript">
</SCRIPT>
<SCRIPT LANGUAGE="JavaScript">
function feedCookie(){
cookieValue= ReadCookie("JavaTest");
document.cooktest2.setString(cookieValue);
}
function bakeCookie(){
WriteCookie("JavaTest", document.inputPlace.words.value);
}
function cookieChange(original, replacement) {
alert("The Java applet has requested that the cookie be changed
      from " + original + " to " + replacement + ".");
WriteCookie("JavaTest", replacement);
}
</SCRIPT>
<APPLET CODE="cooktest2.class" NAME="cooktest2" WIDTH=150
            HEIGHT=25 MAYSCRIPT>
</APPLET><BR>
<FORM NAME="inputPlace">
<INPUT TYPE="text" SIZE=30 NAME="words"><BR>
<INPUT TYPE="button" VALUE="Set Cookie" onClick="bakeCookie()">
<INPUT TYPE="button" VALUE="Feed Applet" onClick="feedCookie()">
</FORM>
</BODY></HTML>
```

When first run, this example looks like its predecessor, as shown in Figure 9-1. The real change takes place after the **Feed Applet** button is pressed. As shown in Figure 9-4, the cookie value has `"Java:"` prepended to it to indicate that the applet is doing more than passively receiving data, and the user receives an alert box announcing the change to the cookie.

As shown in Figure 9-5, this application of LiveConnect will also work in Internet Explorer 4. Remember, however, that Java-to-JavaScript communication only works in Version 4 of Internet Explorer. Internet Explorer 3 and even the preview releases of Internet Explorer 4 will ignore the call completely.

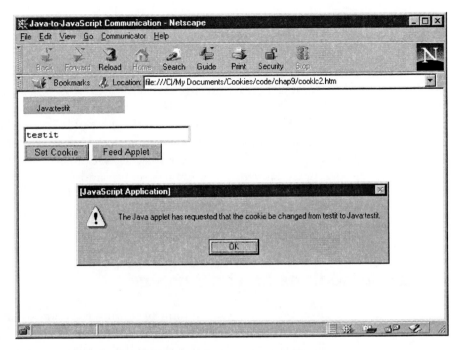

Figure 9-4
LiveConnect in Action—Changing the Cookie in Netscape Communicator

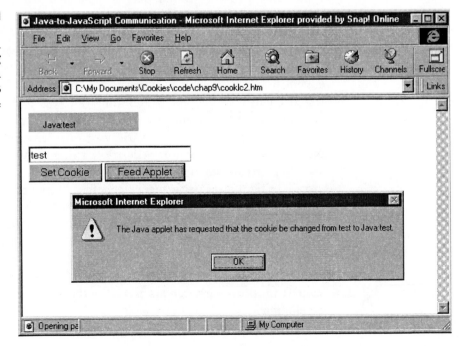

Figure 9-5
LiveConnect in Action—Changing the Cookie in Microsoft Internet Explorer 4

LiveConnect is extremely flexible. Java applets can call JavaScript functions which in turn call Java applet methods. Using this technique, an applet could also call the `feedCookie()` method to get a cookie when it first loads, and use `WriteCookie()` to set a cookie if none was present. An applet could use the JavaScript `jscooklb.js` functions directly for cookie manipulation, as long as the developer has included them in the HTML. Even if the browser did not support Java-to-JavaScript communications, an enterprising developer could create a server application that created a cookie, and then use JavaScript to pass it to the applet. Java applets already have great strength and flexibility. LiveConnect allows JavaScript to add its more intimate knowledge of the browser environment, helping produce capable applications that can customize themselves to meet the needs of individual users.

Java and Cookies on the Server

Java has found a second life away from the compatibility and performance issues of browser implementations. Sun has introduced a servlet API which allows Java programs to perform the same functions as the other server-side applications we have covered. Servlets are much like applets, as they tend to be small, special-purpose programs that work as part of a larger system rather than handling entire tasks by themselves. Servlets give Java developers the full power of Java in an environment that manages considerable portions of the HTTP transaction for them. Servlets can be trusted or untrusted; untrusted servlets run in a server-side sandbox much like the sandbox to which client-side applets are confined—access to file systems, security information, system commands, and network resources is constrained.

Servlets can be used on a variety of different servers, including the Netscape Enterprise Server, Microsoft IIS, and Apache. Sun's own Java Web Server can run trusted servlets as threads of the server application, providing significant performance benefits. All the examples in this section of the chapter have been built for the Java Web Server 1.1 and tested using it. Developers creating servlets for other server platforms should be able to use the same techniques, once they have set up a Java virtual machine and configured their server. The servlet development kit, available at **http://java.sun.com/products/java-server/servlets/index.html**, includes support for third-party servers as well as the core classes needed for servlet development.

Full information on the Java Web Server is available at **http://java. sun.com/products/java-server/webserver/index.html**.

Java servlets are usually small programs like CGI programs, although compiled .jhtml files can use code interspersed with HTML like Active Server Pages. Servlets can also be interspersed to a certain extent with HTML using <SERVLET> elements in parsed HTML files (normally .shtml files, though the server can be configured to parse all HTML), but the examples provided here will be standalone servlets that generate complete pages.

Servlets can also communicate with applets rather than generating HTML, allowing the creation of some powerfully integrated applications. This mechanism could provide a way to pass cookies to applets no more unwieldy than the LiveConnect techniques outlined above.

Java provides request and response objects and a session mechanism much like those in Active Server Pages, though all the method calls and properties are different. The servlet mechanisms for handling cookies deserve special mention as advanced tools—they provide functionality similar to the JavaScript cookie object created in Chapter 4. Sun has added several of the pieces proposed in RFC2109 as well—the Comment field, the Version field, and the MaxAge field instead of Expires. The examples here will demonstrate the cookie and session maintenance mechanisms of Java only; additional information about servlets will be provided only insofar as it is necessary to create the demonstrations.

Sun made the Cookie class much more rational with Version 1.1 of their Java Web Server. Unfortunately, this means that a lot of code got broken. The Cookie class used to be sun.servlet.http.Cookie; now it resides at javax.servlet.http.Cookie. The methods for reading and saving the cookie also changed. What would formerly have been written myCookieVal=Cookie.getCookies(request) is now myCookieVal= request.getCookies(). It makes a lot more sense, but it means that servlets written for Java Web Server 1.0's version of the Servlet API no longer work. The classes.zip file in the Java Servlet Development Kit is missing these files; getting them (until Sun updates the JSDK) requires some digging, finding the jws.jar file and adding it to the classpath in place of the classes.zip file. This may continue to be volatile; check the documentation of your server software to make certain that

all cookie calls are accurate. All code in this chapter was built for and
tested with Java Web Server 1.1 beta.

Setting and Showing Cookies

Our first example will test to see if a cookie has been set on the user's computer, and set one if it hasn't been set before. Then it will display the current status of that cookie. This servlet, Cookie1 is fairly complex already,
but demonstrates a number of the basic parts needed to create a functioning servlet.

```
//import declarations
import java.io.*;
import java.util.*;
import javax.servlet.*;
import javax.servlet.http.*;
import javax.servlet.http.Cookie;
//import sun.servlet.http.Cookie; - obsolete!

public class Cookie1 extends HttpServlet {
//set the cookieName for this example
  private static final String cookieName="ServletCookie";

  public void init(ServletConfig conf) throws ServletException {
      //initialize the servlet with the init method
      //of the HttpServlet class
      super.init(conf);
  }

  public void doGet(HttpServletRequest request, HttpServletResponse
          response) throws ServletException, IOException {
      //forward GET requests to default handler
      this.handleRequest(request, response);
  }

  public void doPost(HttpServletRequest request, HttpServletResponse
          response) throws ServletException, IOException {
//forward POST requests to default handler
      this.handleRequest(request, response);
  }

  public void handleRequest(HttpServletRequest request,
          HttpServletResponse response) throws ServletException,
          IOException{
      //initialize variables for cookie work
      Cookie cookies[], workCookie=null;
      //get cookie value from request object
      cookies=request.getCookies();

      if (cookies!=null) {
        //search for appropriate cookie
        for (int i=0; i<cookies.length; i++){
```

```
        //if found, get cookie value with getValue()
         if (cookies[i].getName().equals(cookieName)) {
           workCookie=(Cookie)cookies[i].clone();
           //end if
          }
        //end for
        }
    //end if
    }
    //if not found, set cookie value with addCookie()
    else {
        workCookie=new Cookie(cookieName,"startValue");
        //set cookie path for older browsers
        workCookie.setPath("/");
        //set expiration date: 15 days from now
        workCookie.setMaxAge(15*24*3600);
        response.addCookie(workCookie);
    }

//write the page displaying the cookie value.
ServletOutputStream output = response.getOutputStream();
  response.setContentType("text/html");
  output.println("<HTML>");
  output.println("<HEAD><TITLE>Servlet Test</TITLE></HEAD>");
  output.println("<BODY BGCOLOR=#FFFFFF>");
  output.println("This is a test of the Java servlet cookie
        mechanisms.");
  output.println("Current cookie
value:"+cookieName+"="+workCookie.getValue()+"</BODY></HTML>");
  output.close();
  }
//for informational use - recommended.
  public String getServletInfo(){
     return "Demonstrates Cookies";
  }
}
```

The import declarations are notable mostly for their difference from the usual applet declarations, bringing in some Java utility classes as well as the classes needed to build a servlet and work with cookies. The `cookieName` string is set outside the methods, making it available to all the methods of the class. The `init` routine initializes the servlet using the initialization routine of its parent servlet class. The `doGet()` and `doPost()` methods, which tell the servlet what to do when it receives a GET and POST request respectively, have both been overridden and their arguments passed to the `handleRequest()` method. This servlet is not expecting to receive any data from forms, but this way all users will receive the same message back. Note the exceptions these methods are required to throw for both servlets and their input/output mechanisms. This application does nothing to handle them, but these declarations are required.

The `handleRequest` method is the heart of this servlet, reading cookies, writing cookies, and creating HTML. It starts by creating two Cookie objects and reading the cookie value into the first of them, cookies.

```
public void handleRequest(HttpServletRequest request,
    HttpServletResponse response) throws ServletException,
    IOException{
    //initialize variables for cookie work
    Cookie cookies[], workCookie=null;
    //get cookie value from request object
    cookies=request.getCookies();
```

Next, the method checks to see if there are any cookies available that match the one our program is monitoring. If there are, it stores the value of that cookie in `workCookie`. If not, it creates a new cookie for future monitoring.

```
if (cookies!=null) {
    //search for appropriate cookie
    for (int i=0; i<cookies.length; i++){
    //if found, get cookie value with getValue()
     if (cookies[i].getName().equals(cookieName)) {
       workCookie=(Cookie)cookies[i].clone();
       //end if
       }
    //end for
    }
//end if
}
//if not found, set cookie value with addCookie()
else {
    workCookie=new Cookie(cookieName,"startValue");
    //set cookie path for older browsers
    workCookie.setPath("/");
    //set expiration date: 15 days from now
    workCookie.setMaxAge(15*24*3600);
    response.addCookie(workCookie);
}
```

The last part of the servlet writes an HTML page to the servlet's output stream, creating the servlet's response. Unlike Active Server Pages and CGI, Java requires that all the writing of this page be done to a separate object which takes its value from the response object's `getOutputStream()` method. There are several other ways to perform this buffering in Java; the technique shown here is probably the simplest. When the Output object is closed, the servlet will send its response.

```
//write the page displaying the cookie value.
ServletOutputStream output = response.getOutputStream();
  response.setContentType("text/html");
  output.println("<HTML>");
  output.println("<HEAD><TITLE>Servlet Test</TITLE></HEAD>");
  output.println("<BODY BGCOLOR=#FFFFFF>");
  output.println("This is a test of the Java servlet cookie
       mechanisms.");
  output.println("Current cookie
value:"+cookieName+"="+workCookie.getValue()+"</BODY></HTML>");
  output.close();
  }
```

The last method, `getServletInfo()`, is provided for the use of the server and other tools that may use a description of the servlet in addition to its class name.

```
//for informational use - recommended.
  public String getServletInfo(){
     return "Demonstrates Cookies";
  }
```

This servlet can be compiled using any Java-compliant compiler, though, as noted above, it will require some additional packages including the latest version of the `javax.servlet.http` classes. Once the servlet is compiled, the administrator should add it to the list of available servlets. The Java Web Server provides a convenient tool for adding servlets, shown in Figure 9-6.

Figure 9-6
Adding the Cookie1 Servlet to the Java Web Server

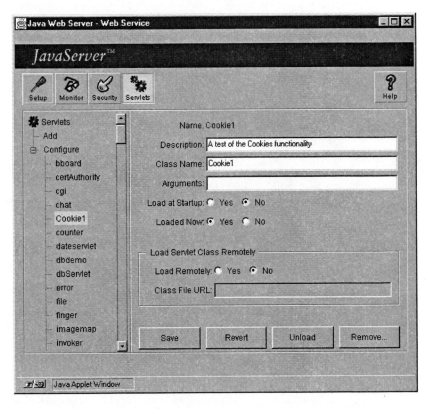

Once the servlet has been added, it can be reached with a Web Browser. Testing this servlet with Netscape produces the results shown in Figure 9-7.

The results should be the same in any browser; the servlet is only sending back HTML. There is no Java sent back in this example, or in any others. Our second cookie example is a utility function, displaying the values of all the cookies available to the server. The same loop used above to search for a cookie is used here to display all of them. Developers having trouble with servlet cookies may want to use this servlet, or parts of it, for diagnosis.

Figure 9-7
Cookie1 Results
in Netscape
Communicator

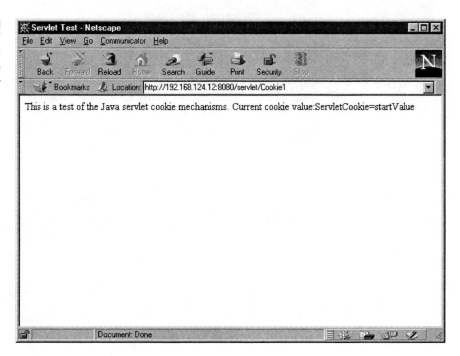

```
import java.io.*;
import java.util.*;
import javax.servlet.*;
import javax.servlet.http.*;
import javax.servlet.http.Cookie;

public class CookieView extends HttpServlet {
  public void init(ServletConfig conf) throws ServletException {
    super.init(conf);
  }

  public void doGet(HttpServletRequest request, HttpServletResponse
       response) throws ServletException, IOException {
    this.handleRequest(request, response);
  }

  public void doPost(HttpServletRequest request, HttpServletResponse
       response) throws ServletException, IOException {
    this.handleRequest(request, response);
```

```
        }

        public void handleRequest(HttpServletRequest request,
            HttpServletResponse response) throws ServletException,
            IOException{

            Cookie cookies[], workCookie=null;

        cookies=request.getCookies();
        String CookieName;
        String CookieValue;

        //open the output
        ServletOutputStream output = response.getOutputStream();
        //set the response type
        response.setContentType("text/html");
        //output the opener
        output.println("<HTML>");
        output.println("<HEAD><TITLE>Cookie View</TITLE></HEAD>");
        output.println("<BODY BGCOLOR=#FFFFFF>");
        if (cookies!=null) {
           for (int i=0; i<cookies.length; i++){
               workCookie=(Cookie)cookies[i].clone();
               CookieName=workCookie.getName();
               CookieValue=workCookie.getValue();
               output.println("Cookie #"+i+":
                       "+CookieName+"="+CookieValue+"<BR>");
           }
        }
        else {
           output.println("No cookies!");
        }
    output.println("</BODY></HTML>");
    output.close();
    }

    public String getServletInfo(){
        return "Cookie Display Servlet";
    }
}
```

After a session of cookie development and servlet exploration, the cookie list might look like Figure 9-8.

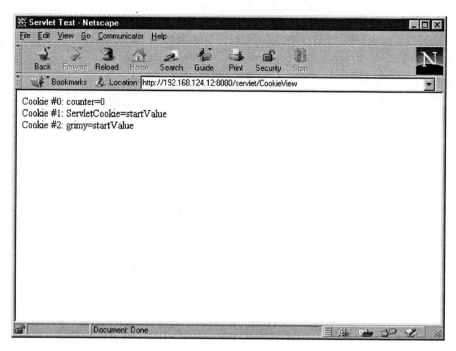

Figure 9-8
Servlet
Cookie Listing

Session Maintenance

In addition to their ability to read and write cookies, the Java Web Server 1.1 and servlets have a sophisticated set of tools for maintaining session status. The session mechanism is flexible enough (with a little effort) to implement URL encoding for users who do not or cannot accept cookies. The Session object can store any Java object that can be kept as a stream, and will store session streams to disk if too many users are connected at once. Sessions will last by default for 30 minutes if there is no user activity.

Sessions are maintained using a set of classes from the `javax.servlet.http` package, and need some administrative setup as well. The Java Web Server 1.1 will enable session tracking by default, but enabling URL rewriting (or encoding, as it frequently known) requires a visit to the administrative server. The **Session Tracking** tab of the **Web Service** control panel has the switch needed to enable URL rewriting, as shown in Figure 9-9. Both sets of radio buttons must be set to **Enabled** for the following examples to work.

Figure 9-9
Enabling Session
Tracking and
URL Rewriting

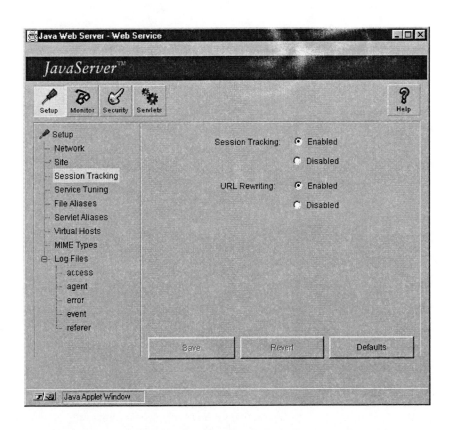

URL Rewriting is turned off by default because it does require more overhead and some duplication of effort. Developers who plan not to use sessions with this server should definitely leave it off. Turning off **Session Tracking** completely will also reduce the number of cookie alerts users receive.

This servlet uses a few of the many tools available to developers using session tracking. Full details of all the methods available are provided in the documentation that comes with the server—check that documentation to make certain that nothing has changed between the beta and the version in current use. The key tool in this project is very simple—the use of the Session object as an associative array. The `session.getValue` and `session.putValue` methods retrieve and enter information in the Session object which be available to future requests made by this user. The Session object itself has a number of properties demonstrated here, which allow developers to determine whether or not the user's browser is accepting cookies, as well as time and date information about the session.

```
import java.io.*;
import java.util.*;
import javax.servlet.*;
import javax.servlet.http.*;
import javax.servlet.http.HttpSession;
import javax.servlet.http.Cookie;

public class sessiondemo extends HttpServlet {

public void init(ServletConfig conf) throws ServletException {
    super.init(conf);
  }

  public void doGet(HttpServletRequest request, HttpServletResponse
        response) throws ServletException, IOException {
    this.handleRequest(request, response);
  }

  public void doPost(HttpServletRequest request, HttpServletResponse
        response) throws ServletException, IOException {
    this.handleRequest(request, response);
  }

  public void handleRequest(HttpServletRequest request,
        HttpServletResponse response) throws ServletException,
        IOException{
    //get the session object
    HttpSession session=request.getSession(true);
    //get the output stream so we can write HTML
    ServletOutputStream output=response.getOutputStream();
    //set the output content type
    response.setContentType("text/html");
    //has this person been here before?  Check counter
    Integer Counter =
(Integer)session.getValue("sessionCount.counter");
    if (Counter==null) {
      Counter = new Integer(1);
    }
    else {
       Counter = new Integer(Counter.intValue() + 1);
    }
    //put the value back in the counter.
    session.putValue("sessionCount.counter",Counter);
    //Write an HTML introduction
    output.println("<HTML><HEAD><TITLE>Session Tracker
            Demonstration</TITLE></HEAD>");
    output.println("<BODY BGCOLOR=#FFFFFF>");
    output.println("<H1>Session Tracking</H1>");
    output.println("<P>This page takes advantage of the Java Web
Server's ability to keep ");
    output.println("session information between visits to a page.
            The session tracking ");
    output.println("can use cookies or URL encoding. If the user
            rejects the cookies or ");
    output.println("is using a browser that won't accept them, a
            properly built servlet ");
    output.println("can take advantage of the JWS to use URL encoding
            instead. The JWS ");
    output.println("handles all the munging, and, given proper
            support, won't cause any ");
```

```
        output.println("problems with other kinds of pages.<P>");

        output.println("<H2>Session-specific Information</H2>");
        output.println("You've been here " + Counter + " times.<BR>");
        output.println("Your session ID is " +
                request.getRequestedSessionId()+"<BR>");
        output.println("Your session ID from the cookie is " +
                request.isRequestedSessionIdFromCookie()+"<BR>");
        output.println("Your session ID from the URL encoding is " +
                request.isRequestedSessionIdFromUrl()+"<BR>");
        output.println("Cookie-supported session: " +
                session.isCookieSupportDetermined()+"<BR>");
        output.println("Your session began at: " +
                new Date(session.getCreationTime())+"<BR>");
        output.println("Your session was last accessed at: " +
                new Date(session.getLastAccessedTime())+"<BR>");
        //encode URL; all URLs in document should receive
        //this treatment.
        output.println("Click <A HREF='"+response.encodeUrl("/servlet/
                sessiondemo")+"'>here</A> to reload the page.");
        output.println("The system will encode your URL if necessary.");
    }
    public String getServletInfo() {
        return "Session demonstration, Java Web Server 1.1";
    }
}
```

The first time users load this page, they are presented with a cookie and the
server also encodes the URL, just in case a user rejects the cookie. The
server is not completely certain of a user's status, as shown in Figure 9-10.

Figure 9-10
A Session Just
Beginning—
Status not yet
Determined

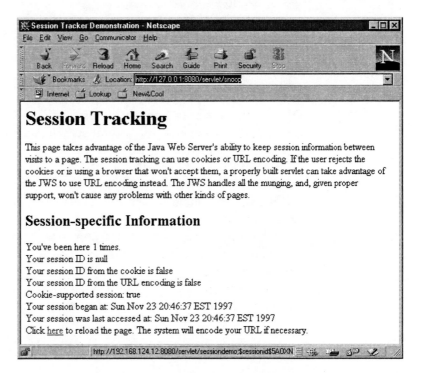

The second time this page is loaded (if the user clicks the **here** at the bottom of the page) the server has received both the cookie and the URL encoding, as shown in Figure 9-11.

Figure 9-11
A Session that
Received both
Cookies and URL
Encoding

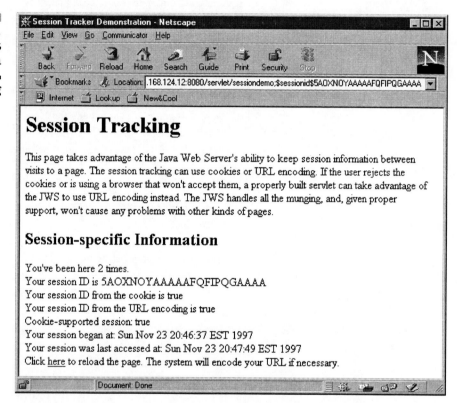

Now that the server knows this user will accept cookies, it no longer encodes URLs; cookies will become its sole means of maintaining state for the session. Clicking on **here** again produces the session information shown in Figure 9-12.

Although the Java Web Server is new, relatively untried technology, it offers a strong complement to the client-side applications Java has previously specialized in. Java is much less friendly than the scripting languages used elsewhere in this book, but has power beyond any of their capacities. (Diehard Perl fans may disagree, of course, but I doubt the legions of JavaScripters and the VBScripters will be too inclined to tout their language's advantages.) Java is a newcomer to state management, but the tools are fresh, reasonably complete, and certainly competitive.

Figure 9-12
Cookie-based
Session,
no Longer
Encoding URLs

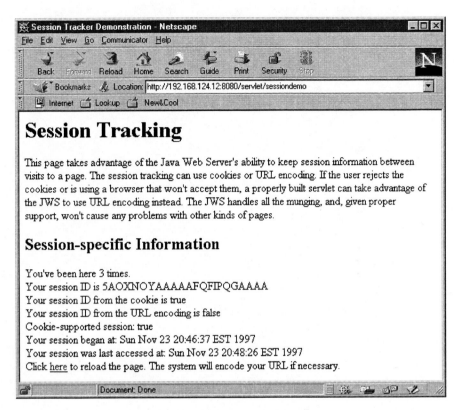

The figure shows a Netscape browser window with the title "Session Tracker Demonstration - Netscape" and the following content:

Session Tracking

This page takes advantage of the Java Web Server's ability to keep session information between visits to a page. The session tracking can use cookies or URL encoding. If the user rejects the cookies or is using a browser that won't accept them, a properly built servlet can take advantage of the JWS to use URL encoding instead. The JWS handles all the munging, and, given proper support, won't cause any problems with other kinds of pages.

Session-specific Information

You've been here 3 times.
Your session ID is 5AOXNOYAAAAAFQFIPQGAAAA
Your session ID from the cookie is true
Your session ID from the URL encoding is false
Cookie-supported session: true
Your session began at: Sun Nov 23 20:46:37 EST 1997
Your session was last accessed at: Sun Nov 23 20:48:26 EST 1997
Click here to reload the page. The system will encode your URL if necessary.

10

Entering the Danger Zone: State Management with Microsoft Site Server

The marketer's dream and the privacy advocate's nightmare meet in many of the tools available as part of Microsoft's Site Server. Site Server is a suite of tools that provide services for large web sites, allowing them to use multiple servers to distribute content, provide community services like voting and conferencing, accept user postings, provide commercial services (in the Enterprise edition), personalize their sites for users, and analyze their usage patterns. The last two services are the ones that make privacy advocates cringe. While personalizing sites can make them more friendly or interesting to the user, the opportunity it provides for data gathering makes possible many of the scenarios that drive users to turn off their cookies completely.

Site Server's tools should be used with caution. Although they give developers great power, that power needs to be used with care and explanation. While the built-in mechanisms of Active Server Pages use cookies, developers need to create their own cookies in order to store data beyond the session. The Microsoft Personalization System (MPS) builds on the tools already available in Active Servers Pages and allows developers easy storage of user data between sessions, with the data linked to the user by a cookie that lasts. Convincing users of the need for the presence of a persistent globally unique ID (GUID) cookie is not always easy, and many sites have yet to apply that cookie to results that clearly benefit the users and not just the site operator. Another of MPS's most controversial features allows developers to create GUIDs that are identical on multiple sites, breaking the rules that prohibit sharing cookie-based information between multiple-domain names. Developers who use this feature, whose setup screen is shown in Figure 10-1, will have much to explain to their users.

Figure 10-1
Assigning a
Master Cookie
Server During
MPS Installation

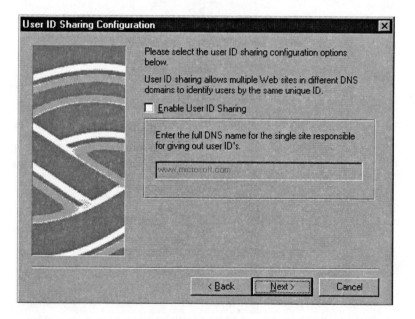

The master cookie server scenario avoids the "third-party server" cookies issue that has arisen with advertising banners. Instead of sending a cookie with a request for a graphic or a part of a page, MPS actually redirects the user to a different server, which checks for a cookie, assigns a cookie if necessary, and redirects the user back to the original server with a message for that server about the cookie set. The original server then assigns a cookie that matches the cookie set by the master server. The result is a set of persistent cookies for different domains, each of which has the same value.

The Commerce Server tools, available in Site Server Enterprise edition, also use persistent cookies to keep track of shopper accounts, affording returning shoppers with convenient access to account information they had provided in previous transactions.

Assembling all the parts that Site Server provides is a difficult task, as we shall see. Composed of an assortment of products from companies bought by Microsoft (notably Interse), Site Server provides a collection of tools rather than the smoothly (or even excessively) integrated experience that Microsoft promotes itself as providing. While a developer could very well use these tools more effectively to gather and analyze user information, the tools are a neglible improvement over those already available for Active Server Pages development. Future versions may, of course, change that.

Despite all these caveats, Site Server and MPS in particular have a lot to offer developers, especially those working on the intranet. Building custom interfaces that address the needs of individual users is easy with these tools, and can in some cases spare developers the need for databases and other costly tools. MPS also works well with authentication systems, allowing them to be used in place of cookies. Developers who need to create sites that present themselves differently to different sets of users will find the tools MPS offers difficult to match, at least for commercial out-of-the-box solutions.

Site Server, especially in the Enterprise edition, makes far greater demands on server hardware and software than do Active Server Pages. Using it requires Intel or Alpha computers running Windows NT Server 4.0, updated with the latest service pack. Microsoft recommends at least 64MB of RAM and a 133Mhz Pentium chip, and the data files produced by MPS and the other Site Server components can rapidly grow enormous on sites with a lot of traffic. While developers can run ASP on Windows 95 machines, using Site Server requires making a considerable investment. Many of Site Server Enterprise's features, like content replication and commerce tools, are for applications that tend to require heavy horsepower anyway. Developers who need to develop sites that use state management but run on smaller (and cheaper) servers should use the Active Server Pages cookie creation and management techniques described in Chapter 8.

From Sessions to Users

While Active Server Pages provide built-in tools for tracking sessions with users, MPS adds to those capabilities with tools for tracking users. The greatest change is that cookies created by MPS are persistent, while those used to maintain Session objects are transient, expiring at the end of the user's browser session. Developers can still use the Session object in their ASP development, taking advantage of its ability to store more kinds of information and destroy that information at the end of the browser session, and avoiding the potential cost of storing large amounts of user data on the server. Still, many of the Session object's uses are more effectively performed by the MPS PropertyDatabase server component.

By default, the PropertyDatabase server component relies on a persistent cookie to connect the personalization information that it stores to a particular user. The server may seem to bombard the user with cookies at first, but after a visit it will settle down, much the way that Active Server Pages stop sending cookies once they have determined that a cookie has been set. The cookie setting begins when an instance of the `MPS.PropertyDatabase` component is created by an Active Server Page.

```
<% set upd =Server.CreateObject("MPS.PropertyDatabase") %>
```

Remember, creating an instance of an object or control in VBScript requires the use of the set statement, and failing to use one will cause an error. JavaScript does not require a set statement.

When the User Property Database component is initialized, it turns on buffering. When Active Server Pages are buffered, nothing is returned to the client's browser until the entire program has finished executing or has stopped because of an error. This allows developers to set headers anywhere in the document. For this to work, the set statement must appear before any HTML is written to the page. Response.buffer=TRUE does the same thing.

Setting the cookie is a two-step process—the MPS server will send a temporary cookie to test the waters, and then set a permanent cookie once it learns if the first cookie has been accepted. For most sites, this will involve an entryway that makes an empty call to an MPS component to set the temporary cookie before the user moves into areas that contain personalized information. Pages that need to use user ID information immediately can give users who are not yet "registered" a redirect response, sending them either to the same page again (which fulfills the need for two requests) or to a registration page (which allows the site to collect more information.) The code below can perform either of those functions.

```
<% redirection=Request.ServerVariables("SCRIPT_NAME")
   'change the value of redirection to a
   'registration page if preferred
   set upd=Server.CreateObject("MPS.PropertyDatabase")
   'check for value for PrevVisit
   if upd("PrevVisit") <> "TRUE" then
      upd("PrevVisit") = "TRUE"
      Response.redirect(redirection)
   end if %>
```

Redirecting users who are rejecting cookies to the same page can set up a loop where the server sends cookies, the user refuses them, and the server tries again. Except in situations where the developer can count on users accepting cookies (generally intranets), this technique should be avoided. Sending users to other pages keeps the loop from developing and keeps cookie rejectors from getting strange delays and pages that will not load at all.

Once the cookie has been set, using the MPS User Property Database (UPD) is much like using the ASP Session object. The syntax for the MPS database is similar to that used for the Session object to store values. There are some limitations, however. The UPD cannot hold arrays (directly) or objects, though there are several tools for storing the values in an array. Effectively, the UPD holds a large number of name-value pairs related to a particular user, all of which are kept on the server and connected to the user by the GUID cookie stored in the user's browser. Apart from the fact that the information is stored on the server, providing some security, as well as avoiding transfer time and a barrage of cookies, the UPD provides functionality very similar to that of a large set of persistent cookies.

The UPD is not a relational database. When MPS is installed, it requests a directory (on a file server, not just a drive) to which it can store its personalization data. The installation program creates 1,000 folders in which MPS will store personalization information in separate files, one per user. While this hashing may yield some economies for the MPS system itself, it makes it fairly difficult to gather the information and store it in a central database for exploration. Developers who need to gather information in a more structured form will probably need to use the database connectivity resources explored in Chapter 8, at least until Microsoft builds a more complete system for analyzing this information. Perhaps the most significant piece of this puzzle is the GUID which MPS-enabled pages will stamp on users, allowing information to be stored to a database with a unique key for analysis. Combined with the system's ability to stamp users with the same GUID for multiple sites, this aspect of Site Server's technology, not the simple storage of information on the server, provides the real threat to privacy. Using the same GUID and Active Server Pages' database connectivity makes it very easy for multiple sites to store information in a centralized database, combining a wide variety of pieces. Companies that run multiple sites providing different services can use this function to combine information on a wide variety of topics into a single centralized dossier.

Multiple Sites, Same Cookies

Microsoft, with its main company site, MSN, Expedia, Carpoint, Sidewalk, MSNBC, and a variety of other ventures, seems a prime company to take advantage of its own tool. In fact, reading my cookie files today (12/5/97) seems to indicate that they are indeed using it.

```
.microsoft.com      TRUE /    FALSE937422025 MC1
GUID=5b4218ea6dc211d188a908002bb74f65

.msn.com            TRUE /    FALSE912902249 MC1
GUID=5B4218E66DC211D188A908002BB74F65

.msnbc.com          TRUE /    FALSE937396832 MC1
GUID=5b4218e66dc211d188a908002bb74f65

.slate.com          TRUE /    FALSE937396834 MC1
GUID=5b4218e66dc211d188a908002bb74f65
```

The coincidence of cookie values (the first of which is in fact slightly different) does not yet mean that Microsoft is up to something devious; it does, however, mean that they are actively using Site Server's ability to assign the same user ID through master cookie servers that serve multiple domains.

The User Properties Database Object has a number of properties (shown in Table 10-1) and methods (shown in Table 10-2) that developers can use to add information to and read information from the UPD. The ID property and the Item method are the two key tools employed throughout this chapter.

Table 10-1 Properties of the User Properties Database Object	Property	Use
	Defaults	Allows developers to set default values for a number of user properties stored in the UPD with a single URL encoded list of name/value pairs; returns an error if used after a value has already been set. If a UPD value will be critical to the layout of a page, make certain to set a default.
	ID	Stores the current user ID; may be set explicitly to change the ID of the current user or to expose information maintained by another user
	ReadOnly	ReadOnly is FALSE by default. Setting it to TRUE will improve performance, but bar the program from writing to the UPD.
	PropertyString	A read-only value that contains all of the currently set user properties in a single URL-encoded string

Table 10-2 Methods of the User Properties Database Object	Method	Use
	LoadFromString	Loads a series of values from a URL-encoded string
	Item	Retrieves the value of the user property whose name is provided as the argument; (using Item is optional—upd.item("myProp") and upd("myProp") are treated the same way)

Using these methods and properties to manipulate UPD information is much simpler than reading and writing values in a relational database. Instead of making complex SQL calls and managing recordsets, developers can use the simpler associative arrays provided by the UPD to keep track of information.

The Default property appears to be useful only when a database is first opened. As soon as a UPD value has been set or referenced, the Default property becomes unavailable and will return an error. If values need to be set after the UPD has been referenced, the LoadFromString() method is a better option. Defaults can be useful for establishing a base set of values when a new user arrives, using a single URL-encoded string to set multiple values simultaneously. For instance, upd.defaults="cookies= tasty&needmilk=yes" would provide a default value of tasty for upd(cookies) and yes for upd(needmilk).

The ID property allows the script to set and retrieve the user's ID. This is most useful for exposing UPD values to multiple users, and will be covered in greater depth below. The ReadOnly property is a useful tool for accelerating programs that only read from the UPD—setting it to TRUE will reduce the amount of overhead MPS imposes on transactions. Finally, the PropertyString property contains all of the name-value pairs of this user's UPD in URL-encoded form, which makes it easy to put all of the values in a URL query string for processing by a script.

The UPD's LoadFromString method is useful for setting a large number of UPD values at a single stroke. It accepts a URL-encoded string as its argument, and, like the Default property above, breaks it down into name-value pairs. Unlike Defaults, LoadFromString can be used at any time on a UPD; the values set will override any current values. Query strings returned from forms can be processed in bulk using LoadFromString, though the personalization example below will demonstrate some of its limitations as well.

The Item method is constantly used but rarely written out. The Item method allows developers to set and retrieve values corresponding to a name, but can be abbreviated. For instance both of the following references will return the same value:

```
upd.item("myName")
upd("myName")
```

The results of the Item method have their own set of properties, shown in Table 10-3, which make it easy to determine if an item has no value, one value, or multiple values, and to manipulate multiple values.

	Method	Use
Table 10-3 Properties of UPD Items	Count	Returns the number of values held in a UPD item; empty items return 0, single-value items return 1, and multi-value items return the number of values included in the item.
	Append	Adds a value to a multi-value UPD item
	Remove	Removes a value from a multi-value UPD item
	Item	Retrieves the value of a multi-value UPD item; like the Item property of the UPD itself, Item is optional. upd.item("myProp").item(3) is treated the same as upd("MyProp")(3)

Multi-valued UPD items aren't quite like arrays. They can be read much like arrays, but their shape can change regularly, and the items inside of them will shift as values are appended and removed. It is generally a bad idea to assume that the values in a multi-value item will always stay at the same position in situations where any values are being removed or appended. The multiple values of the items should always be addressed by number; they have no separate names.

Creating a new multi-value item is the same as creating a single-value item, except that additional values may be added with the Append method. For example, the following code creates a multi-value item named "multival" containing the values "first", "second", and "third".

```
'Clear the variable to avoid appending to old values
upd("multival")=Empty
'Append values to the variable to create array
upd("multival").append("first")
upd("multival").append("second")
upd("multival").append("third")
```

At this point, upd("multival").count would return three. The value of upd("multival")(1) is "first", and upd("multival")(2) is "second". If the program then called upd("multival").Remove(2), however, upd("multival")(1) would remain "first", upd("multival")(2) would be "third"—as the value slid to the second position—and upd("multival")(3) would return an undefined value. A call to upd("multival").count would return two. Append calls add their arguments to the end of the value list, and Remove calls pull them out of the list, reducing the count by one and shifting all values down so that no emptied value leaves behind a gap.

The Dangers of Caching

Microsoft takes extra pains to point out a particular danger of using personalized Web pages—users behind proxy servers may end up seeing each other's personal information. If a proxy server caches a page with information meant for one user and a different user coming through the same proxy server requests that same URL, the proxy server will probably feed the second user the information it has received for the first. While this strategy works very well for static Web pages, it causes problems for dynamic pages, especially pages that contain potentially private information.

There are two solutions to this problem. The better solution, if developers can count on their users' proxy servers and browsers to support HTTP 1.1, is to add the following script:

```
<% Response.AddHeader("Cache-Control", "private")
   Response.Expires=30 %>
```

continued

This tells the browser to cache the page for up to 30 minutes, reducing repetitive downloads, while preventing proxy servers from caching the page at all, protecting it from being inadvertently shared. The other solution, which is more drastic but more commonly used, is to keep the page from being cached at all. This has the advantage of working with HTTP 1.0 as well as HTTP 1.1, and will probably be the recommended solution until HTTP 1.1 becomes dominant.

```
<% Response.Expires=0 %>
```

Especially for commercial sites, developers should make certain not to slip on cache control. Buyers will probably be extraordinarily unhappy if they get someone else's invoice at the end of a transaction, even if their order was processed correctly otherwise.

Personalizing a Site

The Microsoft Personalization System is an excellent tool for creating personalized sites. An ISP or a content provider can give users access to their own personalized pages with a minimum of effort. This example demonstrates using the UPD to store basic information like username and location, preferred background and text colors, a set of files to be displayed on the page, and a set of links chosen by the user for inclusion on the page. Connecting the fine grain of information that can be collected through the UPD to the volumes of data that can be stored on the server makes it possible to build personalized information systems from a set of components.

The site includes two pages, plus a number of files—one page displays the personalized information, and one page provides the registration and personalization services. The display page is actually the index page for the site, but it redirects users to the personalization page if they have not visited before or are not currently submitting personalization information. The registration page is a form that collects the current personalization settings from the UPD, sets defaults if necessary, and passes the new settings to the display page for implementation. Despite the intertwining of the two pages, the registration page is the logical place to start, as it sets the stage for the display page.

The first thing the registration page (`register.asp`) does is check to see if users have previously established personalization settings. If they have not, it sets defaults with the `LoadFromString` method. (The Default property can only be used when the database has just been created)

```
<% set upd =Server.CreateObject("MPS.PropertyDatabase")
   bgcolor=upd("bgColor")
   if bgColor="" then
   'set default values
upd.LoadFromString("name=Guest&bgColor=white&txtColor=black&news=
   on&sports=on&weather=on&target1=Netscape&link1=www.netscape.
   com&target2=Microsoft&link2=www.microsoft.com&target3=IBM&link3=
   www.ibm.com")
   end if
%>
```

The remainder of the page is a form that uses this information for defaults and collects additional information from the user:

```
<HTML>
<HEAD><TITLE>Personalize your page!</TITLE></HEAD>
<BODY BGCOLOR=#FFFFFF>
<H2>Personalize Your Page!</H2>
<P>Welcome to the Cookie Network's Page Personalization Demonstration.
With only two Active Server Pages, we can build you a slightly
customized page that will greet you each time you visit.
<FORM ACTION="display.asp" METHOD=GET>
<P>Background Color:
<SELECT NAME="bgColor">
<OPTION SELECTED>White
<OPTION>Black
<OPTION>Red
<OPTION>Green
<OPTION>Blue
<OPTION>Yellow
<OPTION>Orange
<OPTION>Brown
</SELECT></P>
<P>Text Color:
<SELECT NAME="txtColor">
<OPTION>White
<OPTION SELECTED>Black
<OPTION>Red
<OPTION>Green
<OPTION>Blue
<OPTION>Yellow
<OPTION>Orange
<OPTION>Brown
</SELECT></P>
<P>Show News:<INPUT TYPE="CHECKBOX" NAME="news"
<% if upd("news")="on" then%>CHECKED<% end if %>><BR>
Show Sports:<INPUT TYPE="CHECKBOX" NAME="sports" <% if
upd("sports")="on" then%>CHECKED<% end if %>><BR>
Show Weather:<INPUT TYPE="CHECKBOX" NAME="weather"
<% if upd("weather")="on" then%>CHECKED<% end if %>></P>
<P>Links:<BR>
<% for count=1 to 3
   TargetName="target"&count%>
Link #<%=count%>:<INPUT TYPE="TEXT" VALUE="<%=upd("target"&count)%>"
   NAME="target<%=count%>">
<INPUT TYPE="TEXT" VALUE="<%=upd("link"&count)%>"
          NAME="link<%=count%>">
```

```
<BR>
<% next %>
<INPUT TYPE="SUBMIT" VALUE="Personalize">
</FORM>
</BODY></HTML>
```

The display page (`display.asp`) applies this information. When it first loads, it checks to see if a query string is present. If one is available, it sets the values of the UPD entry for this user to the values in the query string. Note the explicit assignment of the checkbox variables, needed to compensate for the way browsers fail to report unchecked checkboxes. If there is no query string and no `bgcolor` value (a new user), the display page redirects the user to the registration page.

```
<% set upd =Server.CreateObject("MPS.PropertyDatabase")
   ValueString=Request.QueryString
   'checks to make sure no one overloads
   'query string to crash ASP.
   if len(ValueString)>600 then ValueString=""
   if ValueString<>"" then
      upd.LoadFromString(ValueString)
      'compensate for non-reporting of checkboxes
      upd("news")=Request.QueryString("news")
      upd("sports")=Request.QueryString("sports")
      upd("weather")=Request.QueryString("weather")
   end if
   'if still no bgcolor value, redirect
   if upd("bgColor")="" then
       Response.redirect("register.asp")
   end if
   %>
<HTML>
<HEAD><TITLE>Personalized Page</TITLE></HEAD>
<BODY BGCOLOR="<%=upd("bgColor")%>" TEXT="<%=upd("txtColor")%>">
<P>This is your page. Your colors, your content.</P>
<!--Only displays included files if appropriate -->
<% if upd("news")="on" then%>
<!--#include file="news.inc"-->
<% end if
   if upd("sports")="on" then%>
<!--#include file="sports.inc"-->
<% end if
   if upd("weather")="on" then%>
<!--#include file="weather.inc"-->
<% end if %>
<P>Your links:</P>
<% for count=1 to 3 %>
<A HREF = "http://<%= upd("link"&count) %>"><%=
        upd("target"&count)%></A><BR>
<% next %>
<A HREF="register.asp">Change your personalization settings.</A>
</BODY></HTML>
```

The server will parse the server-side includes whether or not they are necessary, adding to overhead. Because IIS parses all includes without determining whether or not they will be necessary, there is no way around this at present. The includes will, of course, be dropped from the file sent to the user's browser if they have unchecked the box for that section.

Because all this runs on the server, it can be used reliably with any browser that accepts cookies and supports forms and colors. Figures 10-2 and 10-3 show what the registration screen and display page look like on a Macintosh running Internet Explorer 3.0; Figure 10-4 shows the display page on a Windows 95 version of Netscape Navigator.

Figure 10-2
Registration Screen, Macintosh Internet Explorer

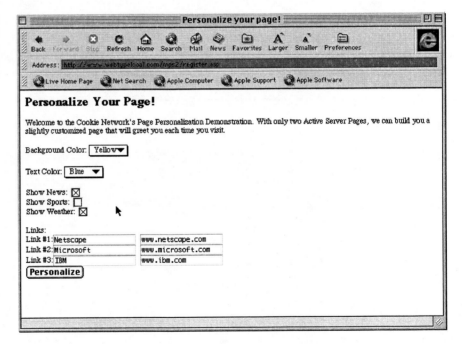

Most simple uses of MPS will take advantage of a combination of forms and the UPD to create pages that meet user needs. More sophisticated applications can update values in the UPD to reflect the pages the user has visited and mark sites of interest; the link values, for instance, can be changed anywhere in the site. The UPD provides a useful set of tools for simple personalization applications.

Figure 10-3
Display Screen,
Macintosh
Internet Explorer

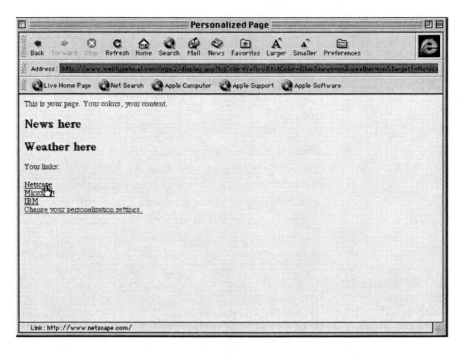

Figure 10-4
Display Screen,
Windows 95
Netscape
Communicator

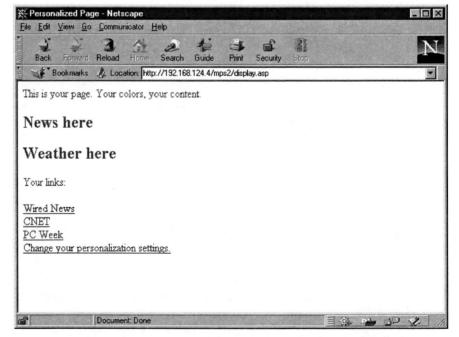

Rebuilding the Maze

Using the MPS makes creating simple border-control applications much easier. Instead of calling out to an external database for persistent storage, the developer can just store values in the UPD. Instead of making complex ODBC calls with SQL, a program can just refer to the UPD to find out whether or not a user is permitted in a particular area. The maze example presented in previous chapters becomes extremely easy to implement when the UPD is used instead of a database. The `global.asa` file can remain blank, and the code used is far simpler. The frontdoor page still exists to support the Microsoft Personalization System's need for two hits before settling down to work with a new user, but overall the architecture has been much simplified.

The new `frontdoor.asp` file checks to see if users have visited before. If they have not, it locks all the doors. No calls to databases or processing of recordsets is required:

```
<% set upd=Server.CreateObject("MPS.PropertyDatabase")
    if upd("MazeVisit") <> "TRUE" then
        upd("MazeVisit") = "TRUE"
        upd("m1")="unlocked"
        for i=2 to 9
        room="m" & i
        upd(room)="locked"
        next
    end if %>
<HTML>
<HEAD><TITLE>Personal Information Collection</TITLE></HEAD>
<BODY BGCOLOR=#FFFFFF>
<FORM ACTION="InfoSubmit.asp" METHOD="GET">
Your Name: <INPUT TYPE="Text" NAME="UserName" SIZE=25 VALUE="<%=
upd("UserName")%>" ><BR>
<INPUT TYPE="SUBMIT" VALUE="Submit information">
</FORM>
</BODY></HTML>
```

The `InfoSubmit.asp` page adds the username to the UPD if necessary, and welcomes users to the maze:

```
<%set upd=Server.CreateObject("MPS.PropertyDatabase")%>
<!-- #include file="redirect.inc" -->
<%
upd("UserName")=Request.QueryString("UserName")
 %>
<HTML>
<HEAD><TITLE>Thank you for joining.</TITLE></HEAD>
<BODY BGCOLOR="#FFFFFF">
<P>Hello, <%= upd("UserName") %></P>
<P>Enter the <A HREF="maze1.asp">Maze</A>.
</BODY></HTML>
```

Note the inclusion of `redirect.inc` at the top of the page. This file includes code that will be used on all of the maze pages to check for new visitors and send them to the `frontdoor.asp` file so they can be properly outfitted for their explorations:

```
<%
    redirection="frontDoor.asp"
    if upd("MazeVisit") <> "TRUE" then
    Response.redirect(redirection)
    end if
%>
```

 Make very certain not to include multiple assignments of the same variable name to the `MPS.PropertyDatabase` control. ASP pages will return strange errors; my test server locked up and would not respond to requests after several hits on a page with that error. The easiest way to avoid this is to make all UPD assigments in the main page, performing only processing in the included files.

The maze pages themselves remain extremely simple, as shown in `maze1.asp`:

```
<% Page=1
    Unlock=7
    Connect1=6
    Connect2=7
    Connect3=8
%>
set upd=Server.CreateObject("MPS.PropertyDatabase")
<!--#include file="mazeCode.inc"-->
```

The code used to run the maze now uses the UPD values rather than session values to handle the unlocking of doors:

```
<%
set upd=Server.CreateObject("MPS.PropertyDatabase")
permissions=upd.item("m" & page)
if permissions<>"unlocked" then
    Response.Write("I'm sorry, but you don't have that key.<BR>")
    Response.Write("You can go back to the
            <A HREF='maze1.asp'>beginning</A> if you like.")
else
    Response.Write("<P>Welcome to room #" & Page &".</P>")
    permissionNew=upd("m" & unlock)
    if permissionNew<>"unlocked" then
        Response.Write("<P>You now have key #" & unlock &".</P>")
    end if
    upd("m" & unlock)="unlocked"
    Response.Write("<P>From here you may visit:</P>")
```

```
Response.Write("<A HREF='maze" & Connect1 &".asp'>Room Number "
        & Connect1 & "</A><BR>")
Response.Write("<A HREF='maze" & Connect2 &".asp'>Room Number "
        & Connect2 & "</A><BR>")
Response.Write("<A HREF='maze" & Connect3 &".asp'>Room Number "
        & Connect3 & "</A><BR>")
Response.Write("<P>Frustrated? <A HREF='quit.asp'>Quit</A> and
        come back later.</P>")
end if
%>
```

The winning page is a little more complex than the rest of the maze pages, because it behaves differently:

```
<% Page=9
    set upd=Server.CreateObject("MPS.PropertyDatabase")
    permission=upd("m" & page)
    if permission<>"unlocked" then %>
I'm sorry, but you don't have that key.<BR>
You can go back to the <A HREF='maze1.asp'>beginning</A> if you like.
<% else %>
<HTML>
<HEAD><TITLE>Congratulations!</TITLE></HEAD>
<BODY BGCOLOR=#FFFFFF>
<P>You found all the keys!</P>
<P>To leave the maze, <A HREF="quit.asp">quit</A>.</P>
</BODY></HTML>
<% end if %>
```

The greatest improvements, however, are in the global.asa and quit.asp files. The global.asa file can in fact be left blank! (A token call to the Session object will turn off the flood of ASPSESSION cookies, but is not necessary to the operation of the maze.) Instead of writing out records to the database, the quit.asp file is simple HTML, and could even be renamed quit.htm:

```
<HTML>
<HEAD><TITLE>Come back again!</TITLE></HEAD>
<BODY BGCOLOR=#FFFFFF>
<P>All your permissions will be kept for your next visit.</P>
<P>Thank you for participating.</P>
</BODY></HTML>
```

This much simpler version of the maze behaves the same way as and looks identical to that presented in Chapter 8, with similar checks at every move between pages. Still, because it avoids the complications of the database solution for persistent storage, it manages to remain far more readable and easier to implement. This version uses a naming convention for multiple items; a single item can also contain multiple values if a developer finds that more flexible in a given situation. MPS is simple, relatively easy to use, and quite reliable when users and developers are cooperative.

There are a few disadvantages to this approach to border control. The most important is that it is difficult to create a central management platform for user permissions. With the database/Session object combination, the values were still stored in a centralized, easily manipulated relational database. If an administrator wants to give a particular user access to an area of the site, he just looks up the user in the database and modifies the privileges. Building tools that do this quickly and easily is not difficult. Creating tools that do this with the UPD is more complex, as the data from users is spread out in unmarked files in 1,000 folders. Given a database that stores GUIDs and some basic information about the users, the permissions can be administered through ASP, but the task is still complicated rather than simplified by the use of the UPD. The UPD is good for casual use, where users can be trusted to run their own show, but not as useful in more structured situations. Still, as the next section will demonstrate, the UPD can be harnessed to a database, making it possible to share information and store it in a structured way..

Connecting to a Database—
Sharing Personalized Information

Connecting the UPD to a database opens up a whole new set of possibilities, transforming personalization information into public information or at least easily used information. Before the UPD, Active Server Pages that needed to store large chunks of information persistently could either load it all into cookies or store it in a database. As the maze example demonstrates, that is no longer necessary. Database connections are still important, however, for any use of the personalization information that goes beyond customizing pages during a session with a particular user. Pouring the UPD information—even if only the user ID—into a database makes it possible to analyze, interpret, and appropriate the information without having to comb through thousands of files to get it.

For a company building an intranet, this could provide a simple way to create a directory for information that is public but does not normally get stored in directory structures. In this example, a `Connection` site wants to allow users to register a Web site they've created and allow others to explore these sites on a person-by-person basis.

If you plan to make UPD data public, make certain that users are aware of this before they find their data open to the world. Most users at this point in the Web's development assume that the information they provide to a site is visible to the owners of that site, but don't expect to see it posted where the whole world can see it. Full disclosure of the intentions of a site collecting data is always a good idea, but in these situations it is even more important.

The first page to build is the registration page, register.asp. Although users will enter through the welcome.asp page, it will redirect new users to the registration page. The registration page is a form that collects the user's first name, and last name, and the address of a Web site the user would like to make public. The registration page uses the UPD to supply defaults if a previously registered user is revisiting the page to make changes.

```
<%set upd = Server.CreateObject("MPS.PropertyDatabase")
%>
<HTML>
<HEAD>
<TITLE>Register for the Connection!</TITLE>
</HEAD>
<BODY BGCOLOR=#FFFFFF>
<P>Register here for the Connection, the easy way to show off and
share your skills. At the Connection, you provide links to a web site
you've created. All information is open to the public.</P>
<FORM ACTION="welcome.asp" METHOD="GET">
First Name:<INPUT TYPE=TEXT NAME="FirstName" SIZE=50
VALUE=<%=upd("FirstName")%>><BR>
Last Name:<INPUT TYPE=TEXT NAME="LastName" SIZE=50 VALUE=<%=
            upd("LastName")%>><BR>
Personal Web Site Name: http://<INPUT TYPE=TEXT NAME="SiteAddr"
            SIZE=100 VALUE=<%=upd("SiteAddr")%>><BR>
<INPUT TYPE="SUBMIT" VALUE="Submit">
</FORM>
</BODY></HTML>
```

The welcome page handles several tasks. First, it checks to see if the user has submitted information from the registration form. If so, it adds the first and last names (but not other information) to the database. Next, it checks to see if the user is properly registered. If not, the user is sent back to the registration form. Finally, the page displays the Welcome message and invites the user to explore the site.

```
<!-- #include virtual="/ASPSAMP/SAMPLES/ADOVBS.INC" -->
<% set upd =Server.CreateObject("MPS.PropertyDatabase")
    FirstName=upd("FirstName")
    ValueString=Request.QueryString
    if len(ValueString)>600 then ValueString=""
    if ValueString<>"" then
        upd.LoadFromString(ValueString)
        set DataObj=Server.CreateObject("ADODB.Connection")
        'Choose a Mode - in this case, read and write.
        DataObj.Mode=adModeReadWrite
        'Open the System DSN
        DataObj.Open "ASPtest"
        'Delete any previous records
```

```
        SQLtext="DELETE Registration.GlobalUID FROM Registration WHERE
                (((Registration.GlobalUID)='" & upd.ID & "'));"
        DataObj.Execute SQLtext, numChanged, adCmdText
        'Add a new record
        SQLtext="INSERT INTO Registration
(GlobalUID,FirstName,LastName) VALUES ('" & upd.ID &"','" &
            upd("FirstName") & "','" & upd("LastName") &"')"
DataObj.Execute SQLtext, numChanged, adCmdText

        'Close the database connection
        DataObj.Close

    end if
    if upd("FirstName")="" then Response.redirect("register.asp")
    %>
<HTML>
<HEAD><TITLE>Welcome to the Connection!</TITLE></HEAD>
<BODY BGCOLOR=#FFFFFF>
<H2>The Connection</H2>
<P>Welcome to the Connection, <%=upd("FirstName") & " " &
upd("LastName")%>. At the Connection, we use an ID cookie to keep
track of your identity. On the <A HREF="register.asp">registration
page</A>, you can provide a public web site location that others
can see. </P>
<P>Remember - <EM>other people can see anything you enter on this
                site!</EM></P>
<P>From here, you may:<BR>
<A HREF="search.asp">Search the directory</A><BR>
<A HREF="http://<%=upd("SiteAddr")%>">Visit your current site</A><BR>
<A HREF="register.asp">Change your entry</A><BR>
</BODY></HTML>
```

Developers who use Access for their back end should avoid naming their ID field GUID. Access appears to use this name internally and making references to it can produce mysterious errors. If you really need to use GUID, make certain to enclose the name in brackets—[GUID] instead of GUID—in all SQL calls.

The directory page (search.asp) checks to make sure the user is registered. If so, it brings up a list of all users from the database, using each user's ID value as a query string for the view page to use. The listing requires a call to an outside database because the UPD provides no facilities for looping through its potentially enormous list of users.

```
<!-- #include virtual="/ASPSAMP/SAMPLES/ADOVBS.INC" -->
<%      set upd = Server.CreateObject("MPS.PropertyDatabase")
        if upd("FirstName")="" then Response.redirect("register.asp")%>
<HTML>
<HEAD><TITLE>Directory</TITLE>
<BODY BGCOLOR=#FFFFFF>
<P>Explore the sites of the users below!</P>
<%
```

```
            'Create Data Access object
             set DataObj=Server.CreateObject("ADODB.Connection")
             set RcdSetObj=Server.CreateObject("ADODB.Recordset")
            'Choose a Mode - in this case, read and write.
             DataObj.Mode=adModeReadWrite
            'Open the System DSN
             DataObj.Open "ASPtest"
            'Get all records
             SQLtext="SELECT Registration.GlobalUID, Registration.LastName,
                     Registration.FirstName FROM Registration ORDER BY
                     Registration.LastName, Registration.FirstName;"
             RcdSetObj.Open SQLText, DataObj, adOpenKeySet, adCmdText

             do until RcdSetObj.EOF
    %>
    <A HREF="view.asp?<%=RcdSetObj("GlobalUID")%>"><%=
         RcdSetObj("FirstName")%> <%=RcdSetObj("LastName")%><BR>

    <%       RcdSetObj.MoveNext
             Loop

            'Close the database connection
             DataObj.Close
        %>
    <P><A HREF="welcome.asp">Return to the Welcome page.</A></P>
    </BODY></HTML>
```

The view page uses only the UPD ID value in the query string, making no reference at all to the relational database. The page displays the information contained in the directory on this particular user; more information could certainly be added. The use of the ID property, not the user viewing the page, sets the viewupd object to display the chosen user's information. This property must be set before any values are referenced. Changing this ID value does not modify any cookies sent to the viewing user or change the ID—it only changes which UPD entries will be displayed.

```
<% set viewupd =Server.CreateObject("MPS.PropertyDatabase")
   viewupd.ID=Request.QueryString
   if viewupd("FirstName")="" then Response.redirect("welcome.asp")
%>
<HTML>
<HEAD><TITLE>Information for <%=viewupd("FirstName")%> <%=viewupd
      ("LastName")%></TITLE></HEAD>
<BODY BGCOLOR=#FFFFFF>
<H2><%=viewupd("FirstName")%> <%=viewupd("LastName")%></H2>
<P>You can visit <%=viewupd("FirstName")%> <%=viewupd
      ("LastName")%>'s web site at:<BR>
<A HREF="http://<%=viewupd("SiteAddr")%>"><%=viewupd("SiteAddr")%>
      </A></P>
<P><A HREF="welcome.asp">Return to the top level</A> | <A
         HREF="search.asp">Return to the directory</A></P>
</BODY></HTML>
```

A user's first visit leads to the registration page, shown in Figure 10-5. After that form is filled out, the user receives the welcome shown in Figure 10-6.

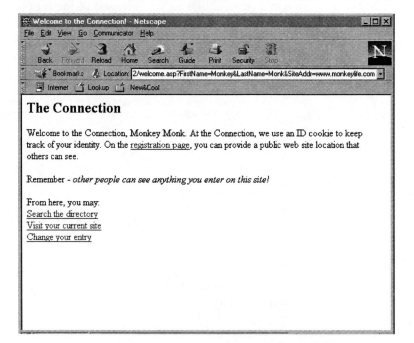

Figure 10-5
Registering for
the Connection

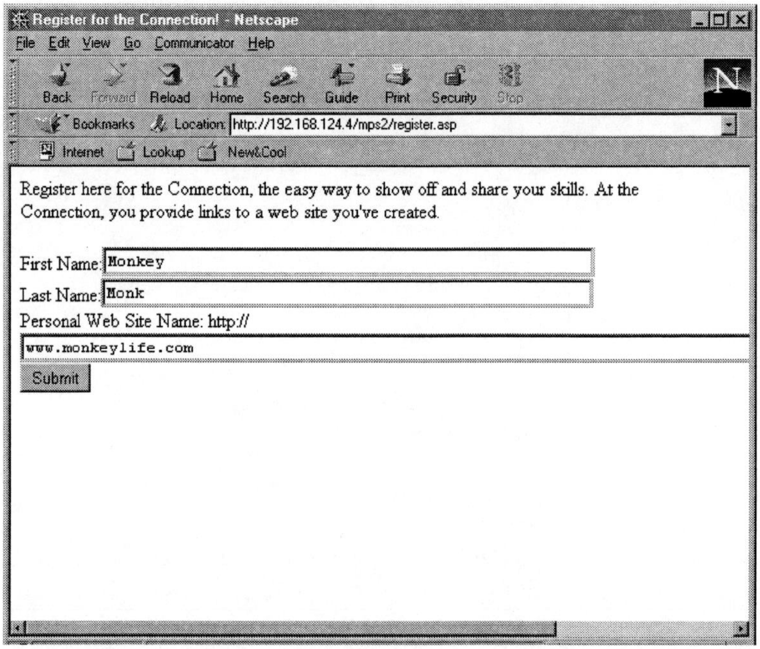

Figure 10-6
Welcome to the
Connection

If a user clicks on **Search the Directory**, a list of all registered users, will appear, as shown in Figure 10-7. All user links are to the same page, `view.asp`, but contain different query strings identifying the user whose information should be displayed as shown in Figure 10-8.

Figure 10-7
The Directory

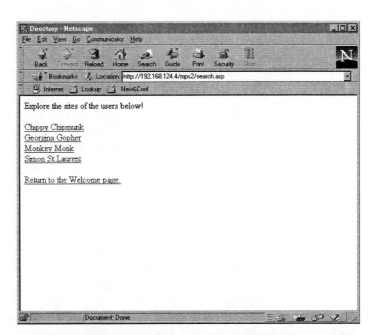

Figure 10-8
Viewing
Another User's
Information

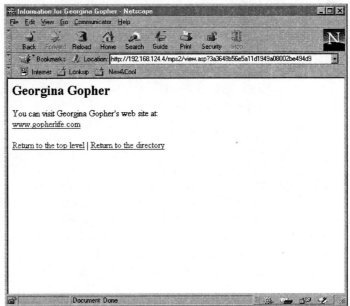

Connecting the UPD to a database is not very difficult, though it also is not automatic. A good rule for developers creating public data sites like the one above is to store in the database only the information needed for the directory search avoiding unnecessary duplication of information between the UPD and the database. Of course, marketers who want to analyze all the information they can collect are probably going to put every bit of information they can into the relational database. Because all the Active Server Page code runs on the server, it is not (except by accident) available to users. As a result, there is no way to tell what the owners do with information submitted to a site that uses the Microsoft Personalization System. The information may stay in the relatively inaccessible but speedy UPD, or it may be stored in a relational database and conglomerated with thousands of other records and log files to create demographic snapshots of users visiting the site.

IDs and Usage Analyst

Following a user through a site is no longer a matter of interpreting IP addresses and visit times to estimate user paths, or manually logging visits to a database; instead, analysis software, like the Usage Analyst included with Site Server, can collect user identity information directly through the log. Usage Analyst is a sprawling program that imports log files into relational databases (Access or SQL Server) and provides a set of analysis tools. The details of how to operate Usage Analyst's three modules and its variety of reports (which can be customized in the Enterprise edition) deserve their own book. This section examines only the relatively small parts of Usage Analyst that take use cookies. Because IIS 4.0 does a much better job of integrating these parts and allowing developers to log cookies, the discussion focuses on IIS 4.0, which includes Usage Analyst in the Site Server Express package.

Although the documentation that comes with Microsoft Personalization Server suggests that it enhances the IIS log to include MPS user GUIDs, the readme file indicates that this is not the case. Making IIS 3.0 keep track of cookies in the log requires downloading the hyperext_log.dll (or mss_log.dll) file from Microsoft, modifying a series of registry entries, and restarting the server. Usage Analyst will supply its own different cookie to the user to track them. Details are provided in the Usage Analyst readme file. Note also that this file is only available for Intel machines; Alpha server administrators should use IIS 4.0's built-in abilities to generate logs that show cookies.

Creating a log that includes cookies is easy in IIS 4.0. Open the Internet Services Management console and find the list of servers, shown in Figure 10-9.

Figure 10-9
Internet Services
Manager, IIS 4.0

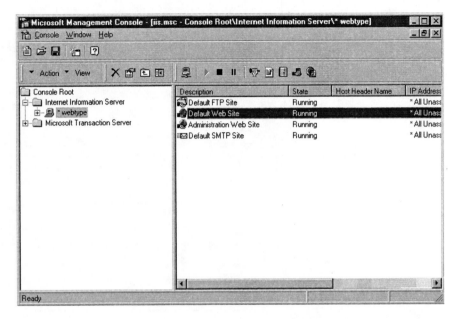

Right-click on the **Default Server** (or the particular server you need to customize) and select **Properties**. In the Properties box, the **Web site** tab will include a list of logging formats, shown in Figure 10-10. Select **W3C Extended Log File Format** and click the **Properties** button.

In the tabs that appear, select **Extended Properties**. This tab offers a wide variety of logging possibilities, shown in Figure 10-11.

What Microsoft calls the **W3C Extended Log File Format** is based on a W3C working draft dated March 23, 1996. It is not a W3C recommendation. The specification is available at **http://www.w3.org/TR/WD-logfile. html**.

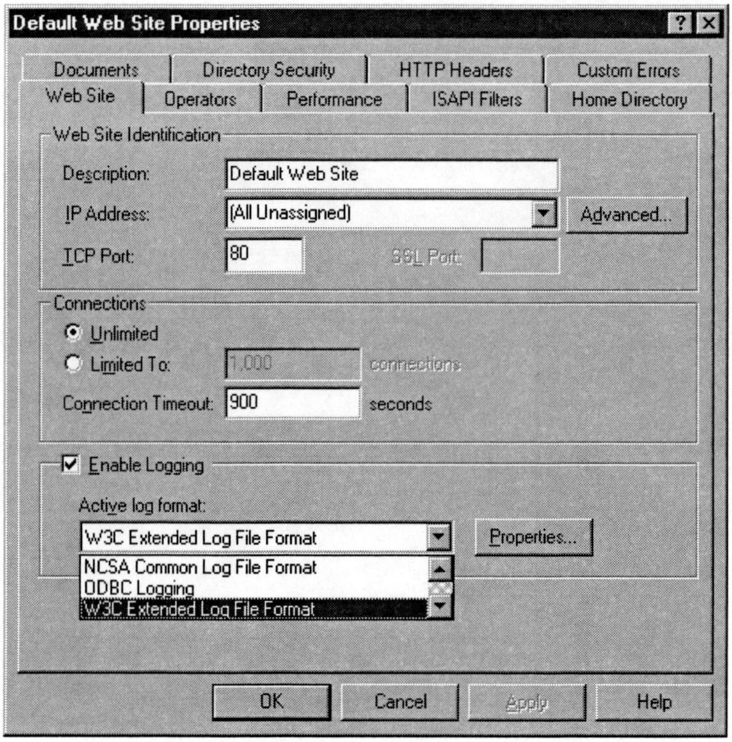

Figure 10-10
Selecting a
Log Format

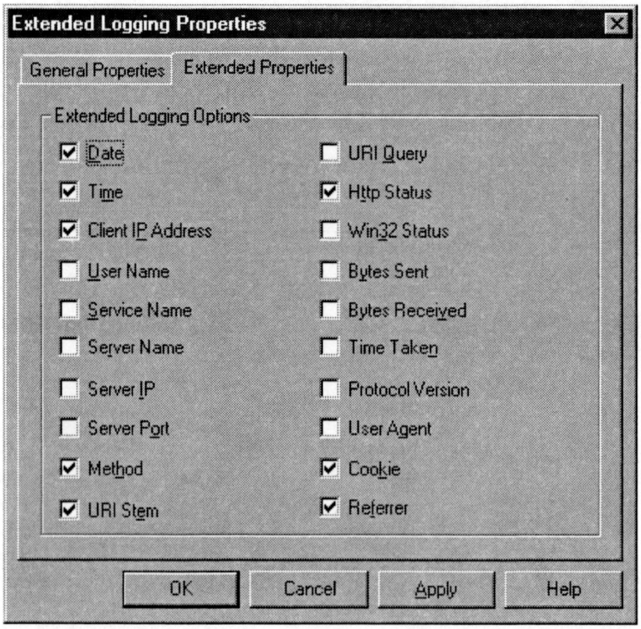

Default Web Site Properties

| Documents | Directory Security | HTTP Headers | Custom Errors |
| Web Site | Operators | Performance | ISAPI Filters | Home Directory |

Web Site Identification

Description: Default Web Site

IP Address: (All Unassigned) ▾   Advanced...

TCP Port: 80   SSL Port:

Connections
◉ Unlimited
○ Limited To: 1,000 connections
Connection Timeout: 900 seconds

☑ Enable Logging

Active log format:
W3C Extended Log File Format ▾   Properties...

NCSA Common Log File Format
ODBC Logging
W3C Extended Log File Format

OK   Cancel   Apply   Help

Figure 10-11
W3C Extended
Log File Format
Possibilities

Extended Logging Properties

General Properties | Extended Properties

Extended Logging Options

☑ Date   ☐ URI Query
☑ Time   ☑ Http Status
☑ Client IP Address ☐ Win32 Status
☐ User Name   ☐ Bytes Sent
☐ Service Name   ☐ Bytes Received
☐ Server Name   ☐ Time Taken
☐ Server IP   ☐ Protocol Version
☐ Server Port   ☐ User Agent
☑ Method   ☑ Cookie
☑ URI Stem   ☑ Referrer

OK   Cancel   Apply   Help

Checking **Cookies** will force the system to keep all cookies received in the log. The W3C format is actually stored in two separate files; one is a "standard" log file that most analysis programs will be able to handle, the other is an extended file. A sample of the extended file follows:

```
#Version: 1.0
#Date: 1997-12-07 20:54:26
#Fields: time c-ip cs-method cs-uri-stem sc-status cs(Cookie)
  cs(Referer)
20:58:00 192.168.124.11 GET /mps2/index.html 200
  MC1=GUID=c35f842d6d1311d1949808002be494d9 -
20:58:47 192.168.124.11 GET /mps2/ index.html 200
  MC1=GUID=c35f842d6d1311d1949808002be494d9 -
21:02:49 192.168.124.11 GET / index.html 200
  MC1=GUID=710bd7946dcc11d1949908002be494d9;+ASPSESSIONIDQGGQQGXZ=BPG
  PCGIBNHHDOKPDKJGDBMKK -
21:06:29 192.168.124.15 GET /dhtml/ index.html 200
  MC1=GUID=710bd7976dcc11d1949908002be494d9 -
21:07:20 192.168.124.15 GET /index.html 200
  MC1=GUID=710bd7976dcc11d1949908002be494d9 -
21:07:20 192.168.124.15 GET / index.html 200
  MC1=GUID=710bd7976dcc11d1949908002be494d9 -
21:10:28 127.0.0.1 GET /chap8/maze/frontDoor.asp 200
  ASPSESSIONIDQGGQQGXZ=MOGPCGIBDECCDKAFHDIEBEMF
  http://localhost/chap8/maze/
21:10:47 127.0.0.1 GET /chap8/maze/InfoSubmit.asp 200
  ASPSESSIONIDQGGQQGXZ=MOGPCGIBDECCDKAFHDIEBEMF
  http://localhost/chap8/maze/frontDoor.asp
21:10:50 127.0.0.1 GET /chap8/maze/maze1.asp 200
  ASPSESSIONIDQGGQQGXZ=MOGPCGIBDECCDKAFHDIEBEMF;+UserID=1404
  http://localhost/chap8/maze/InfoSubmit.asp?UserName=gleeful
21:10:53 127.0.0.1 GET /chap8/maze/maze7.asp 200
  ASPSESSIONIDQGGQQGXZ=MOGPCGIBDECCDKAFHDIEBEMF;+UserID=1404
  http://localhost/chap8/maze/maze1.asp
21:11:01 127.0.0.1 GET /chap8/maze/maze6.asp 200
  ASPSESSIONIDQGGQQGXZ=MOGPCGIBDECCDKAFHDIEBEMF;+UserID=1404
  http://localhost/chap8/maze/maze1.asp
21:11:07 127.0.0.1 GET /chap8/maze/maze7.asp 200
  ASPSESSIONIDQGGQQGXZ=MOGPCGIBDECCDKAFHDIEBEMF;+UserID=1404
  http://localhost/chap8/maze/maze1.asp
21:11:07 127.0.0.1 GET /chap8/maze/maze3.asp 200
  ASPSESSIONIDQGGQQGXZ=MOGPCGIBDECCDKAFHDIEBEMF;+UserID=1404
  http://localhost/chap8/maze/maze7.asp
21:11:11 127.0.0.1 GET /chap8/maze/maze8.asp 200
  ASPSESSIONIDQGGQQGXZ=MOGPCGIBDECCDKAFHDIEBEMF;+UserID=1404
  http://localhost/chap8/maze/maze3.asp
21:11:28 127.0.0.1 GET /chap8/maze/maze6.asp 200
```

Cookies make up a significant portion of this log; even the non-persistent ASPSESSIONID cookies make regular, constant appearances. This information, once imported into a database, can be used for fairly sophisticated tracking of user preferences—especially when combined with the information gathered by MPS.

Microsoft Personalization System maintains its own logs of all UPD transactions in "PropDB" files that are useful for debugging. It also maintains a UPDnames.log file that contains a list of all current names set for any user in the database. At present, Usage Analyst cannot examine these.

Fortunately, Usage Analyst's default set of reports is reasonably benign. The user detail report shows information about conglomerated user behavior, not the paths of individual users through the Web site, as shown in Figure 10-12.

Figure 10-12
Usage Analyst's
Default User
Detail Report
Structure

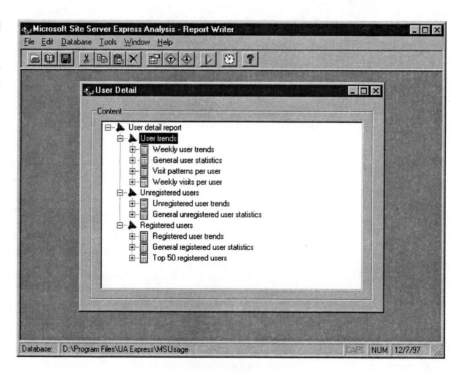

The material contained in these reports is similarly ordinary. Most of the information presented is averages and groupings, as shown in Figure 10-13. When a server only has four visitors (my test server is on a local network), the information could perhaps be traced to individuals, but there is very little damage it could do.

Even the information presented on registered users is quite ordinary. The "Top 50 Registered Users" list comes into play only for sites that require authentication, and the summary of registered user behavior (shown in Figure 10-14) is reasonably innocuous.

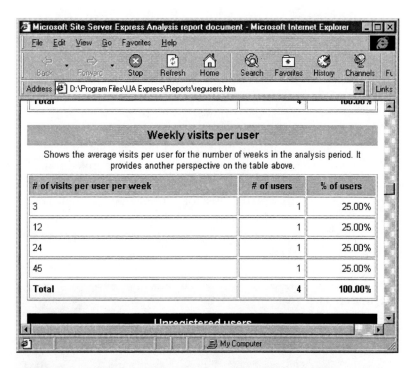

Figure 10-13
Weekly Visits
per User

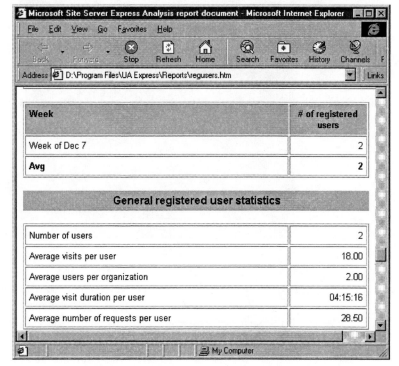

Figure 10-14
Registered User
Statistics

What, Me Worry?

Throughout this book I have tried to present a balanced view of cookies. Cookies are not the demonic privacy destroyers some privacy advocates have claimed, but neither are they harmless trinkets that help programmers overcome a minor glitch in the ways of the Web. The tools described in this chapter are, at present, mostly harmless. Still, they represent some very significant steps toward the creation of Web site-owned dossiers on users, unsuspecting or otherwise. The collection of information itself is fairly harmless, as long as it moulders in inaccessible files that no one reads. The structured collection and analysis of that data, however, is another matter entirely. Figure 10-15 shows a small beginning of that structuring—a table containing cookie information in the `msusage.mdb` file that Usage Analyst collects.

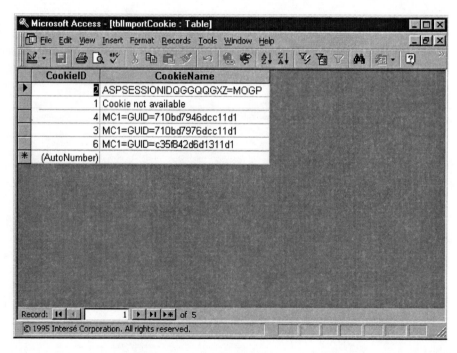

The tools presented in this chapter are not yet particularly frightening. These tools are just the first few steps toward tools that will make it possible for developers to handle all the state management demonstrated in this book with an integrated system that makes developers' lives easier while giving marketers considerably more information to apply toward generating sales. All the tools presented here that stored information in client cookies, dropped it into databases and file systems, and pulled it out again when it was called for are only intermediate steps toward more comprehensive systems. Those larger system will be easier to work with than the demonstrations presented here, storing information in structured formats that handle much of the overhead of all the tools discussed above. More important, perhaps, those systems will be tightly integrated with the new log file formats that can better connect stored information to records sharing the user's path through a site. Armed with the user information entered directly into a site through forms, and a detailed report of which parts of a site received the most attention from particular users, the telemarketing, direct mail, and direct email brigades may have more information than they know how to use.

The next release of Site Server, due out in Spring 1998, may provide more effective tools. Microsoft has already announced its plans to make Usage Analyst and Microsoft Personalization System do a better job of cooperating, thus bringing together the log file analysis and the gathering of personal information. When these systems' improved tools are combined with their ability to allow sites to share user ID values across domains, users may be in for some difficult decisions. Developers may also face a tougher time getting users to accept cookies, especially on the Internet, if this growing integration leads to abuse.

CHAPTER **11**

Cookies
and the Future:
Architectures
and Technologies

Most of the examples in this book have demonstrated a
technology rather archaic by Web standards. In practice,
cookies have changed little since their introduction in
1995, despite the slow movement toward the more-
advanced cookies described in RFC 2109. In answer to the
complaints of both developers and consumers, new technologies are emerging that may one day replace the cookie
with a better, stronger, and safer structure. As the debates
about privacy rage on, vendors coming from several areas
in the computing world are developing tools that do a better job of both storing and protecting user information—
and informing users of their activities. Not all of these
tools behave as transparently to the user as do cookies, but
each has its own advantage in a slowly crowding field.

Cookie Successors and Alternatives

Cookies can work well for many applications, but developers have long been looking for better tools. The most obvious successor to the current version of cookies Netscape Cookies is the Version 1 cookie presented in RFC 2109. RFC 2109 has faced a snail-like adoption process, as momentum builds only very slowly. Even seemingly simple matters like the comment field (for explaining to users what a cookie is supposed to do) can be subject to surprising contention. A large number of developers would prefer to see cookies left on all the time, without the possibility of user intervention. Development becomes much simpler, and developers are assured that their products will work as planned. Allowing users to reject cookies requires considerably more error checking and more explanation as well. Developers whose cookies exist only to help complete a transaction have been tarred with the brush of the privacy invader; many of them are finding one of their key tools rejected by concerned users. Presenting users with a dialog box that asks if they really want a cookie does little to help this situation, from the programmer's perspective.

This is an unusual situation for programmers. While they may have learned to deal with users' typing in bogus data and abusing programs in strange ways, allowing users to reject a tool and its associated data is an innovative concept, though not necessarily a welcome one. As a result, many sites have given up on cookies—why develop a site that only half the users can visit, and then not reliably? Help desks answering calls from users who wiped out their cookie files and now cannot get into sites have a complicated situation to explain, one that is not easily remedied.

Sites that need to maintain state across a large number of transactions are slowly turning to other alternatives. The simplest of these is authentication. Once a user has entered a username and password, the browser will keep track of it for the duration of the session, much as a cookie does. Once a user has been authenticated, the REMOTE_USER variable provides information as unique as a cookie's—as long as only one user has access to each name. In combination with server-side information collection, using techniques similar to those shown in this book with cookies, a site can build up a significant collection of personalized details, including border-crossing and site-personalization information, shopping carts, and all kinds of other data. The problem, of course, is the overhead of assigning usernames and passwords. Some sites have automated this process effectively—for discussion forums, for instance. Still, setting up a user account is more effort than setting a cookie, and requires more effort on the user's part. (Users have to remember the password, among other things.) Authentication does have one significant advantage, though—the user can log in from any browser anywhere and have the same set of information applied to a visit. Cookies, of course, work only for the particular browser on which they were set.

More-secure alternatives to authentication are also growing. Authentication using certificates and digital signatures provides a much more secure route than either cookies or basic authentication can, but also requires more effort on the part of the user. Setting up a certificate system or digital signature service still takes more knowledge than many users have. While these tools are useful (and their prices are falling rapidly), they remain beyond the reach of the average developer.

The main issue all these alternatives address is providing a postive identification of the user—creating a passport, in effect. The various alternatives lack cookies' ability to store a wide variety of information on the client, but do a much better job of identifying the user, making it easier to store information on the server. How that information is collected and used remains a matter of contention, however. Fortunately, a new set of standards just arriving may address many of these needs—and some of the concerns of privacy advocates as well.

Open Profiling System (OPS) and the Platform for Privacy Preferences (P3P)

In June 1997, Microsoft announced its endorsement of the Open Profiling System proposed by Netscape, Firefly (a profile management company), and VeriSign (a digital signature provider). At the height of the browser war rhetoric, both companies agreed to collaborate on a key issue facing browsers: how to encourage users to provide personal information without leaving them worried about how that information will be used. At the same time, these tools will provide a better architecture for uniquely identifying users, addressing many of the same state management issues as cookies do. OPS was submitted to the World Wide Web Consortium (W3C) as a framework and a set of standards. (See **http://www.w3.org/Submission/1997/6** for the full submission.)

OPS uses a `Set-Profile` header much like cookies use a `Set-Cookie` header, but it carries a much richer set of information. Instead of holding a few thousand bytes of name-value pairs available to only one site, a profile carries a somewhat standardized set of fields available (with user permission) to any number of sites. According to the Netscape press release of May 27, 1997,

Personal Profiles contain a wide range of descriptive information about an individual, such as name, address, zip code, phone number, and email address. Personal Profiles can also contain information on an individual's age, marital status, interests, hobbies, and user identification/password. Internet sites and software products that support OPS and Personal Profiles will enable users to be aware of and in control of what profile information they divulge to Internet sites. In addition, OPS enables users to grant permission to specific Internet sites to share their Personal Profiles with other Internet sites.

This does not sound truly promising; the press release is clearly written to whet the appetites of marketers everywhere. OPS is important as a tool for increasing the transparency of Web transactions, sparing users the constant retyping of personal information, and setting standards that prevent sites from sharing information unless enabled by the user.

The W3C is moving forward, with the OPS creators, on its own Platform for Privacy Preferences (P3P). While the W3C shares the interest of Netscape and Microsoft in making Web transactions easier, its focus on privacy gives its efforts a friendlier ring to consumers. As the W3C puts it, "P3P was initially focussed on enabling the expression of privacy practices and preferences. OPS's focus was on the secure storage, transport, and control of user data." As the two projects overlap, the P3P project has come to address the issues presented by OPS and will probably eventually supersede it. OPS is not yet implemented in any major browser, as it was released just after Netscape had finished Communicator 4, but it may appear in future browsers. The P3P recommendations are themselves a work in progress. (For more information on P3P, visit **http://www.w3.org/P3P/**.)

Neither OPS or P3P is finalized, but there is already one implementation ready for at least preliminary examination: Microsoft's Profile Assistant, available as a part of Internet Explorer 4.0 for Windows 95. Profile Assistant can be accessed through either the Internet control panel of Windows 95 or the **View...Internet Options...** menu selection in Internet Explorer 4.0 under the content tab, as shown in Figure 11-1.

If the buttons in the Personal Information area are dimmed out, it is probably because Internet Explorer 4.0 was installed using the **Browser Only** option. Profile Assistant is only available to users who chose the Standard or Full installation options.

Figure 11-1
The Content Tab,
Home of the
Profile Assistant

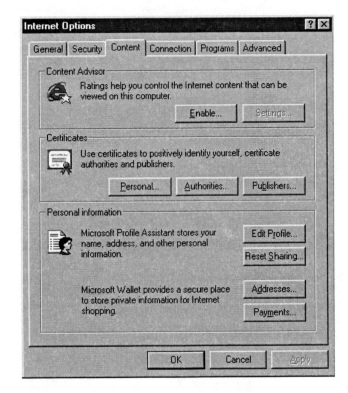

Editing the Profile brings up a tabbed dialog box in which users can announce all kinds of information about their identity, as shown in Figures 11-2 through 11-4.

Figure 11-2
Personal
Information
Collected by the
Profile Assistant

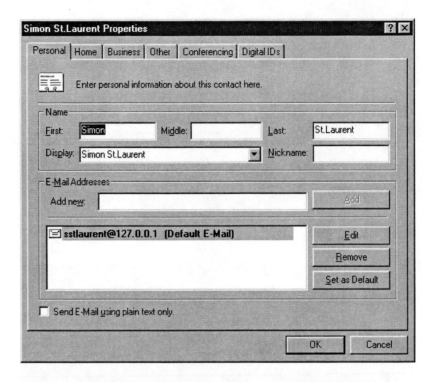

Figure 11-2
Personal
Information
Collected by the
Profile Assistant

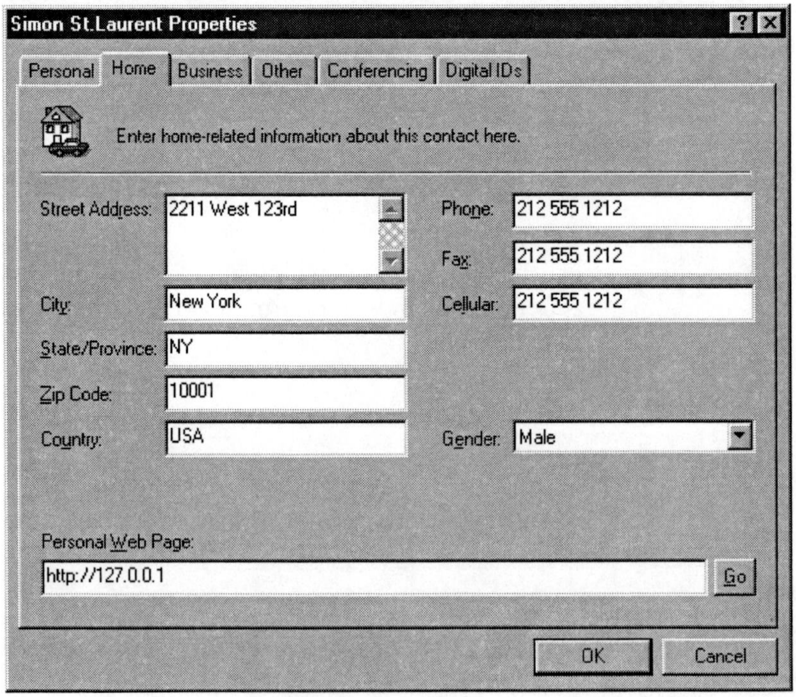

Figure 11-3
Home Information
Collected by the
Profile Assistant

Figure 11-4
Business
Information
Collected by the
Profile Assistant

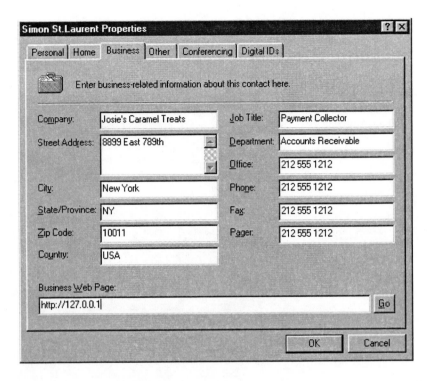

It is certainly a marketer's dream. Once a user has given permission to a site to access information, that site can access updates as well, every time a user visits. Users should probably click the **Reset Sharing...** button periodically, to clear all sharing information. While it might be nice to have site-by-site and item-by-item control over this information (like the control Microsoft provides over cookies in Internet Explorer for the Macintosh), Profile Assistant developers have not yet gotten that far. The current dialog box is shown in Figure 11-5.

Figure 11-5
Yes/No Options
for Resetting
Sharing

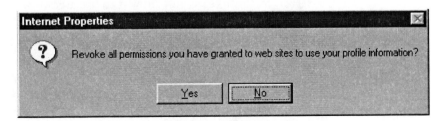

A second tab is a memo space where users can write anything; conferencing is useful for sites that use the Microsoft conferencing tools, and the Digital IDs tool affords users a place to manage their certificates. Microsoft also provides a "wallet" for electronic commerce. Some of the information it contains duplicates information in the Profile Assistant, as shown in Figure 11-6, but other details are clearly aimed at commerce and are kept only in the wallet, as shown in Figure 11-7.

Figure 11-6
The Address
Space in
Microsoft Wallet

Once the information is stored in the browser, sites can access it through the userProfile object in JavaScript or VBScript, though access requires the permission of the user. A program like that below can pull out key information and put it into forms or cookies for transmission to the server, or, in this case, just show it to the user.

```
<HTML><HEAD>
<TITLE>Generating a request</TITLE>
</HEAD><BODY BGCOLOR=#FFFFFF>
<H1>Collecting...</H1>
<SCRIPT>
//only works in IE 4.0
//all code subject to change with
//new specs from the W3C.
//This is an example only; it is probably
//not a good idea to model code on this
//example until the spec is settled.
var profile=navigator.userProfile;

profile.clearRequest();
```

Figure 11-7
Credit Card
Collection in
Microsoft Wallet

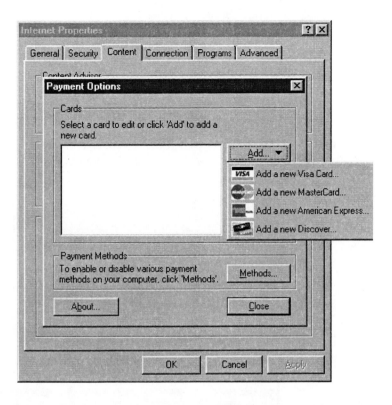

```
profile.addRequest("Vcard.FirstName");
profile.addRequest("Vcard.LastName");
profile.addRequest("Vcard.Email");

profile.doReadRequest(1,"Simon Inc.");

document.write(profile.getAttribute("Vcard.FirstName")+"!");
document.write("<P>I know your last name
is:"+profile.getAttribute("Vcard.LastName"));
document.writeln("<P>I know your email
is:"+profile.getAttribute("Vcard.Email"));
</SCRIPT>
</BODY></HTML>
```

A user who loads this page will be prompted about releasing information to
the server making the request, as shown in Figure 11-8. If the request is
granted, the user will be presented with the screen in Figure 11-9. If the
request is denied, the profile attributes will be blank.

Figure 11-8
Profile Request

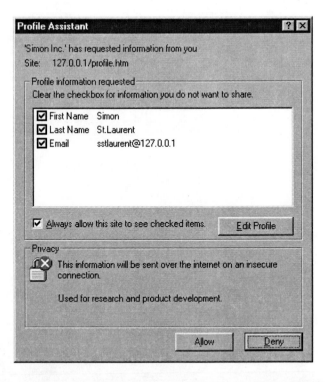

Figure 11-9
Results of
that Request

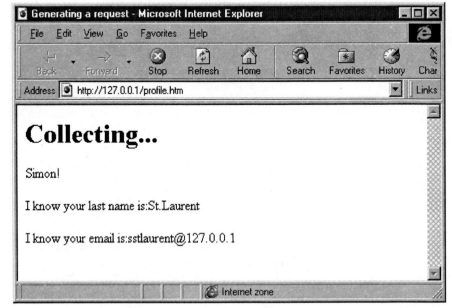

All this is subject to change as the P3P moves through the W3C's working group, but it does provide the best sign yet available of which direction browsers are moving on personal information.

Beyond HTTP

HTTP may not last forever as the predominant mode of information transfer on the Web. Alternative protocols starting to appear offer developers more control over state. While this control has been possible since the very arrival of the Web (HTTP is only one of a number of protocols for making transfers over TCP/IP networks, many of which maintain state), the growth of Java applets and applications has accelerated the trend. An applet might be loaded over HTTP into a Web browser, for instance, and then set up its own connection to the server using its own protocols. As long as the applet, not the browser, is managing the transaction, it is reasonably easy to maintain state and allow programs to communicate over networks.

Microsoft's distributed COM technologies and Sun's RMI (Remote Method Invocation) offer similar tools for making these kinds of connections, and both sets of tools can also program TCP/IP sockets directly. The fate of HTTP alternatives may well be decided by the outcome of the battle between Microsoft and Sun, though other alternatives may appear. For now, HTTP is a widely respected, reasonably uncontested standard, so it will probably remain predominant. It may need some patching (cookies are themselves a patch), but it has proven remarkably resilient over the years.

Identity for Sale

The larger issue surrounding these controversies is not the transfer of data over the Web; it is the use of that information after the transfer. Data collection companies—from direct-mail specialists to credit bureaus—have already irritated millions of people with junk mail, telephone calls, denied loans, and email spam, and consumers are not especially enthusiastic about creating more problems for themselves. Information sent to one company—on a warranty registration card, for instance—can appear in hundreds of other places as the information is repeatedly sold. Even government information can be ransacked for names and addresses, as recent battles over voter registration lists and driver's license information have shown.

Cookies by themselves are innocent of the charges brought against them, if only because, unlike guns, they are not directly capable of much. The people who use cookies, however, can employ a fairly weak tool to connect a wide variety of information to particular identities, fattening them for sale. Cookies do not collect the information by themselves and ship it off to unscrupulous marketers; they do, however, provide the glue that holds together a marketer's profile. Better tools for creating profiles are in the works, but cookies will probably bear a stigma for years to come.

Regulating what is done with information is extraordinarily difficult. In the United States, the Federal Trade Commission has held hearings and consulted with companies to see what can be done. In the interest of avoiding direct regulation, many companies (including McGraw-Hill, the parent company of the publisher of this book) have issued strict guidelines defining what they will and will not do with the information they collect. Other companies lurking in the shadows remain quieter, but the largest companies, those capable of gluing the most pieces together, have at least made public statements that should provide a modicum of protection for personal information. Whether this situation will last is an open question; any clear failure of industry self-regulation will likely provoke a backlash and possibly a strong set of goverment regulations.

The problems remain, however, even if the government steps in. Information is gathered all over the world, and tracing its movements in the flood of data moving through the Internet is nearly impossible. A provider in Finland could flout U.S. regulations quite happily, and if the European Union or Finland produced similar rules, it would not be difficult to move a site from a hosting service in Finland to one in the Cayman Islands or Madagascar or Russia. An Internet connection is an Internet connection, wherever the servers may live, and regulating this distributed network is incredibly difficult.

With or without government intervention, a credibility problem remains. The OPS and P3P standards provide guidelines for companies collecting information, but auditing mechanisms have not yet appeared and there are few ways to check up on companies. It may occasionally become clear that a product or site is flaunting the established rules, as Microsoft has with Site Server's ability to assign the same cookie value to multiple domains, but that still does not present evidence of wrongdoing. Once the information is in the server, it may be combined with information gathered at other sites, or it may be living in isolation, following all the guidelines laid down by self-regulation.

Until these issues are resolved, cookies will remain bones of contention. They have a bright future as a much-needed patch to the HTTP protocol, but there are still storm clouds on the horizon. Solving one problem, that of state maintenance, has created many others, including those of privacy and the value of personal information. Until the latter issues are resolved, programmers who choose to use cookies will face a public relations battle over the use of a much-needed tool.

Index

About
the Author

Simon St.Laurent is an experienced Web developer who has been involved with hypertext since 1989 and the World Wide Web since 1994. He has worked for a number of multimedia and Web design firms on projects for clients from start-up small businesses to Fortune 500 companies. Currently he is on the staff of Systems Integration and Support Services, Inc. St.Laurent is also the author of *Dynamic HTML: A Primer*. He lives in Greensboro, North Carolina.

Cookie
Recipe

Sift or mix together:

2½ cups all purpose flour

1¼ teaspoons salt

1¼ teaspoons baking soda

Mix together until combined:

1 cup softened unsalted butter (2 sticks)

¾ cup granulated sugar

⅔ cup packed dark brown sugar

Add flour mixture to butter/sugar mixture

Add:

2 teaspoons vanilla

2 eggs, one at a time

By hand, stir in:

1 cup semi-sweet chocolate chips

⅓ cup milk chocolate chips

⅓ cup white chocolate chips

⅓ cup butterscotch chips

(½ cup chopped nuts—optional)

Place level tablespoons of dough on ungreased cookie sheets—12 to a sheet.
Bake at 375 degrees for 10 minutes. Let cool for 2 minutes on cookie sheet.
Remove to wire rack to cool completely.
Makes 4 to 4 1/2 dozen cookies.

$28.66